THE FLOOD FROM HEAVEN

Eberhard Zangger

The Flood from Heaven

Deciphering the Atlantis Legend

WITH A FOREWORD BY
Anthony Snodgrass
(Laurence Professor of Classical Archaeology,
University of Cambridge)

William Morrow and Company, Inc.
New York

First published in 1992 in Great Britain by Sidgwick &
Jackson Limited

Grateful acknowledgment is made for permission to
reprint from the following:

Plato, *Timaeus* and *Critias, Volume 1X,* R. G. Bury,
trans. Cambridge, Mass.: Harvard University Press, 1929.
Reprinted by permission of the publishers and the Loeb
Classical Library.

It is the policy of William Morrow and Company, Inc.,
and its imprints and affiliates, recognizing the importance
of preserving what has been written, to print the books
we publish on acid-free paper, and we exert our best
efforts to that end.

Library of Congress Cataloging-in-Publication Data

Zangger, Eberhard.
The flood from heaven: deciphering the Atlantis legend /
Eberhard Zangger.
p. cm.
Includes bibliographical references and index.

ISBN 0-688-11350-8

1. Atlantis. I. Title.
GN75I.Z36 1992
398.23′4—dc20
92-1304 CIP

Printed in the United States of America

First U.S. Edition

1 2 3 4 5 6 7 8 9 10

CONTENTS

The general interest felt in any subject necessarily diminishes when the discussion of it has been long protracted without leading to any satisfactory results.

Such has been the fate of the controversy respecting the site of Troy. By an extraordinary chain of consequences, attempts to ascertain the site of the city have led many to doubt its existence altogether. A writer who comes forward at this stage of the controversy evidently labors under many disadvantages. He finds a large class of those who ought to be his readers totally indisposed to attend to his discussions. He has to encounter the suspicions of another class, who, having once been imposed upon, suspect some latent fraud, some *dolus Danaum* in everything that bears the name and superscription of Troy. The few who retain full faith in the investigation are generally attached to some of the existing hypotheses and will perhaps be found more inaccessible to new ideas than confirmed skeptics. In short, between those who have their minds preoccupied and those who distrust all speculations on the subject, it may be doubted whether a new topographical theory, however satisfactory, be likely to meet with a better reception than the project of a new Greek expedition. Whether the author of this small publication has decided wisely in giving it to the press, under these discouraging circumstances, must be determined by the event.

Charles MacLaren's *A Dissertation on the Topography of the Plain of Troy* (1822) argued for over 270 pages, first of all, that Troy must have existed and, secondly, that its location must have been on the mount called Hisarlık, precisely where Heinrich Schliemann "discovered" Troy, forty-eight years later.

FOREWORD

This is a book that will provoke and stimulate, but not in quite the way that many readers will expect, the way familiar from earlier works on the Atlantis story. The stimulation will be widespread, but the provocation will be mainly directed at two groups of people: those who believe that the Atlantis legend poses no problem, because it is nothing but an imaginative fantasy of Plato's; and those (a smaller group) who believe that there is a problem, but that they themselves have already solved it. Dr. Zangger does not belong to either group. The case that he advances in this book is one that moves from scientific observations to new hypotheses: it is not a claim to have discovered the final truth.

He argues, first, that the Atlantis story was meant by Plato as an account of something historical, however much distorted and misrepresented; as pure fiction, its length and specificity of detail would have been purposeless. In his dialogue the *Timaeus*, Plato has the speaker Critias twice emphasize that his story is about something that actually happened; and he has Socrates himself welcome the story on that understanding. This is certainly *prima facie* evidence for what Plato believed; we may perhaps recall the words of Lewis Carroll: "What I tell you three times is true."

As for the innumerable earlier attempts to identify and locate the historical Atlantis, Dr. Zangger very soon parts company with them and their methods. He shows how conditioned they are by the cultural and scientific climate of their own times. Unlike them, he came to his view not by trying to fit the scientific and archaeological observations (or a selection of them) into a pre-existing theory but by *starting* from such observations.

This is not, then, another ploy in the well-known game of "Confound the Experts." It cannot be, since Dr. Zangger is himself an expert. The natural sciences have gradually come to play a central role in the understanding of prehistory, not just through technical application in archaeology but in their own right. This is true even for episodes of later prehistory like those of the Aegean Late Bronze Age. The author's field is geoarchaeology, the study of the relationship between human and geomorphological processes, and this stands alongside paleobotany, dendrochronology, seismology, vulcanology, climatology and several other disciplines, without which, we now realize, any account of the processes that

ix

shaped and swept away the civilizations of Crete, Mycenae and Troy will be partial and rather superficial.

But at the same time, Dr. Zangger has immersed himself in the texts of Plato, the only fountainhead of the Atlantis story, and in the secondary literature interpreting those texts. As a scientist, he commands a body of evidence with a firm basis in fact, but of debatable relevance to the matter under discussion; in Plato he has a source of unquestionable relevance but dubious basis in fact. To effect a *rapprochement* between two such diverse bodies of information is a delicate but not an impossible task. Just as the human impact of the observed natural phenomena can be estimated in the one case, so can the genuine scientific insights be picked out from the literary account in the other.

To do so, however, involves questioning the received wisdom of more than one discipline. It is this that makes the book a daring venture. Classical philology and the natural sciences are alike in that they discourage iconoclasts: imaginativeness is tolerated, but not widely emulated. These are subjects for the "convergent" intellect, the type that excels in finding the right answer to the kind of questions that *have* a right answer; "divergers," by contrast, are those with the very different aptitude for finding multiple answers to questions that are open-ended. Yet the history of these and other disciplines shows that, every so often, a major advance has been achieved through the kind of imaginative leap of which the divergers are more readily capable. Merely to question established preconceptions has a liberating effect: the pioneers may lose their way, but still leave a trail which others can follow to success.

But there is a frontier, universally if intuitively perceived, at which the imaginative strays over into the crankish. That is what makes this dangerous territory. I do not think that there are many authors who would take the risk of assembling the arguments against their own case, as Dr. Zangger does in his concluding chapter, nor that a genuine crank would begin that chapter with two definitions of crankiness. These are two obvious signs that what we see in this book is not more special pleading, not yet another charge of the hobby-horse brigade, but something rarer and infinitely more interesting: the operation of a divergent intellect in a world of convergers.

Rather than proposing a "correct solution" for the problem of Atlantis, rather than even arguing for the existence of such a solution, it is a plea for freedom to think along new lines. It is in the

Bronze Age city of Troy that Dr. Zangger finds the most plausible model for the account of the vanished splendors of Atlantis, but there are no triumphant claims for a total correspondence. Perhaps the greatest attraction of Troy is the clear glimpse that has been given, within the last few years, of the secrets which it still holds. This is especially true of the Trojan plain around the citadel. The reader who follows Dr. Zangger's account of his own discoveries, in corresponding locations, in the plain around the citadel of Tiryns on the Greek mainland, will begin to share his excitement as to what the future may bring to light.

The book contains a series of specific arguments which some will want to counter. I, for one, have to say that I find the case advanced in the *Odyssey* chapter over-ambitious. But a better response would be to pursue the many new ideas advanced here, possibly in different directions from that followed by the author, to see whether they lead to insights equally novel and fruitful. The challenge is a widely directed one: this is a book well informed enough to engage the experts in several disciplines, yet so readable as to attract at the same time the general reader.

Anthony Snodgrass

CHAPTER ONE

SERENDIPITY

Nobody could say that we had not been warned. Summers in Greece are inevitably hot, but in August 1987 the country was expecting an unprecedented heat wave. I had just bought what seemed to be the last available electric fan in Athens before the suffocating smog descended. With an ambivalent feeling of satisfaction about this acquisition and knowing that I could cross out another item from my "to do" list, but sorry for all those people who would be trying in vain to match my luck during the imminent heat wave, I left the store carrying the booty in a plastic bag.

Athens never changes. It consists of hundreds of thousands of unattractive, concrete, six-story buildings with no green in between. The streets are always bursting with cars and the air is full of clamor and pollutants. I was heading aimlessly toward Syntagma Square in the center of the city. There was one more errand to run before I was released from my duties in the city. One of my Greek friends, an orange-plantation owner from the Argolid, had obtained government permission to export a certain kind of agricultural produce. But the permit only showed the Latin name of the plant (*Carduus*), and nobody could tell what that meant. He had asked me to identify the plant during my visit to Athens. The archaeological libraries which I know, however, turned out to be useless at providing any further clues in this pursuit.

Near Syntagma, I passed a German bookshop which I had never noticed before. It occurred to me that they might have two or three of the common plant-classification books. Besides, at that time I was living in the United States and usually thinking in English, and while in Greece, I had to converse in Greek. The German bookstore thus seemed like a welcome haven, where I would be able to talk in my mother tongue for a little while.

Unfortunately, it turned out that none of the books I had in mind was carried by the shop; but the owner, a charming and extremely supportive lady, was not going to give up the search,

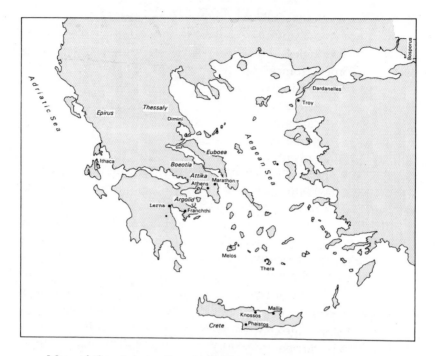

Map of the Aegean Sea, including ancient settlements and place names mentioned in the text.

once I had explained my query. Since no other customers were present, she was able to dedicate all her time and attention to the problem. After about twenty minutes, we finally identified it as a thistle (γαίδουράγκαθα or donkey thistle), one of the most abundant and undesirable plants in Greece. Somebody was evidently trying to make fun of my friend.

After all these efforts, it was clear that I could not leave the shop without buying something, so I politely asked if I could browse through the shelves once more to look for some leisure reading. I sometimes spend up to an hour in a bookshop searching, often in vain, for interesting reading matter. German bookstores abroad tend to have a selection of classics which one either knows inside-out or for which one could not care less. I spent an embarrassingly long time in front of a revolving bookshelf turning it round and round while the salesperson became increasingly irritated. In order to bring this ridiculous situation to an end, I grabbed a book called *Stories of Atlantis*, which had caught my eye at least twenty times while I was spinning the stand.

I did not know anything about Atlantis beyond conventional wisdom. Nevertheless, I was sure that it had never existed and that many, in some instances honorable, people were making fools of themselves by claiming to have found it in various places all over the world. I am a geoarchaeologist, though, and it is part of my job to locate lost landscapes and settlements. I had already found sensible explanations for one or two myths and may have thought subconsciously that, eventually, I should try to tackle this, the biggest of all archaeological problems. A good geoarchaeologist should be able to find, if not Atlantis itself, at least an explanation for the legend.

NAUPLION: FIRST CONTACTS WITH THE MYTH

A few hours later I was back in Nauplion, alone in the dig house of the German excavation campaign at Tiryns, one of the most important Late Bronze Age citadels in the Aegean. There was no urgent fieldwork to be carried out, and I was looking forward to a few days off, during which I could prepare a lecture for the Swedish Archaeological School in Athens. My investigation of the Bronze Age landscape changes of the Argolid had been completed earlier that year, and I had returned in the summer only to conduct a special study of the immediate vicinity of Tiryns itself.

Equipping my room to suit my needs required another busy day of errands and work. I improved the bed by putting wooden boards under the mattress, installed a bizarre system of adapters and power supplies to feed my laptop computer and the priceless fan and stocked up the refrigerator with food. Finally, I was prepared for the worst.

The heat struck without mercy. For two weeks the thermometer that I had attached to a shady place on the roof did not drop below 116°F during the day and 95°F at night. I spent the days in monotonous agony, covered in sweat, gasping for breath, meandering between bed, desk, sink and toilet. Fortunately, I realized that the hottest time of the day is best spent at the beach. Within fifteen minutes one can get from Nauplion to a deserted, sandy beach a couple of miles long. It was during one of these noon escapes from the heat that I finally took out *Stories of Atlantis* for my first encounter with the lost continent.

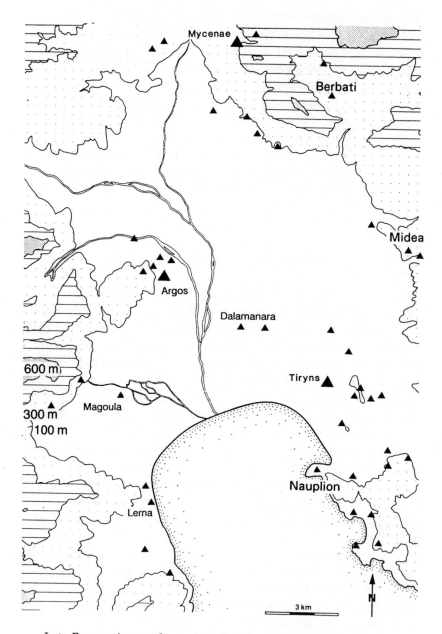

Late Bronze Age settlements in the Argive Plain (after Kilian 1982).

Having arranged towel and body in the sun to my personal satisfaction, protected myself with sunblock, hat and sunglasses, I was prepared for a long and, I hoped, delightful reading adventure. From the introduction I learned that the whole Atlantis myth is based on one single source: a text fragment by Plato. The book provided a translation of parts of this Plato text which I read with great fascination. I was no longer surprised that this narrative had captivated so many people. What an outstanding piece of literature it is, the story of a continent lost eleven thousand years ago, a civilization of great wealth, military power, discipline and technical achievement destroyed by a single, natural catastrophe—proof provided by no less an authority than Plato. But what a vast disappointment the book became for me when it turned out to be a collection of fictional fragments by various authors who had visions of lost continents. To the present day I have not read it fully.

In geoarchaeology, every source of information can become meaningful: two boulders touching in the wall of a clay pit may be significant, as well as an unusual shape of a contour in a topographic map. A dark sediment layer in a drill core may mean something or a bright spot on a satellite image; the plants in an ancient engraving or a microscopic fossil in a stream gravel; a roof-tile fragment in a roadside trench or reed motifs in the paintings on an ancient vase; one single adjective in a hexameter by Homer or an obscure place-name—all these details may provide indications of the past. Geoarchaeological fieldwork consists of collecting such seemingly trivial and completely unrelated pieces of information and linking them to create a rational synthesis. Creating this synthesis may thus have more in common with Hercule Poirot's detective ingenuity than with the mathematical skills required by most sciences. However, in this pursuit of the best possible reconstruction of the past, one must always, *always* avoid secondary sources. Never follow other people's lines of thought in trying to break new ground, because the author himself and scores of his readers will have gone the same way already without success. From secondary sources one is more likely to learn about the character and attitude of an author than to gain original information about a subject. From my perspective, the book was therefore useless.

As a scientist I was (and still am) strongly opposed to explaining the demises of civilizations by natural catastrophes. How many historical examples are there of cultures that were wiped out in a single, natural stroke? How much more change has been wrought by internal system collapses, political upheavals and wars? In any case, my first flirtation with the Atlantis myth ended as abruptly as it had started. The story did not make sense at all. Nowhere in the world was there an ancient civilization of such high standards nine thousand years before Classical Greece. How could it have been involved in a war with the Athenians, as Plato said, if Greece's entire population at that time consisted of little more than a ship-load of late Paleolithic Cro-Magnon cave dwellers, eking out a basic existence on the same low level as their African ancestors two million years before? There was no way I could clarify this myth. I reached the conclusion that it belonged to the genre of paradise fictions, those myths praising a past golden age when everything was more glorious.

(By the way, many scholars have come to the same judgment and I could have adopted this viewpoint by considering secondary sources.)

THE TIRYNS PROJECT (1)

Tiryns is one of the most fascinating archaeological sites I have ever seen, and I had several reasons to be interested in a careful investigation of it. Firstly, Tiryns is the only Late Bronze Age settlement in the Argolid that is surrounded by coastal plain and not isolated on a hilltop. Secondly, nobody has ever been able to find out what the town outside the citadel looked like. Thirdly, there is a remarkable dam one or two miles east of it, which was constructed over three thousand years ago in order to redirect a stream away from the city. During my general work in the Argolid I had not found the reason for this engineering feat. Finally, Tiryns is being excavated by teams from the German Archaeological Institute, who had been generously supporting my Argolid Project without requesting any special investigation of their site itself.

The citadel sits on what is only a fifty-six-foot-high limestone knoll about one mile from the present shore. For a geologist, this is an extremely attractive position. While the sites on hilltops are in erosional environments, where more and more material is carried away with time, Tiryns is in a depositional environment, where sediment accumulates, burying and preserving previous surface

6

soils. At such sites the evolution of the landscape can be recon-structed by determining the stratigraphy around them, in much the same way as the sequence of habitation is determined from the layers in an archaeological excavation. While archaeologists dig trenches to expose the stratigraphy, geoarchaeologists usually take cores from holes drilled into the ground in order to cover a wider terrain and longer periods of time.

Before the end of the heat wave, another graduate student from Stanford University arrived to assist me during the fieldwork. He was not bothered by the heat, and we started to work in spite of temperatures way beyond 104°F. On the second day, we had finished two reasonably long cores just before one o'clock. I some-what reluctantly suggested that we would have another go on condition that we found a *good* site. On a hot summer day in Greece, a good coring site is, first of all, a shady coring site. Therefore, I was looking for a place protected from the sun for another few hours and I found it below a large tree approximately two hundred yards east of the Tiryns walls—a tree that already dominated the area in photographs taken sixty-five years previously.

Unsuspectingly, I was about to unearth what may one day be considered the most important auger core in Mediterranean arch-aeology. I found a string of ceramics to a depth of about sixteen feet. A number of subsequent cores produced similar results, and later archaeological examination revealed that these deposits and their associated pottery dated from a very short period in the Late Bronze Age. The sediments were laid down during a devastating flood, which near the end of the Late Helladic IIIB period—c.1300–1200 B.C. (hereafter LH IIIB)—buried parts of the lower town of Tiryns under several feet of mud. The dam and river conversion east of the citadel had been constructed to prevent any further catastrophes of this kind.

A CLUE IN HEIDELBERG

Three years after my fieldwork in Tiryns I returned to the results of this coring campaign to prepare it for publication. I had meanwhile moved from California to England and was now living in Cam-bridge, where I conducted research into the global aspects of recent environmental change. Although much had happened since

August 1987, the fascination of my discovery at Tiryns did not dwindle. When I presented this study to my departments in Stanford and Cambridge and at international conferences at Baltimore and Heidelberg, I kept expecting somebody to get up and introduce a completely new model for the end of the Bronze Age, initiated by these discoveries. I felt that the geoarchaeological work at Tiryns must bear implications that might solve much more important questions in the field. Although my lectures were well received, nothing of this kind ever happened.

Knowing that my presentation in Heidelberg would be the last opportunity to argue about this project before publication, I used a coffee break to stimulate a discussion with several renowned archaeologists.

"One hundred and twenty years have passed since Schliemann's discovery of Troy," I said, "but what has been found out in the meantime? We don't know what caused the demise of the Achaeans. We don't know whether the Trojan War took place. Can we believe Homer or can we not? Archaeologists do make sweeping conclusions—but only outside their own field. Some explain the end of the Mycenaean era by long-lasting drought; others believe that a depositional event which in fact never happened has radically changed the landscapes all around the Mediterranean during the past two thousand years—and everybody seems to believe them, at least for a decade or two. Many excavators reconstruct shorelines without any conclusive evidence, and just about everyone thinks the tilted wall in his trench records a devastating earthquake."

Bernard Knapp, a friend of mine who specializes in the study of Bronze Age trade in the Eastern Mediterranean, was about to lose control; he found it difficult to bear an ill-informed scientist criticizing archaeological research. According to him, much progress had been made in other areas of archaeological research of which I was totally unaware. He said that I had just expressed some, perhaps justifiable, criticism of one narrow field, Aegean prehistory, which has indeed been dominated by somewhat conservative scholars who do seem to have gone in circles for a rather long time.

"Narrow field?" I responded, "The Bronze Age Mediterranean—it's all that I happen to be interested in." James Muhly, Professor of Ancient Near Eastern and Eastern Mediterranean History at the University of Pennsylvania, added, smiling benignly about this dispute,

8

"It might be worse than you say, Eberhard. If the Trojan War did indeed take place, we would not even be sure which Troy was destroyed by it: VIh or VIIa. One is assumed to have fallen during an earthquake and the other one during a fire. How does one distinguish these two from the effects of war? If you are interested in scrutinizing natural catastrophes detected by archaeologists, you may want to look at Troy too. It may need some careful scientific examination."

As I indicated earlier, I do not generally believe in the political effects of natural disasters, and it seemed that too many events occurred around the Aegean between c. 1250 and 1100 B.C., which, according to current knowledge, appear largely unrelated. From sources of different disciplines, such as archaeology, geology, mythology and poetry, one can produce a list of events which should have occurred during a period of only 100 to 150 years:

1.   The destruction of Troy VIh by earthquakes
2.   The mobilization and preparation for war in Mycenaean Greece and Troy
3.   The construction of the final Mycenaean citadels
4.   The Trojan War
5.   The destruction of Troy VIIa by fire
6.   The destruction of Mycenae and Tiryns by earthquakes
7.   An immense flood catastrophe at Tiryns
8.   The construction of the dam near Tiryns
9.   The destruction and abandonment of most Mycenaean residences
10. The Mycenaean demise and
11. The collapse of the Hittite empire

Elsewhere revolutionary changes occurred throughout the eastern Mediterranean: in Egypt, Kanaan and Cyprus. Yet, in contrast to these upheavals, subsequent centuries were rather quiet.

If, in physical sciences, a theory to explain a phenomenon requires many unusual and largely independent parameters to become plausible, the proposed theory is most likely wrong. Given a choice between different routes, nature would always follow the simplest one. "Research" means re-searching this simplest way. An intuitive ability to find this straightforward answer may therefore be the most valuable virtue any scientist can have. If a phenomenon seems to be complex *and* real, a skilled scientist will nevertheless be able to explain it lucidly. Thus, my premise was that there might well be a simple and rational explanation for the eastern Mediterranean revolutions of *c.* 1200 B.C.

THE BREAKTHROUGH

It was Easter and there was splendid sunshine. My wife and a friend who spent the holidays with us went on a canoeing trip from Cambridge to Grantchester. But I returned home to edit the monograph on my work in the Argolid for publication by the German Archaeological Institute. Using a "brainstorming" technique, I typed out my thoughts, each in a separate paragraph marked by a hyphen. Finally, after a few hours of typing, I had reached the conclusion that Tiryns must have been hit by a simultaneous earthquake and flood, which occurred at the boundary between the LH IIIB and IIIC periods, the onset of the Mycenaean (or Achaean) demise. Perhaps these disasters contributed to the collapse. Then, in the middle of typing this idea, I realized that I might have, inadvertently, begun deciphering the Atlantis legend.

Collapsing into an armchair in the living room, I was overcome simultaneously by excitement and exhaustion. Solutions began falling into place. The flood at Tiryns, the need for a rational answer to the Atlantis legend, the feeling that too much had happened at the end of the Bronze Age—all this could be accommodated by one simple model for the Achaean demise. After about an hour I searched the bookshelf for my first and so far my only book on Atlantis, to begin rereading Plato's original account. The scales fell from my eyes, for he could have actually been providing an altogether faithful account of the Late Bronze Age Aegean, as seen from a foreign perspective. A few problems remained, regarding the timing of the events and the choice of place-names, but it required less than two days of research in the relevant literature to find plausible explanations for most of the discrepancies between the legendary record of the end of Atlantis and the archaeological record of the end of the Aegean Bronze Age. If my conclusions were correct, Plato's account of Atlantis was in fact a retelling of the story of the Trojan War.

DANGERS OF ATLANTIS RESEARCH

Plato described the Atlantis legend as having originated in the sixth century B.C. during a conversation between the Greek statesman Solon and a priest in Saïs, at that time capital of Egypt. After his visit to Egypt, Solon had planned to turn the narrative into an epic poem, but he never succeeded. His unfinished manuscript was handed down over a few generations until Plato, a descendant of Solon, published it a few years before his death in 347 B.C. Although Plato realized the secondary nature of the account, he appears to have been fully convinced of its accuracy. If Plato's suggested transmission is correct, the 2,500-year-old confusion around Atlantis may have resulted from a simple misunderstanding between two very old men, Solon and a Saïtian priest, who were chatting about history and were not quite able to comprehend the meaning of their sources. Solon was fascinated by the story only because he was misguided. If he had realized that the priest was speaking about the Trojan War, he would perhaps not have taken notes of the conversation in his diary.

Why has this episode in Plato's monumental lifework become so fascinating? The answer lies probably in the contrast between Plato's revered credibility and the lack of a plausible historic context for Atlantis. In general we are able to recapitulate and explain Plato's reasoning. Only in the instance of the Atlantis account it seems he either fantasized or possessed knowledge far superior to ours. After thousands of years of failing to provide a satisfactory explanation, most scholars have categorized the Atlantis account as a mere fiction. But there are many indications about the authenticity of the story: firstly, it is inherently logical and, secondly, it is too specific, in fact tediously specific, to be just a simile with some deeper moral. Thirdly, Plato assures the reader of the reliability of his story many times himself. Thus many non-scientists feel that traditional scholarship has failed; and because it has failed in one—arguably important—instance, the fundamental principles of scientific methodology might be questioned altogether. This opened up the ground for scores of "fringe scholars," "cranks" and "lunatics"—as they were then called by an even more aggravated scientific community—to abandon all common sense and hallucinate about lost continents. Today, the Atlantis discussion shows the same division into irrationally arguing, petrified blocs which Charles MacLaren encountered in the debate about Troy 170 years ago.

11

Consequently, the philosopher Harold Cherniss noted that it was "easier to conjure the djin out of the bottle than to get him back again."[1] My work has the perhaps lamentable aim of returning the Atlantis demon to its bottle. It has been a good djin, quite enchanting and utterly harmless, despite its occasional abuse for ideological purposes. Being around for over 2,500 years, however, it has become somewhat exhausted and now deserves to retire for good. I am aware that any affiliation with Atlantis involves certain hazards, as Desmond Lee, one of the Plato translators, realized:

> A preoccupation with Atlantis often leads to a certain craziness, and you have to be on the lookout for this even in works of apparent serious scholarship.[2]

Martin Bernal, however, knows how to distinguish worthless from valuable theories:

> Cranks . . . tend to add new unknown and unknowable factors into their theories: lost continents, men from outer space, planetary collisions etc.[3]

while genuine breakthroughs in science tend to remove these factors rather than to add them. The prime concern of the ideas presented in this book is to remove the unknown and to introduce common sense where it has been lost long ago.

Given the possible explosiveness of any scientific attention to the Atlantis legend and the potential implications of the ideas introduced in this book, it appears crucial to summarize my conclusions: I assume that everything Plato says about the narrative correctly describes his beliefs. Accordingly, the account recollects a manuscript provided by Solon, recounting information received in Egypt. When Plato began the work on *Timaeus* and *Critias*, the two books in which he was going to relate Solon's account of Atlantis, he believed the story to describe the confrontation between an ancient civilization outside the Straits of Gibraltar and Attika, 9,000 years before Solon's time. But Plato never finished *Critias*; one or two paragraphs before the book breaks off in mid-sentence, Plato may have realized what Solon's manuscript was really describing—a clash he was all too familiar with: the Trojan War. At this point the whole concept behind his current project collapsed, and he abandoned it.

According to my interpretation, the story of Atlantis is largely a description of Troy at its peak period (corresponding to Troy VI, around 1300 B.C.), as observed from a foreigner's perspective. The Greek opponents of the Atlanteans were the Achaeans; their culture is sketched at its zenith too; but the demise, accompanied by an earthquake and flood, was also recorded in the account. Sound geological and archaeological observations, introduced in this book, provide evidence of such natural disasters at the onset of the Mycenaean collapse. These events, however, were limited to the Argive Plain, the center of the Mycenaean culture, and by themselves they would not have sufficed to overthrow a healthy community.

Some twenty-five years ago, Rhys Carpenter, a renowned archaeologist, advanced a theory which connected the Mycenaean collapse with long-term climatic change. In the absence of scientific observations, his idea was based on rather tenuous reasoning and anecdotal evidence. Carpenter ruled out a short-term change in weather conditions and proposed the theory of a famine in Greece, caused by drought, which lasted several centuries.[4] But subsequent research found no indications for such a major climatic change, neither in the archaeological record nor in the vegetational history. There are, however, some indications for a short-term (twenty-year) climatic anomaly, centered around 1159 B.C.,[5] triggered by an eruption of Hekla 3, a volcano in southern Iceland. Among the effects attributed to this eruption are high acidity in ice-cores from Greenland, the virtual disappearance of tree-rings in Ireland,[6] an increase of temperature and aridity in Mesopotamia[7] and perhaps even unusual weather conditions and ash rains in China.[8] The Irish dendrochronologist Michael Baillie recently concluded:

> So this 1159 B.C. date for the eruption of Hekla 3 in Iceland has to be borne in mind as at least a trigger event for changes in human affairs – a marker date if ever there was one.[9]

Even citing short-term cataclysmic events such as the eruption of Hekla 3 to explain the end of the Bronze Age does not appear necessary. The political, economic and cultural collapses in the eastern Mediterranean around 1200 B.C. are now generally considered to have been the breakdown of a highly integrated and interdependent economic system—a chain reaction comparable to a domino effect. The discovery of unusual tree-ring patterns and a destructive earthquake and flood in the Argive Plain complies with this model rather than disproves it. These catastrophes became accidentally part of a regional, political demise and probably aggravated it further; in other words, they were more falling dominoes, but the kind of events that were quickly absorbed into ancient lore.

AN OVERVIEW OF THIS BOOK

This book's perspective differs from the two usual approaches to the Atlantis legend, which aim at either proving the historicity of Atlantis or dismissing it.[10] After many thousands of years of research into the history of human ancestors, there is no denying that an accurate framework for the past does exist. Since current understanding of Mediterranean history and known geological processes does not allow for the instantaneous disappearance of a whole continent with an extremely developed culture, the question to be asked should not be "Did Atlantis exist" or "Where was Atlantis?" but "How could Plato's account of the past differ from reality?" As it turns out, a few, but fatal, errors introduced during the transmission and translation of the narrative have distorted it sufficiently to prevent earlier recognition. The present deciphering of Plato's text seemed to me a bit like rearranging jigsaw-puzzle pieces: only a few new pieces have been introduced, some others were false and have been removed; the rest is reassembled in an unprecedented way. Although parts of the puzzle are still incomplete, the interpretations introduced here provide a coherent image that awaits further scrutiny.

Having employed a "unidirectional" approach of reasoning, my argument dashes forward without considering the countless number of other plausible interpretations of the examined sources. This approach is rather dangerous, because it produces the impression that ancient texts or archaeological finds may only be interpreted in one way. On the other hand, it is impossible to discuss all theories that have been brought forward to explain the Atlantis legend, the demise of Late Bronze Age Greece and Homer's Trojan War, and my prime concern is not a synthesis of these previous ideas but the introduction of new ways to look at the past. I would like to show that simple and plausible answers cannot be excluded for even the most complex questions, although the number of scientific publications which have accumulated on the subjects involved has long passed the capacities of any human being.

The emphasis of this book lies in the reconstruction of landscapes and cultures in Bronze Age Greece and at Troy. The arguments sketch parallels between texts and documents, on the one hand, and the environmental record and material culture, on the other. The deciphering of the Atlantis account reveals how ancient legends can be interpreted by employing archaeological knowledge, but such correlation of texts and archaeological record will primarily remain a one-way approach: legends and texts are too often based on subjective and falsified impressions and are not sufficiently reliable to be accepted as fact and applied to our historic knowledge—but they are too valuable to be disregarded altogether.[11]

To provide all the information needed to understand my interpretation of the Atlantis legend, Plato's full account of Timaeus and Critias has been reproduced in the following chapter. The text is a complete and unedited copy, reprinted by permission of the publishers and The Loeb Classical Library from Plato: Timaeus and Critias, Volume IX (translated by R.G. Bury, Harvard University Press, Cambridge, Mass., 1929). The third chapter examines the structure or "anatomy" of these two volumes to unveil Plato's sources: is it more likely that he employed a historic source, as he claimed, or did he wholly invent the story? Whatever the answer to this question, the first and simplest approach in any attempt to comprehend the Atlantis legend must be to trust Plato's word. Only when this avenue of investigation fails should one try a fresh approach from a different angle. As will be shown, the "deciphering" of the narrative may not require Plato's involvement in its composition at all. A very general knowledge of Mediterranean prehistory combined with a healthy portion of common sense may suffice to solve the mystery. Therefore, a brief review of Greek archaeology will be provided in chapter four, emphasizing the interrelation of people and landscape, for these are the primary elements of the account. Thereafter, each paragraph, sentence and clause of Plato's Atlantis text will be looked at as being one piece of the jigsaw puzzle, to be compared with the picture provided by archaeology. A new image of Atlantis will gradually materialize, perhaps stimulating new ideas about eastern Mediterranean prehistory in general.

The sixth chapter reexamines Homer's descriptions of Troy; his Iliad was at least partially vindicated through the discovery of the site, and the unraveling of the Atlantis myth may ensure a similar effect for the *Odyssey*. The seventh chapter presents a new reconstruction of the landscape changes around Troy, based on historical sources, field observations and satellite imagery. The last chapter examines briefly the factors which prevented the decoding of the legend and lists counter-arguments against the ideas presented in this book.

A NOTE ON CITATIONS AND NAMES

References to Plato's *Timaeus* and *Critias* are made in the text using the Stephanus page numbers: *Timaeus* = 17A–91C, *Critias* = 106A–121C. Homer's work is referred to in the text using book and line number in Roman numerals for the *Iliad* and in Arabic numerals for the *Odyssey*. Quotations from Homer are usually taken from the Penguin Classics translation by E.V. Rieu unless they are marked with the name of a different translator. The Late Bronze Age inhabitants of Greece and their civilization are called "Mycenaean" or "Achaean" here, but the latter term is the one I prefer. The name Troy, as used here, usually describes the whole city, which probably extended far beyond the walls of the thus-far excavated citadel, here normally called Ilion.

CHAPTER TWO

PLATO'S
ATLANTIS
ACCOUNT

The following text represents a complete, literal translation of those two passages by Plato, in which Atlantis is described. These are the *only* sources for the legend. Plato presents the story in the form of monologues by a person called Critias, who is recollecting a tale that goes back to the Greek statesman Solon and his visit to Egypt.

TIMAEUS 21E–25D

"In the Delta of Egypt," said Critias, "where, at its head, the 21E
stream of the Nile parts in two, there is a certain district called
Saitic. The chief city in this district is Saïs—the home of King
Amasis—the founder of which, they say, is a goddess whose
Egyptian name is Neïth, and in Greek, as they assert, Athena.
These people profess to be great lovers of Athens and in a
measure akin to our people here. And Solon said that when
he travelled there he was held in great esteem amongst them;
moreover, when he was questioning such of their priests as
were most versed in ancient lore about their early history, he 22A
discovered that neither he himself nor any other Greek knew
anything at all, one might say, about such matters. And on
one occasion, when he wished to draw them on to discourse
on ancient history, he attempted to tell them the most ancient
of our traditions, concerning Phoroneus, who was said to be
the first man, and Niobe; and he went on to tell the legend

17

about Deucalion and Pyrrha after the Flood, and how they   B
survived it, and to give the genealogy of their descendants;
and by recounting the number of years occupied by the
events mentioned he tried to calculate the periods of time.

"Whereupon one of the priests, a prodigiously old man,
said, 'O Solon, Solon, you Greeks are always children: there is
not such a thing as an old Greek.' And on hearing this he
asked, 'What mean you by this saying?' And the priest   C
replied, 'You are young in soul, every one of you. For therein
you possess not a single belief that is ancient and derived from
old tradition, nor yet one science that is hoary with age. And
this is the cause thereof: There have been and there will be
many and diverse destructions of mankind, of which the
greatest are by fire and water, and lesser ones by countless
other means. For in truth the story that is told in your country
as well as in ours, how once upon a time Phaethon, son of
Helios, yoked his father's chariot, and, because he was unable
to drive it along the course taken by his father, burnt up all
that was upon the earth and himself perished by a
thunderbolt—that story, as it is told, has the fashion of a   D
legend, but the truth of it lies in the occurrence of a shifting
of the bodies in the heavens which move round the earth, and
a destruction of the things on the earth by fierce fire, which
recurs at long intervals. At such times all they that dwell on
the mountains and in high and dry places suffer destruction
more than those who dwell near the sea; and in our case the
Nile, our Saviour in other ways, saves us also at such times
from this calamity by rising high. And when, on the other
hand, the Gods purge the earth with a flood of waters, all   E
the herdsmen and shepherds that are in the mountains are
saved, but those in the cities of your land are swept into the
sea by the streams; whereas in our country neither then nor at
any other time does the water pour down over our fields from
above, on the contrary it all tends naturally to well up from
below. Hence it is, for these reasons, that what is here
preserved is reckoned to be the most ancient; the truth being
that in every place where there is no excessive heat or cold to
prevent it there always exists some human stock, now more,
now less in number. And if any event has occurred that   23A
is noble or great or in any way conspicuous, whether it be in
your country or in ours or in some other place of which we

know by report, all such events are recorded from of old and preserved here in our temples; whereas your people and the others are but newly equipped, every time, with letters and all such arts as civilized States require; and when, after the usual interval of years, like a plague, the flood from heaven comes sweeping down afresh upon your people, it leaves none of you but the unlettered and uncultured, so that you become young as ever, with no knowledge of all that happened in old times in this land or in your own. Certainly the genealogies which you related just now, Solon, concerning the people of your country, are little better than children's tales; for, in the first place, you remember but one deluge, though many had occurred previously; and next, you are ignorant of the fact that the noblest and most perfect race amongst men were born in the land where you now dwell, and from them both you yourself are sprung and the whole of your existing city, out of some little seed that chanced to be left over; but this has escaped your notice because for many generations the survivors died with no power to express themselves in writing. For verily at one time, Solon, before the greatest destruction by water, what is now the Athenian State was the bravest in war and supremely well organized also in all other respects. It is said that it possessed the most splendid works of art and the noblest polity of any nation under heaven of which we have heard tell.'

"Upon hearing this, Solon said, that he marvelled, and with the utmost eagerness requested the priest to recount for him in order and exactly all the facts about those citizens of old. The priest then said: 'I begrudged you not the story, Solon; nay, I will tell it, both for your own sake and that of your city, and most of all for the sake of the Goddess who has adopted for her own both your land and this of ours, and has nurtured and trained them—yours first by the space of a thousand years, when she had received the seeds of you from Gê and Hephaestus, and after that ours. And the duration of our civilization as set down in our sacred writings is 8000 years. Of the citizens, then, who lived 9,000 years ago, I will declare to you briefly certain of their laws and the noblest of the deeds they performed: the full account in precise order and detail we shall go through later at our leisure, taking the actual writings. To get a view of their laws, look at the laws here; for

B

C

D

E

24A

19

you will find existing here at the present time your city. You
see, first, how the priestly class is separated off from the rest;
next, the class of craftsmen, of which each sort works by itself
without mixing with any other; then the classes of shepherds,
hunters, and farmers, each distinct and separate. Moreover
the military class here, as no doubt you have noticed, is kept
apart from all the other classes, being enjoined by the law   B
to devote itself solely to the work of training for war. A further
feature is the character of their equipment with shields and
spears; for we were the first of the peoples of Asia to adopt
these weapons, it being the Goddess who instructed us, even
as she instructed you first of all the dwellers in yonder lands.
Again, with regard to wisdom, you perceive, no doubt, the law
here—how much attention it has devoted from the very   C
beginning to the Cosmic Order, by discovering all the effects
which the divine causes produce upon human life, down to
divination and the art of medicine which aims at health, and
by its mastery also of all the other subsidiary studies. So when,
at that time, the Goddess had furnished you, before all others,
with all this orderly and regular system, she established your
State, choosing the spot wherein you were born since she
perceived therein a climate duly blended, and how that it
would bring forth men of supreme wisdom. So it was that   D
the Goddess, being herself both a lover of war and a lover of
wisdom, chose the spot which was likely to bring forth men
most like unto herself, and this first she established.
Wherefore you lived under the rule of such laws as these—
yea, and laws still better—and you surpassed all men in every
virtue, as became those who were offspring and nurslings of
gods. Many, in truth, and great are the achievements of your
State, which are a marvel to men as they are here recorded;
but there is one which stands out above all both for   E
magnitude and for nobleness. For it is related in our records
how once upon a time your State stayed the course of a
mighty host, which, starting from a distant point in the
Atlantic ocean, was insolently advancing to attack the whole of
Europe, and Asia to boot. For the ocean there was at that time
navigable; for in front of the mouth which you Greeks call, as
you say, "the pillars of Heracles," there lay an island which was
larger than Libya and Asia together; and it was possible, for
the travellers of that time to cross from it to the other islands,

and from the islands to the whole of the continent over   25A
against them which encompasses that veritable ocean. For all
that we have here, lying within the mouth of which we speak,
is evidently a haven having a narrow entrance; but that
yonder is a real ocean, and the land surrounding it may most
rightly be called, in the fullest and truest sense, a continent.
Now in this island of Atlantis there existed a confederation of
kings, of great and marvellous power, which held sway over
all the island, and over many other islands also and parts of
the continent; and, moreover, of the lands here within the   B
Straits they ruled over Libya as far as Egypt, and over Europe
as far as Tuscany. So this host, being all gathered together,
made an attempt one time to enslave by one single onslaught
both your country and ours and the whole of the territory
within the Straits. And then it was, Solon, that the manhood
of your State showed itself conspicuous for valour and might
in the sight of all that world. For it stood pre-eminent above
all in gallantry and all warlike arts, and acting partly as leader   C
of the Greeks, and partly standing alone by itself when
deserted by all others, after encountering the deadliest perils,
it defeated the invaders and reared a trophy; whereby it saved
from slavery such as were not as yet enslaved, and all the rest
of us who dwell within the bounds of Heracles it
ungrudgingly set free. But at a later time there occurred
portentous earthquakes and floods, and one grievous day and
night befell them, when the whole body of your warriors was
swallowed up by the earth, and the island of Atlantis in like   D
manner was swallowed up by the sea and vanished; wherefore
also the ocean at that spot has now become impassable and
unsearchable, being blocked up by the shoal mud which the
island created as it settled down.'"

The first part of Plato's Atlantis account as recollected by Critias
from notes of Solon ends here. Plato continues to talk about
Atlantis in the subsequent book, which he named after the
speaker. Although the first half of the book *Critias* describes
ancient Attika and not Atlantis, I include it here, because it is
generally considered part of the Atlantis account.

CRITIAS 108E–121C

"Now first of all we must recall the fact that 9,000 is the sum   108E
of years since the war occurred, as is recorded, between the
dwellers beyond the pillars of Heracles and all that dwelt
within them; which war we have now to relate in detail. It was
stated that this city of ours was in command of the one side
and fought through the whole of the war, and in command of
the other side were the kings of the island of Atlantis, which
we said was an island larger than Libya and Asia once upon a
time, but now lies sunk by earthquakes and has created a   109A
barrier of impassable mud which prevents those who are
sailing out from here to the ocean beyond from proceeding
further. Now as regards the numerous barbaric tribes and all
the Hellenic nations that then existed, the sequel of our story,
when it is, as it were, unrolled, will disclose what happened in
each locality, but the facts about the Athenians of that age and
the enemies with whom they fought we must necessarily
describe first, at the outset—the military power, that is to say,
of each and their forms of government. And of these two we
must give the priority in our account to the state of Athens.

"Once upon a time the gods were taking over by lot the   B
whole earth according to its regions—not according to the
results of strife: for it would not be reasonable to suppose that
the gods were ignorant of their own several rights, nor yet
that they attempted to obtain for themselves by means of
strife a possession to which others, as they knew, had a better
claim. So by just allotments they received each one his own,
and they settled their countries, and when they had settled
them, they reared us up, even as herdsmen rear their flocks,
to be their cattle and nurslings; only it was not our bodies that
they constrained by bodily force, like shepherds guiding their   C
flocks with stroke of staff, but they directed from the stern
where the living creature is easiest to turn about, laying hold
on the soul by persuasion, as by a rudder, according to their
own disposition; and thus they drove and steered all the
mortal kind. Now in other regions others of the gods had
their allotments and ordered the affairs, but inasmuch as
Hephaestus and Athena were a like nature, being born of the
same father, and agreeing, moreover, in their love of wisdom
and of craftsmanship, they both took for their joint portion

this land of ours as being naturally congenial and adapted   D
for virtue and for wisdom, and therein they planted as native
to the soil men of virtue and ordained to their mind the mode
of government. And of these citizens the names are
preserved, but their works have vanished owing to the
repeated destruction of their successors and the length of the
intervening periods. For, as was said before, the stock that
survived on each occasion was a remnant of unlettered
mountaineers which had heard the names only of the rulers,
and but little besides of their works. So though they gladly   E
passed on these names to their descendants, concerning the
mighty deeds and the laws of their predecessors they had no
knowledge, save for some invariably obscure reports; and
since, moreover, they and their children for many
generations were themselves in want of the necessaries of life,
their attention was given to their own needs and all their talk
was about them, and in consequence they paid no regard   110A
to the happenings of bygone ages. For legendary lore and the
investigation of antiquity are visitants that come to cities in
company with leisure, when they see that men are already
furnished with the necessaries of life, and not before.

"In this way, then, the names of ancients, without their
works, have been preserved. And for evidence of what I say I
point to the statement of Solon, that the Egyptian priests, in
describing the war of that period, mentioned most of those   B
names—such as those of Cecrops and Erechtheus and
Erichthonius and Erysichthon and most of the other names
which are recorded of the various heroes before Theseus—
and in like manner also the names of the women. Moreover,
the habit and figure of the goddess indicate that in the case of
all animals, male and female, that herd together, every species   C
is naturally capable of practising as a whole and in common its
own proper excellence.

"Now at that time there dwelt in this country not only the
other classes of the citizens who were occupied in the
handicrafts and in the raising of food from the soil, but also
the military class, which had been separated off at the
commencement by divine heroes and dwelt apart. It was
supplied with all that was required for its sustenance and
training, and none of its members possessed any private
property; and from the rest of the citizens they claimed to   D

receive nothing beyond a sufficiency of sustenance; and they
practised all those pursuits which were mentioned yesterday,
in the description of our proposed 'Guardians.' Moreover,
what was related about our country was plausible and true,
namely, that, in the first place, it had its boundaries at that
time marked off by the Isthmus, and on the inland side
reaching to the heights of Cithaeron and Parnes; and that the
boundaries ran down with Oropia on the right, and on the   E
seaward side they shut off the Asopus on the left; and that all
other lands were surpassed by ours in goodness of soil, so that
it was actually able at that period to support a large host which
was exempt from the labours of husbandry. And of its
goodness a strong proof is this: what is now left of our soil
rivals any other in being all productive and abundant in crops
and rich in pasturage for all kinds of cattle; and at that
period, in addition to their fine quality it produced these   111A
things in vast quantity. How, then, is this statement plausible,
and what residue of the land then existing serves to confirm
the truth? The whole of the land lies like a promontory
jutting out from the rest of the continent far into the sea; and
all the cup of the sea round about it is, as it happens, of a great
depth. Consequently, since many great convulsions took place
during the 9,000 years—for such was the number of years
from that time to this—the soil which has kept breaking away   B
from the high lands during these ages and these disasters,
forms no pile of sediment worth mentioning, as in other
regions, but keeps sliding away ceaselessly and disappearing
in the deep. And, just as happens in small islands, what now
remains compared with what then existed is like the skeleton
of a sick man, all the fat and soft earth having wasted away,
and only the bare framework of the land being left. But at
that epoch the country was unimpaired, and for its mountains   C
it had high arable hills, and in place of the 'moorlands,' as
they are now called, it contained plains full of rich soil; and it
had much forest-land in its mountains, of which there are
visible signs even to this day; for there are some mountains
which now have nothing but food for bees, but they had trees
no very long time ago, and the rafters from those felled there
to roof the largest buildings are still sound. And besides, there
were many lofty trees of cultivated species; and it produced
boundless pasturage for flocks. Moreover, it was enriched by

the yearly rains from Zeus, which were not lost to it, as now,   D
by flowing from the bare land into the sea; but the soil it had
was deep, and therein it received the water, storing it up in
the retentive loamy soil; and by drawing off into the hollows
from the heights the water that was there absorbed, it
provided all the various districts with abundant supplies of
springwaters and streams, whereof the shrines which still
remain even now, at the spots where the fountains formerly
existed, are signs which testify that our present description of
the land is true.

"Such, then, was the natural condition of the rest of the   E
country, and it was ornamented as you would expect from
genuine husbandmen who made husbandry their sole task,
and who were also men of taste and of native talent, and
possessed of most excellent land and a great abundance of
water, and also, above the land, a climate of most happily
tempered seasons. And as to the city, this is the way in which it
was laid out at that time. In the first place, the Acropolis, as it
existed then, was different from what it is now. For as it is   112A
now, the action of a single night of extraordinary rain has
crumbled it away and made it bare of soil, when earthquakes
occurred simultaneously with the third of the disastrous
floods which preceded the destructive deluge in the time of
Deucalion. But in its former extent, at an earlier period, it
went down towards the Eridanus and the Ilissus, and
embraced within it the Pnyx, and had the Lycabettus as its
boundary over against the Pnyx; and it was all rich in soil and,
save for a small space, level on the top. And its outer parts,   B
under its slopes, were inhabited by the craftsmen and by such
of the husbandmen as had their farms close by; but on the
topmost part only the military class by itself had its dwelling
round about the temple of Athene and Hephaestus,
surrounding themselves with a single ring-fence, which
formed, as it were, the enclosure of a single dwelling. On the
northward side of it they had established their public
dwellings and winter mess-rooms, and all the arrangements in
the way of buildings which were required for the community   C
life of themselves and the priests; but all was devoid of gold or
silver, of which they made no use anywhere; on the contrary,
they aimed at the mean between luxurious display and
meanness, and built themselves tasteful houses, wherein they

25

and their children's children grew old and handed them on in
succession unaltered to others like themselves. As for the
southward parts, when they vacated their gardens and
gymnasia and mess-rooms as was natural in summer, they
used them for these purposes. And near the place of the
present Acropolis there was one spring—which was choked   D
up by the earthquakes so that but small tricklings of it are now
left round about; but to the men of that time it afforded a
plentiful stream for them all, being well tempered both for
winter and summer. In this fashion, then, they dwelt, acting
as guardians of their own citizens and as leaders, by their own
consent, of the rest of the Greeks; and they watched carefully
that their own numbers, of both men and women, who were
neither too young nor too old to fight, should remain for all
time as nearly as possible the same, namely, about 20,000.

"So it was that these men, being themselves of the character   E
described and always justly administering in some such
fashion both their own land and Hellas, were famous
throughout all Europe and Asia both for their bodily beauty
and for the perfection of their moral excellence, and were of
all men then living the most renowned. And now, if we have
not lost recollection of what we heard when we were still
children, we will frankly impart to you all, as friends, our
story of the men who warred against our Athenians, what
their state was and how it originally came about.

"But before I begin my account, there is still a small point   113A
which I ought to explain, lest you should be surprised at
frequently hearing Greek names given to barbarians. The
reason for this you shall now learn. Since Solon was planning
to make use of the story for his own poetry, he had found, on
investigating the meaning of the names, that those Egyptians
who had first written them down had translated them into
their own tongue. So he himself in turn recovered the original
sense of each name and, rendering it into our tongue, wrote it
down so. And these very writings were in the possession of my   B
grandfather and are actually now in mine, and when I was a
child I learnt them all by heart. Therefore if the names you
hear are just like our local names, do not be at all astonished;
for now you know the reason for them. The story then told
was a long one, and it began something like this.

"Like as we previously stated concerning the allotments of

the Gods, that they portioned out the whole earth, here into
larger allotments and there into smaller, and provided for   C
themselves shrines and sacrifices, even so Poseidon took for
his allotment the island of Atlantis and settled therein the
children whom he had begotten of a mortal woman in a
region of the island of the following description. Bordering
on the sea and extending through the centre of the whole
island there was a plain, which is said to have been the fairest
of all plains and highly fertile; and, moreover, near the plain,
over against its centre, at a distance of about 50 stades, there
stood a mountain that was low on all sides. Thereon dwelt one
of the natives originally sprung from the earth, Evenor by
name, with his wife Leucippe; and they had for offspring an   D
only-begotten daughter, Cleito. And when this damsel was
now come to marriageable age, her mother died and also her
father; and Poseidon, being smitten with desire for her,
wedded her; and to make the hill whereon she dwelt
impregnable he broke it off all round about; and he made
circular belts of sea and land enclosing one another
alternately, some greater, some smaller, two being of land and
three of sea, which he carved as it were out of the midst of the
island; and these belts were at even distances on all sides, so as
to be impassable for man; for at that time neither ships nor   E
sailing were as yet in existence. And Poseidon himself set in
order with ease, as a god would, the central island, bringing
up from beneath the earth two springs of waters, the one
flowing warm from its source, the other cold, and producing
out of the earth all kind of food in plenty. And he begat five
pairs of twin sons and reared them up; and when he had
divided all the island of Atlantis into ten portions, he assigned
to the first-born of the eldest sons his mother's dwelling and
the allotment surrounding it, which was the largest and best;   114A
and him he appointed to be king over the rest, and the others
to be rulers, granting to each the rule over many men and a
large tract of country. And to all of them he gave names,
giving to him that was eldest and king the name after which
the whole island was called and the sea spoken of as the
Atlantic, because the first king who then reigned had the
name of Atlas. And the name of his younger twin-brother,   B
who had for his portion the extremity of the island near the
pillars of Heracles up to the part of the country now called

27

Gadeira after the name of that region, was Eumelus in Greek, but in the native tongue Gadeirus—which fact may have given its title to the country. And of the pair that were born next he called the one Ampheres and the other Evaemon; and of the third pair the elder was named Mneseus and the younger Autochthon; and of the fourth pair, he called the first Elasippus and the second Mestor; and of the fifth pair, Azaes was the name given to the elder, and Diaprepês to the second. So all these, themselves and their descendants, dwelt for many generations bearing rule over many other islands throughout the sea, and holding sway besides, as was previously stated, over the Mediterranean peoples as far as Egypt and Tuscany.

C

"Now a large family of distinguished sons sprang from Atlas; but it was the eldest, who, as king, always passed on the sceptre to the eldest of his sons, and thus they preserved the sovereignty for many generations; and the wealth they possessed was so immense that the like had never been seen before in any royal house nor will ever easily be seen again; and they were provided with everything of which provision was needed either in the city or throughout the rest of the country. For because of their headship they had a large supply of imports from abroad, and the island itself furnished most of the requirements of daily life—metals, to begin with, both the hard kind and the fusible kind, which are extracted by mining, and also that kind which is now known only by name but was more than a name then, there being mines of it in many places of the island—I mean 'orichalcum,' which was the most precious of the metals then known, except gold. It brought forth also in abundance all the timbers that a forest provides for the labours of carpenters; and of animals it produced a sufficiency, both tame and wild. Moreover, it contained a very large stock of elephants; for there was an ample food-supply not only for all the other animals which haunt the marshes and lakes and rivers, or the mountains or the plains, but likewise also for this animal, which of its nature is the largest and most voracious. And in addition to all this, it produced and brought to perfection all those sweet-scented stuffs which the earth produces now, whether made of roots or herbs or trees, or of liquid gums derived from flowers or fruits. The cultivated fruit also, and the dry, which serves us

D

E

115A

28

for nutriment, and all the other kinds that we use for our meals—the various species of which are comprehended under the name 'vegetables'—and all the produce of trees which affords liquid and solid food and unguents, and the fruit of the orchard trees, so hard to store, which is grown for the sake of amusement and pleasure, and all the after-dinner fruits that we serve up as welcome remedies for the sufferer from repletion—all these that hallowed island, as it lay then beneath the sun, produced in marvellous beauty and endless abundance. And thus, receiving from the earth all these products, they furnished forth their temples and royal dwellings, their harbours and their docks, and all the rest of their country, ordering all in the fashion following.

B

C

"First of all they bridged over the circles of sea which surrounded the ancient metropolis, making thereby a road towards and from the royal palace. And they had built the palace at the very beginning where the settlement was first made by their God and their ancestors; and as each king received it from his predecessors, he added to its adornment and did all he could to surpass the king before him, until finally they made of it an abode amazing to behold for the magnitude and beauty of the workmanship. For, beginning at the sea, they bored a channel right through the outermost circle, which was three plethra in breadth, one hundred feet in depth, and fifty stades in length; and thus they made the entrance to it from the sea like that to a harbour by opening out a mouth large enough for the greatest ships to sail through. Moreover, through the circles of land, which divided those of sea, over against the bridges they opened out a channel leading from circle to circle, large enough to give passage to a single trireme; and this they roofed over above so that the sea-way was subterranean; for the lips of the land circles were raised sufficient height above the level of the sea. The greatest of the circles into which a boring was made for the sea was three stades in breadth, and the circle of land next to it was of equal breadth; and of the second pair of circles that of water was two stades in breadth and that of dry land equal again to the preceding one of the water; and the circle which ran round the central island itself was of a stade's breadth. And this island, wherein stood the royal palace, was of five stades in diameter. Now the island and the circles and

D

E

116A

the bridge, which was a plethrum in breadth, they
encompassed round about, on this side and on that, with a
wall of stone; and upon the bridges on each side, over against
the passages for the sea, they erected towers and gates. And
the stone they quarried beneath the central island all round,
and from beneath the outer and inner circles, some of it being
white, some black, and some red; and while quarrying it they   B
constructed two inner docks, hollowed out and roofed over by
the native rock. And of the buildings some they framed of
one simple colour, in others they wove a pattern of many
colours by blending the stones for the sake of ornament so as
to confer upon the buildings a natural charm. And they
covered with brass, as though with plaster, all the
circumference of the wall which surrounded the outermost
circle; and that of the inner one they coated with tin; and that
which encompassed the acropolis itself with orichalcum which   C
sparkled like fire.

"The royal palace within the acropolis was arranged in this
manner. In the centre there stood a temple sacred to Cleito
and Poseidon, which was reserved as holy ground, and
encircled with a wall of gold; this being the very spot where at
the beginning they had generated and brought to birth the
family of the ten royal lines. Thither also they brought year by
year from all the ten allotments their seasonable offerings to
do sacrifice to each of those princes. And the temple of   D
Poseidon himself was a stade in length, three plethra in
breadth, and of a height which appeared symmetrical
therewith; and there was something of the barbaric in its
appearance. All the exterior of the temple they coated with
silver, save only the pinnacles, and these they coated with
gold. As to the interior, they made the roof all of ivory in
appearance, variegated with gold and silver and orichalcum,
and all the rest of the walls and pillars and floors they covered
with orichalcum. And they placed therein golden statues, one
being that of the God standing on a chariot and driving six
winged steeds, his own figure so tall as to touch the ridge of   E
the roof, and round about him a hundred Nereids on
dolphins (for that was the number of them as men then
believed); and it contained also many other images, the votive
offerings of private men. And outside, round about the
temple, there stood images in gold of all the princes, both

themselves and their wives, as many as were descended from
the ten kings, together with many other votive offerings both
of the kings and of private persons not only from the State
itself but also from all the foreign peoples over whom they
ruled. And the altar, in respect of its size and its
workmanship, harmonized with its surroundings; and the   117A
royal palace likewise was such as befitted the greatness of the
kingdom, and equally befitted the splendour of the temples.

"The springs they made use of one kind being of cold,
another of warm water, were of abundant volume, and each
kind was wonderfully well adapted for use because of the
neutral taste and excellence of its waters; and these they
surrounded with buildings and with plantations of trees such
as suited the waters; and, moreover, they set reservoirs round   B
about, some under the open sky, and others under cover to
supply hot baths in the winter; they put separate baths for the
kings and for the private citizens, besides others for women,
and others again for horses and all other beasts of burden,
fitting out each in an appropriate manner. And the
outflowing water they conducted to the sacred grove of
Poseidon, which contained trees of all kinds that were of
marvellous beauty and height because of the richness of the
soil; and by means of channels they led the water to the outer
circles over against the bridges. And there they had
constructed many temples for gods, and many gardens and   C
many exercising grounds, some for men and some set apart
for horses, in each of the circular belts of island; and besides
the rest they had in the centre of the large island a race course
laid out for horses, which was a stade in width, while as to
length, a strip which ran round the whole circumference was
reserved for equestrian contests. And round about it, on this
side and on that, were barracks for the greater part of the
spearmen; but the guard-house of the more trusty of them
was posted in the smaller circle, which was nearer the acropolis;   D
while those who were the most trustworthy of all
had dwellings granted to them within the acropolis round
about the persons of the kings.

"And the shipyards were full of triremes and all the
tackling that belongs to triremes, and they were all amply
equipped.

"Such then was the state of things round about the abode of

the kings. And after crossing the three outer harbours, one E
found a wall which began at the sea and ran round in a circle,
at a uniform distance of fifty stades from the largest circle and
harbour, and its ends converged at the seaward mouth of the
channel. The whole of this wall had numerous houses built on
to it, set close together; while the sea-way and the largest
harbour were filled with ships and merchants coming from all
quarters, which by reason of their multitude caused clamour
and tumult of every description and an unceasing din night
and day.

"Now as regards the city and environs of the ancient
dwelling we have now wellnigh completed the description as it
was originally given. We must endeavour next to repeat the 118A
account of the rest of the country, what its natural character
was, and in what fashion it was ordered. In the first place,
then, according to the account, the whole region rose sheer
out of the sea to a great height, but the part about the city was
all a smooth plain, enclosing it round about, and being itself
encircled by mountains which stretched as far as to the sea;
and this plain had a level surface and was a rectangle in shape,
being 3,000 stades long on either side and 2,000 stades wide at
its centre, reckoning upwards from the sea. And this region, B
all along the island, faced towards the south and was sheltered
from the northern blasts. And the mountains which
surrounded it were at that time celebrated as surpassing all
that now exist in number, magnitude and beauty; for they
had upon them many rich villages of country folk, and
streams and lakes and meadows which furnished ample
nutriment to all the animals both tame and wild, and timber
of various sizes and descriptions, abundantly sufficient for the
needs of all and every craft.

"Now as the result of natural forces, together with the C
labours of many kings which extended over many ages, the
condition of the plain was this. It was originally a quadrangle,
rectilinear for the most part, and elongated; and what it
lacked of this shape they made right by means of a trench dug
round about it. Now, as regards the depth of this trench and
its breadth and length, it seems incredible that it should be so
large as the account states, considering that it was made by
hand, and in addition to all the other operations, but none the
less we must report what we heard: it was dug out to the D

depth of a plethrum and to a uniform breadth of a stade, and
since it was dug round the whole plain its consequent length
was 10,000 stades. It received the streams which came down
from the mountains and after circling round the plain, and
coming towards the city on this side and on that, it discharged
them thereabouts into the sea. And on the inland side of the
city the channels were cut in straight lines, of about 100 feet in
width, across the plain, and these discharged themselves into
the trench on the seaward side, the distance between each
being 100 stades. It was in this way that they conveyed to the   E
city the timber from the mountains and transported also on
boats the seasons' products, by cutting transverse passages
from one channel to the next and also to the city. And they
cropped the land twice a year, making use of the rains from
Heaven in the winter, and the waters that issue from the earth
in summer, by conducting the streams from the trenches.

"As regards their man-power, it was ordained that each
allotment should furnish one man as leader of all men in the
plain who were fit to bear arms; and the size of the allotment   119A
was about ten times ten stades, and the total number of all the
allotments was 60,000; and the number of the men in the
mountains and in the rest of the country was countless,
according to the report, and according to their districts and
villages they were all assigned to these allotments under their
leaders. So it was ordained that each such leader should
provide for war the sixth part of a war-chariot's equipment, so
as to make up 10,000 chariots in all, together with two horses
and mounted men; also a pair of horses without a car, and   B
attached thereto a combatant with a small shield and for
charioteer the rider who springs from horse to horse; and two
hoplites; and archers and slingers, two of each; and
lightarmed slingers and javelin-men, three of each; and four
sailors towards the manning of twelve hundred ships. Such
then were the military dispositions of the royal City; and those
of the other nine varied in various ways, which it would take a
long time to tell.

"Of the magistracies and posts of honour the disposition,   C
ever since the beginning, was this. Each of the ten kings ruled
over the men and most of the laws in his own particular
portion and throughout his own city, punishing and putting
to death whomsoever he willed. But their authority over one

33

another and their mutual relations were governed by the precepts of Poseidon, as handed down to them by the law and by the records inscribed by the first princes on a pillar of orichalcum, which was placed within the temple of Poseidon in the centre of the island; and thither they assembled every fifth year, and then alternately every sixth year—giving equal honour to both the even and the odd—and when thus assembled they took counsel about public affairs and inquired if any had in any way transgressed and gave judgement. And when they were about to give judgement they first gave pledges one to another of the following description. In the sacred precincts of Poseidon there were bulls at large; and the ten princes, being alone by themselves, after praying to the God that they might capture a victim wellpleasing unto him, hunted after the bulls with staves and nooses but with no weapon of iron; and whatsoever bull they captured they led up to the pillar and cut its throat over the top of the pillar, raining down blood on the inscription. And inscribed upon the pillar, besides the laws, was an oath which invoked mighty curses upon them that disobeyed. When, then, they had done sacrifice according to their laws and were consecrating all the limbs of the bull, they mixed a bowl of wine and poured in on behalf of each one a gout of blood, and the rest they carried to the fire, when they had first purged the pillar round about. And after this they drew out from the bowl with golden ladles, and making libation over the fire swore to give judgement according to the laws upon the pillars and to punish whosoever had committed any previous transgression; and, moreover, that henceforth they would not transgress any of the writings willingly, nor govern nor submit to any governor's edict save in accordance with their father's laws. And when each of them had made this invocation both for himself and for his seed after him, he drank of the cup and offered it up as a gift in the temple of the God; and after spending the interval in supping and necessary business, when darkness came on and the sacrificial fire had died down, all the princes robed themselves in most beautiful sable vestments, and sat on the ground beside the cinders of the sacramental victims throughout the night, extinguishing all the fire that was round about the sanctuary; and there they gave and received judgement, if any of them accused any of

D

E

120A

B

C

34

committing any transgression. And when they had given
judgement, they wrote the judgements, when it was light,
upon a golden tablet, and dedicated them together with their
robes as memorials. And there were many other special laws
concerning the peculiar rights of the several princes, whereof
the most important were these: that they should never take
up arms against one another, and that, should anyone
attempt to overthrow in any city their royal house, they
should all lend aid, taking counsel in common, like their   D
forerunners, concerning their policy in war and other
matters, while conceding the leadership to the royal branch of
Atlas; and that the king had no authority to put to death any
of his brother-princes save with the consent of more than half
of the ten.

"Such was the magnitude and character of the power which
existed in those regions at that time; and this power the God
set in array and brought against these regions of ours on some
such pretext as the following, according to the story. For
many generations, so long as the inherited nature of the   E
God remained strong in them, they were submissive to the laws
and kindly disposed to their divine kindred. For the intents of
their hearts were true and in all ways noble, and they showed
gentleness joined with wisdom in dealing with the changes
and chances of life and in their dealings with one another.
Consequently they thought scorn of everything save virtue
and lightly esteemed their rich possessions, bearing with ease
the burden, as it were, of the vast volume of their gold and
other goods; and thus their wealth did not make them drunk   121A
with pride so that they lost control of themselves and went to
ruin; rather, in their soberness of mind they clearly saw that
all these good things are increased by general amity combined
with virtue, whereas the eager pursuit and worship of these
goods not only causes the goods themselves to diminish but
makes virtue also to perish with them. As a result, then, of
such reasoning and of the continuance of their divine nature
all their wealth had grown to such a greatness as we
previously described. But when the portion of divinity within
them was now becoming faint and weak through being
ofttimes blended with a large measure of mortality, whereas   B
the human temper was becoming dominant, then at length
they lost their comeliness, through being unable to bear the

35

burden of their possessions, and became ugly to look upon, in
the eyes of him who has the gift of sight; for they had lost the
fairest of their goods from the most precious of their parts;
but in the eyes of those who have no gift of perceiving what is
the truly happy life, it was then above all that they appeared
to be superlatively fair and blessed, filled as they were with
lawless ambition and power. And Zeus, the God of gods, who
reigns by Law, inasmuch as he has the gift of perceiving such
things, marked how this righteous race was in evil plight, and
desired to inflict punishment upon them, to the end that
when chastised they might strike a truer note. Wherefore he
assembled together all the gods into that abode which they
honour most, standing as it does at the centre of all the
Universe, and beholding all things that partake of generation;
and when he had assembled them, he spake thus: . . ."

CHAPTER THREE

THE ANATOMY OF THE ATLANTIS ACCOUNT

Fundamental challenges to disciplines tend to come from outside. It is customary for students to be introduced to their fields of study gradually, as slowly unfolding mysteries, so that by the time they can see their subject as a whole, they have been so thoroughly imbued with conventional preconceptions and patterns of thought that they are extremely unlikely to be able to question its basic premises.[12]

I realize there is too much hypothesis in what I have suggested. There must be better and even simpler explanations.[13]

THE BELIEVERS

There are two principal ways to interpret Plato's story of Atlantis: either it is predominantly an historical account, with presumably some distortions, or it represents fiction probably based, in some measure, on fact. No one, however, has been able to argue convincingly in which of these two groups Plato's report belongs. Two major obstacles prevented a plausible interpretation of the Atlantis legend: firstly, the enormously diverse expertise required to investigate the account, entailing disciplines such as ancient history, philology, archaeology and paleogeography, and secondly, the "conventional preconceptions and patterns of thought" mentioned at the beginning of this chapter in the quotation by Martin Bernal. Our current attitudes toward Atlantis, even the subconscious feelings of people who never gave any thought to the subject (myself included), stem from a fierce controversy which has raged throughout much of this century. The people involved in the debate can be grouped into advocates of a once existent but possibly misrepresented Atlantis—they are usually called "believers"—and those who assume that Plato invented the whole story; they are called "non-believers." Even within the two camps, however, no consensus of opinion has ever been reached. To understand our predominantly negative gut reactions about any attention to Atlantis, it will be necessary to review briefly the debate that dominated the last century.

One of the most senior scientists ever involved in the Atlantis debate was Spyridon Marinatos, the excavator of Akrotiri on Santorini. He once remarked during an interview with journalist Ernst von Khuon that Atlantis ranks only second to the Bible in terms of numbers of publications.[14] Some people put the number of books dealing with Atlantis at only 100,[15] 2,000[16] or 5,000;[17] others estimate it at 20,000,[18] 25,000[19] or even 50,000.[20] The lost continent has been thought to have existed at over forty locations, including sites in the Caucasus, the Netherlands, the Bahamas, the Arctic, Mongolia, Tunisia, Crimea, Malta, Iran, Australia, Spitzbergen, Ceylon, Brazil, Prussia, North and South America, Bimini, South Africa, Morocco, Nigeria, Heligoland, Portugal, Spain and Greenland.[21] Various faunal phenomena have been attributed to the disappearance of Atlantis, including the suicidal habits of Norwegian lemmings,[22] who—like eels[23]—direct their migratory habits to lost Atlantis. One author, Immanuel Velikovsky, even claimed that Atlantis was destroyed by a comet which later became the planet Venus.[24] Erich von Däniken, finally, moved Atlantis to outer space.[25]

The history of Atlantis interpretations represents an example *par excellence* for the variability of human perception with time. For the last five hundred years many major scientific discoveries and *Zeitgeist* trends were immediately applied to the Atlantis legend. True "Atlantis research" beyond the occasional comment took off after the discovery of the New World. Francisco López da Gómara was the first to suggest (in 1553) that the New World itself must have been Atlantis,[26] while the Jesuit Athanasius Kircher in his book

© 1981 United Feature Syndicate, Inc. Reprinted by permission.

Mundus subterranes (1665) first saw the Azores as Plato's legendary island.[27] Both of these early ideas are still current today. The most influential book ever written on Atlantis appeared in 1882, and it was still in print in 1970: in *Atlantis—The Antediluvian World* Ignatius Donelly used the recent discovery of a submarine mountain ridge in the middle of the North Atlantic to incite the Atlantis discussion.

Another scientific breakthrough that appeared to be relevant for the understanding of the Atlantis account was the discovery of the Late and Middle Bronze Age civilizations in Greece by Heinrich Schliemann and Arthur Evans. In 1909 an anonymous letter entitled "The Lost Continent" appeared in *The Times*, triggering a scientific dispute that still goes on today. The author of the letter, K.T. Frost,[28] revealed himself a few years later in a follow-up article for a scientific journal.[29] These two reports perhaps represent the most rational contributions to the interpretation of Plato's Atlantis account ever produced. Unfortunately, Frost became a victim of Evans's publicity efforts for the excavations on Crete and as a result he understated Schliemann's discovery of the Mycenaean era on the Greek mainland (which Arthur Evans had called Late Minoan III) and concluded that, of all the discoveries made in recent years that of Minoan Crete is the most amazing and the most vital to the reconstruction of the Mediterranean history.[30]

Frost deduced that Plato's Atlantis account rested on an epic poem describing the demise of the Minoan civilization on Crete. His ideas were picked up in the late 1960s, when two further breakthroughs occurred: one was the moon landing by Apollo XI, making people feel that at this stage of technical achievement the world ought to be able to solve its oldest historical riddle. The second was the discovery of an ash layer in the Mediterranean which was thought to be from an eruption of Thera (Santorini), a volcano in the Aegean. A string of books published in 1969 claimed that this eruption caused the sudden downfall of the Minoan culture and that these events were, as Frost had suggested, reflected in the Atlantis account.[31] Over twenty years later, the Santorini hypothesis has lost both its persuasiveness and its supporters, because radiocarbon dating revealed that the eruption of Thera occurred before the peak of the Minoan culture. Nevertheless, some scholars, not including the initial advocates, still maintain that Atlantis reflects impressions of the Minoan civilization.[32]

THE NONBELIEVERS

One discipline, above all others, may appear most liable to provide a satisfactory explanation of the Atlantis enigma: ancient philology. This field has recently produced the most rigorous nonbelievers and their views are largely responsible for our current conventional preconceptions of a fictitious Atlantis. An analysis of philological research into the subject, however, reveals a striking lack of thorough, scientific investigations into the Atlantis account. A pronounced reserve and lack of interest appears to conceal a feeling of embarrassment that such nonsense really exists in ancient literature. Further scrutiny reveals that most philological authorities have restricted their comments on Atlantis to expressions of predominantly disapproving gut reactions, but hardly more than that.[33]

One hundred years ago, before the subject of Atlantis had such a bad image, the experts were much more open-minded. In the first English edition of *Timaeus*, R.D. Archer Hind considered it impossible to determine whether *"Plato has invented the story from beginning to end or whether it really more or less represents some Egyptian information brought home by Solon."*[34] Another influential Plato expert, A.E. Taylor, admits in the very first sentence of his *Commentary on Plato's Timaeus*,[35] that his interpretations were bound to be full of errors. He has only taken up the task of examining the *Timaeus*, because the book would not receive the combined attention of natural scientists, paleogeographers and philologists which it needed before it would be correctly interpreted:

> Either the *Timaeus* must be left uncommented or one who is not an "expert" must do what he can to elucidate it at the risk of making plenty of bad mistakes due to his inexpertness.[36]

Taylor's comments are a combination of brilliant expertise and common sense. He dissects the entire *Timaeus*, including the part on Atlantis, and finds various indications for the historicity of individual components of the account. Although he concludes that there is "no reason to suppose that the whole narrative is more than a fiction of Plato's own," he seems to regret the lack of any other plausible theory. Thus Taylor's work could hardly be interpreted as evidence for the fictional origin of the account, it is more a capitulation of the search for another, unifying explanation. He was later described as having spent a lifetime trying to prove that *every word* Plato wrote was historically based—with the exception of the Atlantis account![37]

In 1937 another Plato authority, Francis Macdonald Cornford seemed slightly more determined in his dismissal of Atlantis; nevertheless he only devoted a footnote[38] to the remark that "serious scholars now agree that Atlantis probably owed its existence entirely to Plato's imagination." He presents no evidence as to why these scholars have come to such a conclusion, and ignores the lively, highly intellectual debate that had occupied the geographic sciences for the two decades prior to the publication of his book.[39] Besides implying that anybody who does not accept this assertion could not be considered a "serious scholar," Cornford also produces a self-contradicting effect in this argument by using the word "probably": either the story rests *entirely* on Plato's imagination, or *probably*, but not both. Such an ambiguity is characteristic of the scientific perspective of the Atlantis account.

An analysis of the philological contributions to the Atlantis controversy shows that at least one-third of the authors infer an historic foundation in Plato's report. Some experts believe Atlantis represents the town of Helike,[40] which was destroyed during an earthquake in 373 B.C., a catastrophe frequently mentioned in ancient texts.[41] Others take it as a reflection on the Persian War (500–478 B.C.)[42] or as impressions of the Sicilian city of Syracuse, which Plato had visited a few times, and of its ruler's residence in particular.[43] Again, others declare that Atlantis should be thought of as part of Athens itself,[44] or that the Atlanteans reflect the lower part of the social soul, while the prehistoric Athenians represent its intellect.[45] Most nonbelievers, however, just consider the account as a "fine piece of literary fiction,"[46] without elaborating on their arguments—frequently admitting that the most obvious reading of the text would be as a factual account.[47]

HOW ABOUT A NEUTRAL APPROACH?

Scholarly discussions of Plato's account usually concentrate on the introduction of *Timaeus* and the final two paragraphs of *Critias*, which are strikingly consistent with Plato's political beliefs,[48] thus suggesting the whole narrative in between could be a "politico-philosophical myth."[49] This conception, however, disregards Plato's insistence, that the narrative represents a genuine historical tradition, as he states on different occasions in the text (20D, 26E). Nor does it explain why Plato's fictional world was mixed with sound scientific observations, for example the soil erosion in ancient Attika and its consequences for hydrology and agriculture. Furthermore, in *Critias*, Plato explicitly stated and frequently implied a genuine interest in prehistory—why would he ridicule his own concerns in the same book by producing such an incredible, inflated fairy tale?[50] Even disbelievers admit that the arguments against a fictional Atlantis outnumber the ones in favor.[51] There is the position of the story in a genuine scientific treatment of the history of the universe, and there are all the perfect matches between the transmission of the account as outlined by Plato and today's knowledge of Solon's travels and Athenian family lines. But there are still more, thus far neglected indications supporting the existence of a non-Platonic manuscript. The account appears plausible, because it expresses the narrator's admiration for the technical achievements in the legendary land and not for their ethical principles or cultic beliefs. It concentrates on providing minutiae about quarrying and shipbuilding, design and layout of architecture and artificial ports—mentioning nothing irrational of the kind usually found in Greek mythology.[52] An inclination toward technical descriptions is unknown in Plato's other work. In order to even think along these lines, Plato would have needed the mind of an engineer—much more so to invent the large number of plausible, but complex elements and their successful functioning together as a whole. Furthermore, the Egyptian priest, who relates the account, though not portrayed in much detail, reveals precisely the slightly pompous attitude one would expect to find in an Egyptian, sixth-century B.C. intellectual talking to a Greek peer.[53] This kind of subtlety is limited to genuine experience[54] or ingenuous artistry (although Plato may have gathered such impressions himself during a possible visit to Egypt).[55] Furthermore, nobody can be certain what the purpose of Plato's fictitious story might have been. Many humanists assume that it was supposed to show Plato's ideal state in action, but Atlantis is depicted as a bizarre, even "barbaric" looking place, where cultic rituals culminated in the brutish cutting up of bulls and the burning of their extremities. Atlantean aristocrats were allowed to murder whomever they wished, apart from peers (in whose cases they had to request permission first). Plato reports little about Atlantis that would make it qualify as an ideal state and therefore never uses this association outside the introduction. The ancient Greek opponent of Atlantis, however, would perhaps qualify as an exemplary state, but it is not the main subject of the narrative. If Atlantis really originated in Plato's mind only, he would have been able to produce a much more suitable story.[56]

Finally, nobody has so far been able to provide a convincing argument for the abrupt end of *Critias*. The prevailing assumption that Plato became tired of his own fiction appears pathetic.[57] Why would Plato want to describe in breathtaking length what Atlantis looked like, including such details as favored desserts and bathroom temperatures, without ever elaborating the philosophy behind this fictional world? The two final paragraphs, before the account breaks off, do mention some divine punishment for the Atlanteans, but these statements are surprisingly superficial and completely disproportionate to the length of the technical descriptions. Some people claim Plato may have maneuvered himself into a corner with his fantastic depiction of a fictional world,[58] but the careful structure of everything Plato wrote bears evidence that he knew the end before he started writing.

There are too many reasons to trust Plato's word and to presume that his comments about the Atlantis account reflect his sincere beliefs. Yet there is only one convincing argument why he should have invented it all, namely the lack of a sensible interpretation of where and what Atlantis could have been. We should not escape from our responsibility to find a sensible explanation by just calling Plato a fraud. Creating a myth out of nothing and to the extent he would have done with this narrative appears to me much more difficult than most disbelievers think. Plato would have had to weave fantasy carefully into the historic account itself, including the facts about Solon and his visit to Egypt, the realistic characterization of the Egyptian priest and the transmission. All of these components are plausible. So, too, is the characterization of the Greek high culture in the story, mentioning, for instance, the existence of writing long before Plato's time. Yet, despite this careful planning, Plato abandoned what could have been the perfect hoax. There are several examples of Plato's caution in handling oral narratives of dubious correctness. Why should he jeopardize his reputation by repeatedly emphasizing the accuracy of what really was a fairy tale? How many great thinkers has the world seen who invented a piece of fiction with the gravity of the Atlantis legend and then claimed again and again that it belonged in the real world—without losing their fame?

Fundamental breakthroughs in sciences have often been little more than assertions of what we would now consider indisputable facts: Newton's laws of mechanics, Wegener's continental drift and Darwin's evolutional relation of apes and humans are just some examples. Solving the Atlantis myth, too, might be achieved by just correlating obvious facts and removing unknowns, rather than introducing them. In the case of Atlantis, accepting the obvious would most likely mean accepting Plato's description of its origin. If Plato's arguments have always been historically based, the Atlantis account should be no exception to that rule. Furthermore, the riddle must be solved by employing the current level of archaeological knowledge only—without introducing sunken land masses and obscure civilizations. Scientific knowledge must be applied to elucidate the Atlantis account and not the other way around! Schliemann's attempt to reconstruct the Bronze Age from the *Iliad* and the *Odyssey* is as unacceptable today as it was 120 years ago (despite a large number of traditional historians who have, in a similar way, scoured Greece trying to recapitulate Pausanias' travels). With luck, we might be able to determine the conditions and moods which led ancient writers to their prose. To accept their writings as historic "fact" or "truth," even in the case of prosaic travel reports, would be naive.

My approach to solving the Atlantis enigma rests on the acceptance of today's historical and archaeological knowledge and on the assumption that Plato correctly described it as information collected abroad by somebody else. Since our understanding of prehistory and geology leaves no room for the existence of a highly civilized continent in the Atlantic Ocean 11,000 years ago, the first two premises require a third supposition: something must be wrong with the story! At least one more detail points in the same direction: the lack of an independent description of Atlantis, apart from Plato's account.[59] If such a fabulous city really existed, there should have been numerous reports of it, considering that it represented a mighty force attempting to suppress everybody else in the eastern Mediterranean.[60]

THE TRANSMISSION

A plausible explanation accommodating all the above premises would be that Plato's Atlantis story represents a "freak" version of a well-known legend describing a place which does indeed play a prominent role in both mythology and archaeology. In one individual line of transmission this story may have become so distorted that its true context was concealed from everybody involved. Fortunately, Plato himself describes in elaborate detail the particular transmission of the story. According to him it originated during a visit by Solon, a Greek merchant, statesman, general and poet, to Saïs, the governmental seat of Egypt in the sixth century B.C. In a conversation with the episcopate leaders in Saïs, Solon was told of unknown ancestors of the Greeks, whose fame extended throughout the eastern Mediterranean. According to the hieroglyphic columns from which the priests retrieved the story, the most remarkable deed of these ancient Greeks was the overthrow of the mighty Atlantis. Solon conveyed the mysterious

Egyptian narrative to Dropides—a relative and *"very dear friend"* (20E)—as emphasized in now lost poems by Solon. Dropides transmitted the story of Atlantis to his son, Critias the elder. Critias the younger, grandson of the former and narrator of the account in Plato's books, first heard about Atlantis during an *Apaturia* feast, held in October in honor of Dionysus, when he was ten years old and his grandfather close to ninety years of age (21B). Critias later emphasized that, as a child, when his grandfather was in possession of Solon's manuscript, he learned Solon's account by heart; but now he owned these writings himself, probably having inherited them (113B).

Plato's description of Critias' first encounter with the Atlantis legend at the *Apaturia* is surprisingly detailed, so vivid indeed that it may reflect an autobiographical experience. After all, Critias' and Plato's family lines were one and the same. Plato himself, as a child, may have learned of the Atlantis account during a family event such as the *Apaturia*. Later, as a renowned philosopher and teacher, he should have had access to the original manuscript, that is, if his description of the source is correct. Toward the end of his life, he could have incorporated the inherited account into his own writings, conceivably to provide a permanent record of a story which had captivated him as a child—a story he considered *"passing strange yet wholly true"* (20D). A truly fascinating story it was, destined to be lost in Plato's family if it was not published by him.

The knowledge of Solon's conversations with the priests in Saïs and the transmission of his notes were limited to this family only—the original manuscript was indeed lost, as were most of the rest of Solon's writings. Painstaking analysis of Athenian family lines[61] has revealed that Plato's proposed handing down of the account was chronologically possible if the conversation which is recollected in *Timaeus* and *Critias* took place at about 420 B.C.[62] At that time, Plato would have been only seven years old. He composed *Timaeus* and *Critias* around 360 B.C. Although Plato's suggested transmission works for the period between Solon's visit to Saïs to the year 420 B.C., to fill the gap of sixty years until the Atlantis account was actually recorded in writing, Plato himself must be introduced as one component of the transmission.

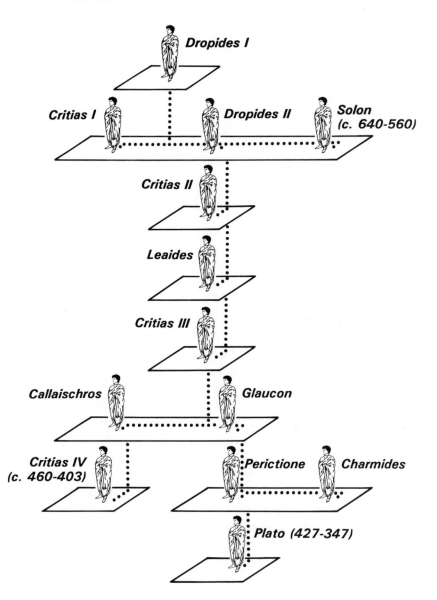

Plato's stemma, one of the longest attested family lines in Athens, allows a comparison between proven lineage and the suggested transmission of the Atlantis account (20E). Solon is said to have passed the story to Dropides II, who related it to his son, Critias II. The grandson of the former, Critias III, is the narrator in Plato's dialogues. (After Davies 1971 and Luce 1978, 76.)

PLATO

Despite the voluminous record of Plato's own writing, which survives to the present day, his personal life has remained relatively
unknown. The only sources of personal information on Plato are
the reports of Plutarch, Diogenes Laërtius and Diodorus Siculus
and his own Epistles, although some of these are forgeries.[63] Plato
(427–347 B.C.) undoubtedly descended from a wealthy, aristocratic
Athenian family. He began his career early by writing tragedies
and soon he became a follower and student of the philosopher
Socrates, whose execution in 399 B.C. had a devastating impact on
Plato. In the aftermath of Socrates' death Plato left his home in
Athens and moved to Megara, Syracuse in Sicily, mainland Italy
and possibly to Egypt and Phoenicia. After his return to Athens he
founded the Academy in 386 B.C. where he taught for twenty
years. In 367 B.C. he was invited to return to Syracuse as an adviser
to the ruling, thirty-year-old Dionysius II. In Syracuse, Plato soon
found himself embroiled in court intrigues and because of this
decided to return promptly to Athens. He moved again to Syracuse
in 361/360 B.C., but this third visit also ended in disaster.

Plato may have felt particularly attracted to southern Italy
because of the flourishing Pythagorean community at Taras. He
derived his philosophical principles to some extent from the doctrines of that group,[64] and his experiences in southern Italy could
have played an important role in the composition of the Atlantis
dialogues. Two of the main speakers in *Timaeus* and *Critias* are
from Sicily and southern Italy, the America of the Hellenic world in
those days.[65] Although Plato had become embroiled in intrigues
during each of his three visits to Magna Graecia—Diodorus Siculus
even relates that Plato ended up being sold as a slave at the end of
his first visit[66]—he returned from these journeys strongly inspired
by the Pythagorean school and may have embarked on the writing
of *Timaeus* and *Critias* just after his last visit to Syracuse in 360
B.C.[67]—although the precise date for the composition is not
actually known. Plato wrote one more voluminous book, the *Laws*,
after he abandoned work on *Critias*.

Plato's writing became common knowledge in antiquity, and
most ancient authors must have been familiar with his unfinished
Critias. A few casual remarks by later writers do not seem to
indicate any excitement about the story. The first to comment on it,
Aristotle (384–322 B.C.), Plato's prime pupil, brought Atlantis into

connection with Troy. Unfortunately, only third-hand knowledge of Aristotle's remarks survives; his precise comments are not preserved. The Greek geographer and historian Strabo (63 B.C.–A.D. 26) wrote in a serious, detailed treatment of the Trojan geography that Aristotle had compared Plato's Atlantis with the defense wall of the Greeks at Troy, saying, that "he who invented it also destroyed it."[68] The comment implies that Aristotle believed in the existence neither of Atlantis nor of a Greek defense wall at Troy (but then again, Aristotle *did* believe that women have fewer teeth than men). Due to the complicated transmission, however, his phrase about Atlantis may have been misunderstood or misquoted.

Aristotle's student Theophrastus (371–287 B.C.), however, considered the Atlantis story as at least partly grounded in fact.[69] The Syrian philosopher, geographer and historian Poseidonios (135–51 B.C.), friend and tutor of Cicero, also argued "that it is possible that the story about the island of Atlantis is not a fiction."[70] Strabo agreed with his view, although he generally considered Poseidonios too much a credulous enthusiast. There are no indications that any of these authors considered Atlantis to be elsewhere than outside the Straits of Gibraltar. A general acceptance of Plato's description could be explained by the presence of similar oral traditions in ancient Greece. Homer's description of Phaeacia, for example, has much in common with Atlantis (see chapter six), and so does Pindar's *Paean*.[71]

The last important representative and head of the Neo-Platonic, Athenian school, Proclus (A.D. 411–485), wrote elaborate comments about the *Timaeus*.[72] He reports the visit of Crantor, a Hellenic Greek, to Saïs, roughly one hundred years after Plato had composed *Timaeus* and *Critias*. Crantor knew the Atlantis account and was its first editor; he was able to visit the Neïth temple where he saw a column like the one mentioned in Plato's text, covered completely with hieroglyphic signs. Learned scribes translated the text for Crantor, and he found it to be in complete agreement with Plato's account. Once again, the interpretation of Proclus' text is ambiguous; he himself considered Crantor's view of an historic Atlantis to be naive, but equally rejected the other extreme that it is fully invented.[73] Since there are no fully reliable vindications of the historicity of the Atlantis account, the validation must be derived from the text itself.

THE CONVERSATION

Like most of Plato's books, *Timaeus* and *Critias* are written as dialogues, although in both cases the person whose name is the title dominates the presentation of ideas. People present during the conversation include Socrates, Timaeus, Critias and Hermocrates. The latter three are contesting for the best contribution to a traditional festival at which renowned epic poems were presented. The conversation between these four interlocutors may have been a public contest with a large audience, because the locality is twice described as a theater (108B, 108D). There is a controversy about the precise event. Some scholars assume that it was, as Proclus said,[74] the lesser *Panathenaea* festival held in early June, just after the *Bendideia*; others suggest the *Plynteria*.[75]

Most of the characters involved in the conversation are real. Socrates (470–399 B.C.), the discussion leader, was Plato's idol and teacher. Socrates, who left no writings of his own, was executed for his beliefs when Plato was twenty-nine years old. Socrates was the dominant character in Plato's life and philosophy; consequently he also assumed the main role in many of Plato's books. Timaeus, after whom the first dialogue of the trilogy was named, is introduced as a native of Locri in southern Italy. Since nothing authentic is known about him beyond the dialogue itself, there is no evidence that he actually lived. Timaeus is characterized as a distinguished scientist who has *"occupied the highest offices and posts of honor in his State"* (20A)—he is assumed to have been at least seventy years old at the time of the conversation.[76]

Most scholars today perceive Critias, the second speaker, to have been the grandfather of the tyrant by the same name; the latter lived from 460 to 403 B.C.[77] The former, who is taking part in the conversation, would have been Plato's own great-grandfather.[78] He is depicted as an old man who finds it easier to remember the long-distant past than what happened yesterday (26B). Critias appears in the earlier dialogues, *Charmides* and *Protagoras*, and was said to have been *"an amateur among philosophers, a philosopher among amateurs."*[79] Socrates may allude to this reputation by stating that *"all of us know, Critias is no amateur in any of the subjects we are discussing"* (20A).[80]

Hermocrates, the fourth person, is depicted as being a young, promising man who has not yet achieved anything notable.[81] There is general agreement that Plato's Hermocrates represents the man who later became a famous general and prominent citizen of Syracuse[82] and who, according to Forsyth, was well known for his anti-Athenian views.[83]

Although the festival and most characters are historical, the discourse, as Plato describes it, certainly never took place. Plato regularly used fictitious dialogues incorporating existing people for pedagogic purposes. Putting imaginary speeches in the mouth of historic characters was a common exercise in his time, practiced by Thucydides too.[84] Nevertheless, considering Plato's abilities and reputation, he must have been trying to set an example in this technique. He chose a date for the discussion that was chronologically coherent with the described transmission (20E). Around 420 B.C. all the characters could have been alive;[85] Socrates would then have been fifty years old, but Critias would have been around ninety,[86] perhaps impersonating the role of his own grandfather when the younger Critias first heard Solon's account. Plato also placed the discussion at a time when he himself was a seven-year-old boy, matching the young Critias's age at the first encounter with the story. Therefore, if the detailed description of the *Apaturia* festival indeed recollects an autobiographical experience of Plato, he has skilfully placed the dialogue at a time when he was the boy who first heard of Atlantis while Critias, the narrator, assumed the role of his own ninety-year-old grandfather of the same name.

PLATO'S INTENDED TRILOGY

Plato indicates unequivocally that Timaeus, Critias and Hermocrates were meant to contribute individually to the festival. Timaeus' presentation is complete, but Critias' stops in the middle of a sentence and the third volume, *Hermocrates*, was never begun,[87] although it was forecast in earlier remarks.[88] The intended trilogy was conceived as a description of the creation of the world and the history of its inhabitants. The contents of the trilogy rested largely on the scientific achievements of the Pythagorean school, and the whole project was apparently meant to express ideas with a distinct western flavor. Plato assigned each speaker, two of whom were westerners, a subject that suited their respective expertise:

Timaeus:	History of the earth
Critias:	Ancient Greece and its opponents abroad
Hermocrates:	Modern history

The first completed book, *Timaeus*, covers seventy-five pages in the Stephanus edition of 1578, from which today's quotation system is derived. The second volume, *Critias*, was left unfinished after fifteen pages in the Stephanus text. If *Critias* and the third book of the trilogy, *Hermocrates*, were intended to equal the first volume in length, Plato had finished just twenty percent of *Critias* and forty percent of the whole trilogy when he aborted the project.

TIMAEUS: PLATO AS A NATURAL SCIENTIST

Interpreting the story of Atlantis is made much easier by carefully examining the text's structure and its position in Plato's lifework. Furthermore, a reconstruction of the unfinished parts of the trilogy seems essential. Plato had just finished the *Politeia*, a ten-volume treatment of politics, when he began writing *Timaeus* and *Critias*. Although traditional interpretations assume that the Atlantis narrative illustrates Plato's ideal state as introduced in *Politeia* (*Republic*), Atlantis is not the focal point of *Timaeus* at all. The account itself covers three pages in Stephanus; most of the remaining seventy-two pages are devoted to the history of the earth and the knowledge of physical sciences and medicine. A list of contents in *Timaeus* stresses the subordinate role of Atlantis, which only appears in the introduction of this book[89] and has no significance for the main body of the text except as a link between *Politeia* and *Critias*.

I. INTRODUCTION
    a. Recollection of Socrates' speech on the ideal state
    b. Socrates' wish to hear about the existence of such a state
    c. *Solon's account of Atlantis*
    d. Critias expresses desire to present the whole story later

II. THE ORIGIN OF THE EARTH
    a. Being and becoming
    b. Body and soul of the earth
    c. Time and planets
    d. Living organisms

The main theme of *Timaeus* is the natural sciences: physics, biology and anatomy—unfamiliar subjects in Plato's writing.[90] The book's purpose is to summarize the best available knowledge of natural sciences, beginning with the creation of the world and its inhabitants. Plato uses this volume to provide what he considers an accurate synopsis of the then known elements of astronomy, the structure of matter, and human psychology and physiology. The book is organized chronologically, the first part dealing with the origin of the universe. Plato carries the reader's imagination to a point *"before the beginning of years,"* when *"the earth was without form and void."*[91] He then describes how the world gradually evolved into a harmonious body.

The merit of the scientific thinking as presented by Plato is disputed amongst Classical historians and philosophers; their judgment of the work ranges from "disaster" to "vindication." A.E. Taylor, however, considered the science in *Timaeus* *"to be in detail exactly what we should expect in a fifth-century Italian Pythagorean who was also a medical man."*[92] Plato is assumed to have derived these doctrines from earlier physicists, such as Empedocles and Alcmaeon; from contemporary Pythagoreans, including his friends Theaetetus and Eudoxus; and from the medical schools of Syracuse (Philistion) and Cos and Cnidos (Diogenes of Apollonia).[93] *Timaeus* may therefore be described as a chiefly eclectic composition of traditional and modern knowledge, possibly modified to suit Plato's own philosophy. In the eyes of the Cambridge scholar G.E.R. Lloyd, *Timaeus* *"is neither a provisional hypothesis, nor a myth in the sense of a baseless fiction,"*[94] but *"a document of first-rate importance in the history of Greek science."*[95] It may have been written to provide a permanent record of the scientific discoveries of Plato's science-oriented friends[96] and thus lacks his original thoughts beyond the strictly teleological view that all natural phenomena belong to an ultimate design.[97]

While most, if not all, of Plato's scientific knowledge presented in the *Timaeus* rests on the achievements of other scholars, many of his philosophical ideas may have been conceived in Socrates' mind first. Isocrates (436–338 B.C.), a contemporary thinker who had opened a rhetoric school in Athens a few years before Plato inaugurated his Academy, even accused the latter of plagiarism, saying that many of his principles rested on descriptions of the Egyptian socio-political system.[98] Proclus reports how Plato was derided by the people, for they knew that he could not be regarded as the genuine inventor of the *Politeia*.[99] According to Proclus' source, Crantor, Plato took the criticism so seriously that he embarked on the Atlantis story, which was indisputably unique.

The introduction of Timaeus first summarizes the preceding work *Politeia*. Next Critias, talking about Solon's experiences in Saïs, suggests a valid candidate for Socrates' ideal state as outlined in *Politeia*. But he declines to provide the complete story until his turn has come, after Timaeus has described the origin of the earth and the creation of man. Critias will then follow him to discuss the legendary achievements of the Greeks' prehistoric ancestors. This arrangement makes perfect sense if Plato considered the Atlantis account to be a historical narrative. As a piece of literary fiction invented by Plato, it could hardly have been more misplaced than in a scientific recollection about the history of the universe. This mismatch has been observed by a few Plato experts:

> I don't think it has been sufficiently noticed what an odd procedure this is. In reply to his comparatively simple question, 'Will my ideal state work?', Socrates has inflicted on him an extremely complex account of the physical world, followed by a piece of imaginary history, followed by an unknown *tertium quid*.[100]

In conclusion, *Timaeus* provides a summary of the current (fifth- and fourth-century B.C.) knowledge of natural sciences derived from various sources and not resting on Plato's own ideas and observations.[101] Atlantis merely appears in the introduction of the book in a subordinate role as a link between the preceding volume, *Politeia*, and the subsequent *Critias*.[102]

CRITIAS AND HERMOCRATES

Having covered most aspects of natural sciences, including the creation of the earth and human beings, the next two volumes, *Critias* and *Hermocrates* were meant to recollect the history from man's first appearance till Plato's time.[103] Only the first fraction of the latter two volumes was completed, and their intended contents must remain speculation. The existing contents of *Critias* has the following structure:

I. INTRODUCTION
    a. Pledge for indulgence
    b. Time scale and catastrophe
II. PREHISTORIC ATTIKA
    a. First settlements
    b. Political boundaries
    c. Soil conditions
    d. The city of Athens
III. ATLANTIS
    a. Nomenclature
    b. *Origins*
    c. *The city*
    d. *The geography*
    e. *Military*
    f. *Political and legal authority*
    g. *Degeneration and punishment*
IV. COUNCIL OF THE GODS

Perhaps the simplest reconstruction of Plato's plans for the remainder would render two synoptic books about history based on the same principle of composition as *Timaeus*. Gathering all available and credible sources of information about the past, Plato probably intended to draw an eclectic and unoriginal picture of history,[104] using his own philosophical perspective. Continuing in chronological order, Critias, as the next speaker, related what was known about prehistoric Greece, the famous predecessors of the

Athenians, their legendary enemies abroad and perhaps the dark ages which preceded the emergence of Classical Greece. Hermocrates, being a contemporary of Plato and a military man, no doubt was assigned the role of discussing the most recent political developments.[105] If Plato really intended to write three books of equal size, much unused historical material would have remained when he discontinued his work on the trilogy. Some of this material, however, seems to appear in his next and final book, the *Laws*.[106]

Just as *Timaeus* rests on principles established by predecessors and contemporaries of Plato, so, too, the remaining prehistoric and historical accounts *Critias* and *Hermocrates* were to be founded on information from extraneous sources, chiefly oral tradition and accounts by chronographers, as John Victor Luce said:

> Plato's method consists in accumulating materials rather than fabricating them. He constructs his account from the resources of a well-stocked mind, not an erratic imagination.[107]

Some of the information planned for incorporation in Plato's books must have been common knowledge in his day. Nevertheless, the intended trilogy would have comprised *"the most ambitious project he had ever conceived,"*[108] because he was entering unfamiliar ground. Contrary to most chronographers, Plato intended to provide a coherent, scientific account of the past. Such a recapitulation would ensure the survival of valuable ideas and oral reports and award Plato an opportunity to present the past in the light of his own doctrines.

To use a geological metaphor, the trilogy resembles a conglomerate with extraneous, non-Platonic theories representing pebbles of various size embedded and indestructibly cemented by Plato's own philosophy. This conglomeratic structure of the text explains why parts of the Atlantis account are fully accepted as traditional and accurate knowledge of ancient Attika, while other parts are clearly identified as Platonic philosophy, and again other parts are labeled as genuine fiction. Despite the solid fusion of matrix and inclusions, the boundaries between individual pebbles and surrounding cement remain sharp, and the different, foreign sources and Plato's own views are still identifiable. A knowledgeable scholar could use colored pencils to circle the various extraneous pieces in the text—and Plato experts have done precisely that, identifying the historical sources used in *Timaeus* and other books

Timaeus   **Critias**   **Hermocrates**

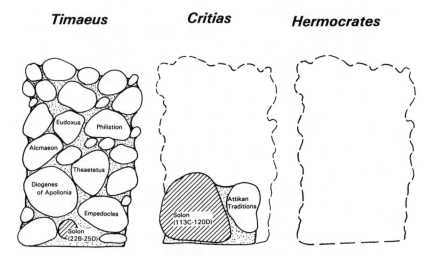

Plato's unfinished trilogy *Timaeus-Critias-Hermocrates* was intended as an "History of the Universe" presenting the observations of earlier and contemporary scholars, such as Eudoxus, Philistion, Alcmaeon and Solon. Thus, it resembled a conglomerate consisting of many pebbles, representing other people's achievements; only the matrix which cemented these pebbles was genuinely Platonic. Solon's account of Atlantis is just one of the alien pieces of information that was incorporated into Plato's work. It plays a minor role in *Timaeus* but was probably intended to be the centerpiece of *Critias*.

by Plato.[109] In principle, the provenance of most if not all of the pebbles has been identified—the one exception being the story of Atlantis. Yet, in this case source and transmission are provided by the author himself.

THE SPECIAL ROLE OF ATLANTIS

From this perspective Atlantis and its place in the trilogy are anything but unusual. It represents one of many non-Platonic elements describing the past. Plato placed it in the proper context of the chronologically ordered *Critias*. Nevertheless, the story stands out, because it exceeds in length any other non-Platonic element in the trilogy. Plato appears unusually excited about this element; perhaps because he knew that he was publishing a curious narrative of controversial reliability. He goes out of his way to ensure its correctness, thereby giving the impression that he himself might have been the only person who fully believed in its accuracy. The story could have meant more to Plato than to others, because he may have known it since childhood. The fact that the account went back to Solon, one of Plato's distant forefathers whom he respected highly, may have played a role too. But most importantly, Solon knew of thus-far-concealed feats by the ancient Athenians, and his account perfectly suited Plato's ideology, since it underlined a teleological view of the world, in which meticulously organized and highly stratified societies flourished, because they resembled *"a living and moving image of the immortal gods"* (37C). Thus, it may have been planned as the central piece of the trilogy, which would explain why Plato placed the whole conversation at around 420 B.C.—in accordance with the transmission of the Atlantis legend. Furthermore, since Atlantis was thought to be a high civilization in the far west, the story suited the overall western theme of the trilogy.

Conceivably, Plato could have introduced others to Solon's report who might have been more critical toward its reliability. Such potentially disappointing reactions are reflected in the lengthy prologue by Critias before he embarks on telling the whole story of Atlantis. Comparing his forthcoming presentation with Timaeus' speech on sciences, Critias remarks:

> It is easier to appear to speak satisfactorily to men about the gods, than to us about the mortals. For when the listeners are in a state of inexperience and complete ignorance about a matter, such a state of mind affords great opportunities to the person who is going to discourse on that matter. (107B)

Critias then goes on to explain how people are easily content with any painting of divinities as long as it bears some remote resemblance to their own images of the gods. But when a painter is portraying mortals, he is quickly criticized for even the smallest of flaws.

> And precisely the same thing happens, as we should notice, in the case of discourses: in respect of what is celestial and divine we are satisfied if the account possesses even a small degree of

likelihood, but we examine with precision what is mortal and human. (107D)

Critias therefore begs for a "greater rather than less measure of indulgence" (108A), perhaps expressing Plato's own insecurities about his attempt to paint a potentially distorted view of a real Atlantis. In the fictional dialogue, Socrates grants Critias permission to tell the story; in the real world, however, Plato never received much understanding from his readers for his failure to trust other people's judgment and to venture outside his own expertise. Human behavior and the validity of Plato's fears have not changed in 2,300 years: today we can smile at his attempt to derive the origin of women from reincarnated cowards and wrongdoers, as he does in the scientific parts of the *Timaeus* (91A), just as he explains rock formation by high air pressure (60D) and the sense of hearing as a process that starts at the head and ends in the liver (67B). But never will he be excused for outlining an ancient civilization in a way that does not absolutely match the historical and archaeological knowledge available in the twentieth century. The picture of Atlantis, despite all its details, was painted with a broad brush in the artistic style of the sixth century B.C., but it has been subjected to the microscopic scrutiny of modern times. Although no one can deny the usefulness of today's electron microscopes, for instance to examine the stomata of a leaf, will they help us to see the forest for the trees? To use the analogy of the conglomerate once more, Plato experts have employed extraordinary care in analyzing the matrix but not the pebble itself.

In the discussion that follows, I regard only *Timaeus* 22B–25D and *Critias* 113C–120D as a genuine, independent, non-Platonic tradition.

STRUCTURE OF THE ATLANTIS ACCOUNT

Plato's description of Atlantis is divided into two parts, both provided by Critias, the man who claims to possess Solon's original manuscript. These two parts, one in *Timaeus* and one in *Critias*, are quite different in style, structure and focus.

1.   *Timaeus* 22B–25D: The first, shorter part of the Atlantis account summarizes the initial meeting between Solon and the Saïtian priests. One priest stressed the lack of historical knowledge in Greece and remarked that Solon does not even know his glorious ancestors. After that, a summary of the achievements of the Greek high culture, the story of their war, and their demise are given. This part of the Atlantis legend is poorly organized: the flood from heaven is mentioned at a number of different places, and the same is true for the selective homicide of leading ranks of the society. The lack of organization may indicate the strictly oral and casual character of the first conversation between Solon and the priests.

2.   *Critias* 113C–120D: In *Timaeus*, the priest indicates his willingness to show Solon the original hieroglyphic writing. The second part of the account, given in *Critias*, may represent a copy of the hieroglyphic text; it is well organized and describes Atlantis with unique attention to detail.

A third, central part, *Critias* 110C–112E, is usually attributed to the Atlantis legend; it describes the geography of ancient Attika including its political boundaries and the effect of deforestation and soil erosion. This is the only part of the Atlantis account which most Classical scholars accept as reflecting empirical observations by laymen or intellectuals who concerned themselves with what we would call natural science. I do not consider this segment to be part of Solon's manuscript; it probably represents another, extraneous piece of information resting on oral tradition. Plato introduced it before Solon's narrative of Atlantis because he thought between the two opponents in the war *"we must give the priority in our account to the state of Athens"* (109A).

The account itself appears stratified like a layer cake: the bottom layer is the true appearance of Atlantis as it really was. The second layer would be the first subjective distortion of this reality by the narrator who reported the story to the Egyptian scribe. Naturally, this narrator could not mention everything he saw; he may have overlooked some important features and omitted others to abbreviate the report. On the other hand, he would have emphasized some minor details that were to him particularly remarkable. The third layer would be the Egyptian scribe's interpretation of the report and his translation into hieroglyphs. There may not have been hieroglyphic signs for all the items observed in the foreign country, forcing the scribe to use similar but not quite correct terms. Fourthly, there is the priest who, translating from hieroglyphic signs to Greek, may have emphasized certain parts in the text more than others. He may also have misinterpreted some of those signs which did not quite accurately fit the original report. Then there is Solon's perception of the whole story and, possibly, his attempt to help with the translation. When he heard the account, Solon may have been as old as eighty; he also was highly excited and could have misinterpreted it. At a later date, he intentionally changed some of the names given by the account, as is explicitly stated by Plato. A next layer would include possible changes made to the story during its transmission from Solon to Plato. Plato's impact on the account is most difficult to assess, but he may well have copied it without introducing any changes. Finally, there are the translations of Plato's Greek text into modern languages. Do these translations really express what Plato meant? The uppermost layer, possibly the toughest to penetrate, is today's *Zeitgeist* and bias. Plato's story of Atlantis unambiguously states that a *Greek* civilization was destroyed by simultaneous earthquakes and floods, yet today's conventional wisdom persistently assumes *Atlantis* was the victim of these catastrophes. Conventional wisdom also says that a tidal wave could have destroyed the ancient civilization, whereas the account clearly describes the flood as having come down from heaven. So there are about eight layers of possible distortion concealing the truth. To reach down to the bottom, the historic truth, appears in most cases to be impossible. In some cases, I shall try to reconstruct how individual pieces of information may have been altered during the translation, but my principal aim is to demonstrate that the *core* of the account could realistically describe a Late Bronze Age civilization in the Mediterranean.

In summary, Plato's incentive to compose such a monumental and extremely difficult trilogy may well have derived from personal struggles in Athens, possibly ignited or exacerbated by Isocrates. To silence his critics, Plato embarked on a vast subject: the history of the earth and the universe, the center of which was a startling revelation, known within Plato's family only. Plato thereby ensured that the trilogy would be more sensational than his previous, book the *Politeia*. To avoid future accusations of plagiarism, Plato clearly acknowledged Solon as the author of the secret family manuscript; furthermore, Solon's credibility provided extra authority to a story which seemed dubious, to say the least. Because the Athens/Atlantis conflict represented Plato's principles so well, he went out of his way to assure the reader that the narrative was historically accurate. To disguise the fact that he was involving himself in an unfamiliar subject, Plato uses one long section of Solon's notes in the introduction of the trilogy, proposing Atlantis as a candidate for Socrates' ideal state; that way he could link this new work to the previous one, the *Politeia*. Socrates also provides an elaborate summary of the *Politeia* to strengthen the link, which nonetheless remains weak.

Making use of a story that was entirely composed by somebody else, Plato accepted the locations and chronologies as described, despite some doubts about the reliability of the account. I suspect that Plato did not interfere with the manuscript at all, because of his concern that oral narratives must not be changed in transmission. If we continue arguing along this avenue, that Plato was not involved in the composition of the original Atlantis account, we are left with just two components to be examined further: the story itself and today's knowledge of Mediterranean archaeology. If any historical equivalent to Atlantis existed, it must be located within this archaeological framework. The next chapter will provide the basic knowledge of human and environmental history that is required to find a reasonable context for Atlantis.

CHAPTER FOUR

THE ANCIENT AEGEAN

At Tiryns a more minute scrutiny of the ruins laid bare by Schliemann brought us to the conclusion that the so-called prehistoric palace was not only . . . later than the Macedonian period, but was in fact a Byzantine re-occupation of the site. . . . I am in excellent Athenian archaeological company in my opinion that the "prehistoric palace" of Tiryns is one of the most extraordinary hallucinations of an unscientific enthusiast which literature can record. *The Times,* 29 April 1886

In a Greek village at five o'clock on a summer afternoon the streets are full of noise and tumult. Most Greek men are independent farmers and merchants, while most Greek women are—somewhat less independently—overseers of a large and lively household. Fully relaxed from a prolonged afternoon nap, gathering in streets and outside shops to pursue their daily rounds, the villagers are joined, of course, by the children, whose school has finished before the siesta. They are now taking over streets and church-yards playing football or basketball in large groups of all ages. Around eight o'clock the landscape changes from the dusty yellow mist that dominated the scenery for most of the day; the sun is painting it now in manifold, delightful colors. The air gives warmth and invites an evening stroll. Men are gathering in the Kafenion to discuss politics; women, in smaller groups, chat outside their homes about events that really matter. At eleven, the villagers are still awake, but the place has become dark, and silence begins to dominate.

ICE AGE TO NEOLITHIC

Three hundred thousand years ago, this was quite different, and what are now obvious moods during the day were then imperceptible. Regardless of the day time, life continued on the same low level of activity—because there was no man-made commotion. The hours passed in silence; after dusk, the scene just got darker—and colder. The cold was of a threatening kind. Mingled with moisture, it penetrated everything, seeking to inhibit life where it could reach it. Although the shape of the landscape was almost identical with today's, its dress, plants and wildlife, were completely different, determined by the cold and aridity. The climate of Greece was as cool and dry as the interior of Alaska today, and covered with a vegetation similar to today's Siberia. The Argolid, the focal point of our interest where, much later, Agamemnon resided with his vassals, was then covered by a steppe of sagebrush (*Artemisia*), a plant which shares its name, derived from a goddess, with the Artemisian mountain range which dominates the western side of the Argolid. Its slopes and foothills then bore pine forests with interspersed oak trees.

The foreground of illustrations drawn to visualize this era is often overcrowded with all kinds of extinct, voracious creatures like the saber-toothed tiger, while volcanoes ceaselessly erupt in the background—but the past was just mute and incomprehensibly long. Every few thousand years the ground shook for several seconds, but not even these earthquakes resulted in a dramatic change, because there was nothing to be damaged and nothing to be lost. Greece became an earthquake-prone country, because the consolidated African continent pushed and moved against Europe at a rate of up to four inches per year. Within 100,000 years over one-half mile of Mediterranean seafloor may have been squeezed into the depths between the continents. The resulting pressure caused the Artemisian mountains to rise at a rate of twenty inches per thousand years.[110] Thus in 100,000 years its peaks grew by over 160 feet. Endless erosion by wind and rain, however, counteracted these processes, enabling the earth to keep a balance between its internal mountain-building processes and its external destructive processes. Although *"everything flows"*—as the philosopher Heraklitos put it—the low speed of the flow renders these changes imperceptible without scientific instruments.

In looking at a particular day only 300,000 years ago, over one hundred million very similar days have passed since. Geologists, juggling with billions of years, often pretend comprehension of such time spans. I fear that, like anybody else, we lack the imagination for such dimensions, but only have become used to speaking about them.

From a geological perspective, the last few million years on earth saw the most radical environmental changes in its entire history, marked by the oscillations of ice ages (glacials) and warm periods (non-glacials). In 100,000-year cycles the average global temperature fluctuated by at least 40°F, causing climate, vegetation and fauna belts to shift hundreds or thousands of miles and sea level to rise and fall with an amplitude of almost four hundred feet.

Apparently very few human beings lived in Greece a few hundred thousand years ago. No clear human record has been found apart from a single skull of an early *Homo sapiens* dated to 240,000–160,000 B.P. (before present). The ancestor of the Neanderthals who inhabited the country in the last ice age had entered the Near East *c.* 60,000 years ago[111] during a mild interval of the last glacial. In Greece, the Neanderthals apparently favored open-air sites in coastal plains with an abundance of plant and animal resources;[112] they chose to live in northern Thessaly, Epirus and the Argolid 50,000 to 32,000 years ago.[113] At that time the climate, although dry and cool, allowed sagebrush steppe with patches of deciduous oaks to cover the plains and small pine forests to occupy higher elevations. Large mammals then living in Greece included elephant, aurochs, deer, steppe ass and Saiga antelope, all of which were hunted by Neanderthals.

Around 30,000 years ago the world plunged into a full glacial, the global climate turned colder and vegetation thinned out, allowing steppe to take over most of the country and limiting lusher vegetation to springs in lower terrain only. The cooling resulted in larger polar ice caps and a global lowering of sea level to *c.* four hundred feet below present, thereby producing considerably increased coastal plains. At that time the Argive Plain stretched six miles farther south, and the Adriatic Sea was dry land, generating three hundred miles of coastal plain. The ice age reached its peak around 20,000 B.P. (before present). Soon thereafter the climate began to improve—the world changed again, and it changed rather quickly. While the ice melted, warmer and especially wetter conditions in Greece allowed trees to invade the sparsely vegetated landscape. Open oak forests containing beech, holly, hornbeam, pistachio and almonds took over at low elevations, and fir and pine forests with evergreen shrubs and trees at higher elevations. Sea level began to rise abruptly c. 13,000 years ago; 5,000 years later it had completed most of its four-hundred-foot increase, and the extensive coastal plains had largely drowned.

At the onset of the full glacial another phase of habitation, now of a completely different character from the Neanderthals, began to inhabit Epirus, Boeotia and the Argolid, where people settled in caves and rock shelters at higher elevations. Although the climatic improvement continued and warm and moist conditions came to prevail, interior Greece may have been abandoned again between 12,500 and 8000 B.P. Only Franchthi Cave in the southern Argolid remained at least seasonally occupied, but more undiscovered sites may well have existed. Franchthi's inhabitants then lived by hunting. Their food consisted mainly of red deer and wild boar, whose abundance indicates the transformation of the interior into denser woodland. The subsistence of the people at Franchthi became gradually more diversified; plants and marine resources were increasingly exploited. Both land snails and marine shellfish were collected[114] and wild plants such as lentils, vetch, pistachio, almonds, wild oats and barley were utilized.[115] Volcanic glass (obsidian), a superb stone from which to make tools, was imported from Melos,[116] far out in the Aegean Sea since the Upper Paleolithic. Certain faunal species such as wild ass and ibex began to disappear,[117] while large tuna, about eight feet long and over 440 pounds, were caught for the first time in the later Mesolithic.[118]

The use of marine resources, the evidence for long-distance transport of obsidian, and the skills required to catch large fish provide indications that the late Mesolithic community was chiefly oriented toward the sea. More, perhaps seasonal, dwellings of these "seafarers" may have existed along the Greek shores, but they would have drowned during the subsequent raising of the sea level. At this time, there are no indications that humans interfered with Greece's interior environment at all. The interior landscape was dominated by drought-resistant evergreen and coniferous woodland made up of warm-temperate forests of black pine, juniper and evergreen oak.[119] Glades and rockier areas were covered with wild olives and evergreen brush of heather, myrtle, pistachio, rhododendron and bulbs,[120] while the wildlife of the interior included brown bear, wolf, fox, hyena[121] and perhaps lion and leopard.

By the seventh millennium B.C. the interior of Greece became settled again. The new inhabitants brought with them the knowledge required to cultivate wheat, barley and pulses and to domesticate cows, pigs, sheep and goats.[122] Not surprisingly, they first utilized the fertile lowlands of Thessaly, where the soil was tillable and able to retain sufficient moisture for agriculture.[123] They introduced grinding stones for cereals and polished axes to open up this land of trees and brush for cultivation and grazing.[124] The first houses were square or rectangular with brushwood roofs. Small villages, never exceeding twenty homes and a population of fifty to three hundred, commonly formed politically and economically independent units.[125] The farmers had storage pits and hearths; they ate fish and shellfish, hare and birds, apple and pear. Initially stock grazing was limited to valley floors cleared for cultivation only;[126] gradually, however, people continued modifying the environment to suit their own needs by clearing more and more of the surrounding hills. A rapidly increasing population was accompanied by human-induced deforestation, incipient overgrazing and the rise and spread of diseases such as malaria, dysentery and hookworm.[127] Pottery was employed from c. 6500 B.C. onward. In the fourth millennium B.C. settlements grew larger and a social structure was increasingly apparent, expressed architecturally in a hierarchy of construction with a main building in the center of the settlement.

A prime archaeological site of the Late Neolithic is Dimini in southeastern Thessaly. The people of Dimini settled near the coast, where the post-glacial sea-level rise had reached its peak, drowning the estuaries and producing natural harbors in abundance.[128] By 3000 B.C., however, the fertile lowlands were completely deforested, ox-drawn plows had come into use[129] and the local forest timber from the woods, still covering the hills, was increasingly exploited for shipbuilding, house beams, tools and charcoal. As a result, the soil lost its dense natural vegetation, became unstable and eroded. The eroded material was carried downslope by streams and dumped in shallow bays, forcing the coast to shift seaward. The site of Dimini, which had been established just above the shore, lies about two miles away from the sea today.[130]

The Neolithic settlement of Dimini was established on a hillock close to the shore. Soon thereafter the shallow bay in front of the site was filled in by sediment, and today the coast lies about two miles from the site (from Zangger 1991b).

THE EARLY BRONZE AGE AND
THE EMERGENCE OF TROY

A new archaeological era began around 3000 B.C. with the first use of bronze in the Aegean. Copper alloys incorporating arsenic had been produced for several centuries in Central Asia,[131] but tin bronze, an alloy of copper and up to ten percent tin, was apparently invented away from these early metallurgical centers. Metals have unique advantages over all other natural resources: they are durable, malleable, and above all reusable. Modern industrial society depends to a large extent on the availability of metals. By combining various elements and using different melting techniques an endless variety of steels and other alloys is today obtainable, each one with its own distinctive characteristics. Already in prehistoric times, human readiness to experiment with alloys, first by combining copper and arsenic, later by utilizing tin bronze,

68

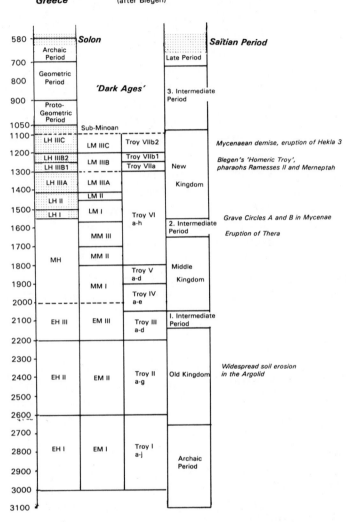

Mainland Greece	Crete	Troy (after Blegen)	Egypt	
580	Solon		Saïtian Period	
Archaic Period		Late Period		
700				
Geometric Period	'Dark Ages'	3. Intermediate Period		
800				
900				
Proto-Geometric Period				
1050	Sub-Minoan			
1100				
LH IIIC	LM IIIC	Troy VIIb2		Mycenaean demise, eruption of Hekla 3
1200				
LH IIIB2	LM IIIB	Troy VIIb1		Blegen's 'Homeric Troy',
LH IIIB1		Troy VIIa	New	pharaohs Ramesses II and Merneptah
1300				
LH IIIA	LM IIIA		Kingdom	
1400				
LH II	LM II			
1500				
LH I	LM I	Troy VI a-h		Grave Circles A and B in Mycenae
1600			2. Intermediate Period	
MM III			Eruption of Thera	
1700				
MM II				
MH				
1800		Troy V a-d	Middle	
MM I			Kingdom	
1900				
		Troy IV a-e		
2000				
2100	EH III	EM III	Troy III a-d	I. Intermediate Period
2200				
2300				Widespread soil erosion
2400	EH II	EM II	Troy II a-g	Old Kingdom	in the Argolid
2500				
2600				
2700				
2800	EH I	EM I	Troy I a-j	Archaic Period
2900				
3000				
3100				

Time chart of some eastern Mediterranean cultures during the Bronze Age (3000–1100 BC) and subsequent centuries. The phases appear as they would be found in an excavation (younger periods above older ones). The Late Bronze Age "Mycenaean period" (c. 1550–1100 B.C.) in mainland Greece is shaded. EM = Early Minoan; MM = Middle Minoan; LM = Late Minoan; EH = Early Helladic; MH = Middle Helladic; LH = Late Helladic. (Chronology for mainland Greece, Crete and Troy after Demakopoulou ed. 1990, for Egypt after Hobson 1990.)

bears witness to the desire for sophisticated metals. At least six metals are known to have been in use during the Bronze Age: gold, silver, lead, copper, tin and iron.[132] Although individual iron objects appeared as early as the third millennium B.C., this metal's potential was not explored until after the end of the Achaean era, evidently due to the lack of the necessary refining techniques.

The fate of one site in particular, Troy, was closely connected with the new era, the "Bronze Age". In the Aegean, tin bronzes first emerged near the Hellespont shortly after Troy had been founded there.[133] Not only did both Troy and the Bronze Age arise roughly simultaneously, they were also going to cease concurrently, about two thousand years later. The area around Troy, the Troad, is particularly rich in metal resources, and a great number of prehistoric copper, lead and gold mines have been found there.[134] Nevertheless, several Trojan tin bronzes seem to have been produced from foreign ores; thus Troy may have been more of a processing and trading center than a production site.[135] Cyprus is regarded as the main supplier of copper,[136] but archaeometallurgists are still uncertain where the tin came from.[137] Currently known sources for tin are today's Afghanistan, Czechoslovakia, Romania, Spain, and Cornwall in Britain.

The beginning of the new era was not accompanied by any drastic changes on the Greek mainland. Low hills near the sea continued to be favored for settlements; such mounds bore two-room houses with gravel roads in between and large central buildings.[138] Especially during EH II, the middle phase of the Early Bronze Age (Early Helladic II), a strong, wealthy agricultural and trading society developed. Wild animals were abundantly used, and the range of domesticated livestock was enlarged to include the horse and the donkey.[139] Vegetables like peas, beans and lentils became more popular, while the overall economy, in addition to domesticated animals, included weaving and a variety of trades, increasingly involving metals such as copper and silver. Among the most remarkable architectural EH II achievements was the "House of Tiles," an impressive central building in fortified Lerna, and a massive circular building, almost ninety feet in diameter, across the bay at Tiryns.

From an environmental perspective the end of the flourishing Early Helladic II resembled the landscape changes seen in the Gulf of Volos at the end of the Neolithic: an increasing population overexploited the natural resources, especially timber. Until then

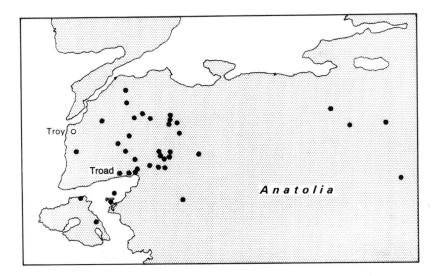

The distribution of ore deposits in northwestern Anatolia shows that the Troad is particularly rich in metal resources. (After Wagner *et al.* 1985.)

the limestone slopes around the Argive Plain may have carried as little as four to eight inches of soil; sufficient, however, to support at least a scant pine forest. With the artificial removal of the trees and the concurrent expansion of intensive pastoralism, the soil became loose and was washed away. Masses of alluvia, several feet thick, accumulated in the coastal plain, pushing the shoreline seaward and deeply burying many prehistoric sites.[140]

Greece had precious little arable land and limited freshwater resources to begin with, but both of these natural assets were severely damaged by prehistoric over-exploitation. Clayey soils tend to retain rainwater for a long time, releasing it slowly and continuously as perennial streams. Barren limestone mountains, however, stripped of their soil cover, are unable to retain water; streams dry up, and downpours, having thus far been a blessing for agriculture, become a terrible threat: in the form of ephemeral flash floods they increase erosion and bury lowlands under mud and water. The earth has no difficulty in renewing its soil once it is lost, but in a dry climate soil regeneration will require a few thousand years of landscape stability. Hence, from a cultural point of view, the Final Neolithic and Early Bronze Age soil erosion in Greece of five thousand years ago arguably represent the most disastrous environmental circumstance ever to have struck that country. Other disasters followed. Toward the end of the third millennium many thriving communities, including Lerna and Tiryns, suffered destruction by human hands. The subsequent inhabitants of these sites were materially less advanced than the earlier society. Their houses were chaotically arranged, irregular and small, with crooked facades and thin walls.[141]

THE MINOAN CULTURE

While the culture on the Greek mainland remained on an inconspicuous level for a few more centuries, dramatic achievements occurred elsewhere in the Aegean. During the twentieth century B.C. the long-standing and thriving agricultural community on Crete evolved into a palatial society. A unique architectural style emerged, with elaborate open palaces reflecting princely, territorially extensive rule. The most famous palace, almost five acres in size, arose at Knossos, but other elite residences of equal or only slightly lesser rank appeared at Phaistos and Mallia.[142] All of these places had previously borne important settlements, providing ground for the assumption that some indigenous clans were able to develop gradually to a higher degree of organization and prosperity. The palaces were formidably organized structures with a central rectangular court and separate areas for reception, domestic life, crafts production, religion and storage. Master artists decorated the palaces with superb frescoes depicting the Minoan style of life: marine and floral motifs in rich colors, birds, monkeys, trees, bulls and goats prevail in the paintings. The tremendous advances in artistry accompanied increasing political power and wealth. Outside the palaces, the standard of living soared, too, as is reflected in municipal drainage systems and roads paved with cobblestones.

The skillful exploitation of agronomic resources combined with extensive husbandry provided the foundation for a healthy agricultural economy. Crete became self-sufficient in most agricultural and craft goods and was able to develop wide trading contacts allowing for exports of pottery, grain and presumably oil and clothes. Although the Minoan culture on Crete was by no means uniform or monolithic, its style of life seems to have been little altered over time.

The Minoan economic success resulted in a need for written records. Pictorial signs, reminiscent of Egyptian hieroglyphs, appeared engraved or painted on pottery, seal stones and presumably on perishable substances such as wax or papyrus. The bulk of inscriptions which survived, however, were scribbled on hand-sized, leaf-shaped clay tablets. Because these were not baked after use, they would have decayed, too, if a conflagration which destroyed the palaces had not hardened them. Consequently all tablets date from the final year of the palaces. The script, today termed Linear A, was written in the language of the people who created the Minoan civilization. Unfortunately, apart from the numerals, Linear A is still undeciphered and the language unrecognized, although it is clear that it was not Greek.[143]

A volcanic eruption in the seventeenth century B.C. destroyed the magnificent three-story houses on Thera, a small island north of Crete, and may have caused some commotion on Crete as well. Nevertheless the apex of Minoan prosperity occurred after this eruption at the end of the sixteenth century. Shortly after 1500 B.C. many Minoan sites were destroyed or abandoned. Finally, from 1450 to 1400 B.C., people from mainland Greece, who thus far lagged behind the Minoan achievements, took control of Knossos and much of Crete. Genuine warrior-graves, containing heavy spearheads and a bronze helmet, report a style of life quite different from that of the Minoans. The symbols of Linear A became transformed into the Greek Linear B to accommodate the language of the mainlanders.

THE ACHAEANS

Contemporary with the final phase of Minoan civilization, a new culture materialized in Greece. Within a few centuries it was to evolve into the first high civilization on the European mainland. Traditionally the first signs of the initial phase of this Late Bronze Age, Mycenaean or Achaean culture were placed in the sixteenth century B.C., but the now accepted radiocarbon dates for the eruption of Thera (1650–1600 B.C.)[144] may require the pottery chronology to be slightly adjusted, possibly dating the early Achaeans to the seventeenth century B.C. Knowledge of the first Achaeans derives mainly from two grave circles at Mycenae. Each circle consisted of single and family graves in deep rectangular shafts covered with wooden beams or stone slabs. The earlier grave circle B still contained much pottery made in Middle Bronze Age tradition, whereas grave goods in circle A showed notable Cretan influence. Some of the upright *stelae* above the graves displayed engraved illustrations including horse-drawn chariots. The graves contained numerous luxury goods, including gold, amber and ivory jewelery, silver mugs, large bronze swords, daggers with exquisite ornaments and the famous death masks of gold and electrum. However, neither the materials used for these precious objects nor the artistic styles in which they were manufactured were native to Greece. Nevertheless, the unique combination of massive armament, horse-drawn chariots, hunting motifs and fine craftsmanship characterizes the onset of a genuine new civilization. The willingness of the Greeks to adopt alien inventions becomes evident from Achaean architecture too: the first palace at Pylos was still reminiscent of Minoan Knossos, Gla's citadel resembled levantine examples,[145] and the defense gallery of the final palace at Tiryns as well as Mycenae's Lion Gate are well matched by similar curiosities at Hattusas in Hittite Anatolia.[146]

The subsequent political and economic success of the Achaean culture rested on coupling skillful artistry and metalworking with long-distance trade and warfare, including the use of advanced weapons such as horse-drawn chariots. The Achaeans developed a distinguished, fine pottery which occurred throughout the Aegean between 1400 and 1250 B.C. (LH IIIA2 to LH IIIB1).[147] Cyprus, Syria, Palestine, Egypt and the west coast of Asia Minor were actively trading with the Achaeans, who may have exchanged hides, timber, wine, olive oil and purple dye[148] for linen, papyrus, rope and stone vessels. The most prominent import commodity, however, must have been raw metal, since neither copper nor tin ores occur in Greece. Finished metal objects, on the other hand, were probably among the most important exports from Greece.

A fourteenth-century B.C. shipwreck near Ulu Burun in southern Turkey provides evidence of the Late Bronze Age trading goods being shipped across the eastern Mediterranean; it contained 100 Canaanite amphorae, one with aromatic resin, logs of ebonylike African blackwood, stone anchors, large storage jars (*pithoi*), some containing the seeds of pomegranates, blue glass ingots, Mesopotamian cylinder seals, a Mycenaean kylix, a mug and a "pilgrim's flask" made of tin, a gold chalice, silver bracelets, a quartz cylinder seal, carved amber beads, ivory and gold scarabs, a hoard of precious scrap metal, hippopotamus' teeth, an elephant's tusk, ostrich eggshells, fragments of tortoiseshell and above all a hinged, wooden writing tablet! The main cargo, however, consisted of two hundred raw copper ingots weighing six tons in total plus finished bronze products such as swords, daggers, arrowheads, chisels, sickle blades and adzes.[149]

Much useful information regarding the Achaean society, economy and administration has been retrieved from the Linear B tablets found on the mainland. Over twelve hundred tablets were recovered from Pylos; more tablets were found at Mycenae, Thebes and Tiryns.[150] The circumstances which enabled the preservation of the tablets in Pylos were similar to the events on Knossos: a fire in *c.* 1200 B.C. destroyed the palace but hardened the clay of the tablets. They bear rather tedious administrative accounts evidently recorded for temporary use only. These inventories, nevertheless, provide a quantitative insight into Achaean economy. For instance, the smiths in the kingdom of Pylos turn out to have been concentrated in groups of up to 26 and totaling nearly 400[151]—a strong indication that Pylos produced a surplus of metal goods for export.

The existence and contents of the Linear B tablets exemplify how meticulously organized and administered the Achaean society must have been. At the top of the hierarchical pyramid stood the king, or *Wanax*, who was surrounded by nobles and who commanded a large number of artisan underlings. The palace architecture was explicitly designed to emphasize the outstanding role of the leader. The main building was a spacious hall, called *megaron*, with a large hearth in its center and four columns around it. A throne was situated on one of the long sides of the wall. Outside the main *megaron* the palace was divided into functional areas.

After the first appearance of early Achaean residences, dispersed over several coasts of southern and central Greece, the kingdoms in the Argive Plain gradually assumed a leading role, turning this area into the "powerhouse" of the Achaean world. The natural setting of the Argive Plain offers everything the rulers could have desired. First of all, the plain itself represents the largest fertile area in the southeast of Greece—facing the directions in which Achaean trade, much like Minoan trade, aimed. Moreover, the plain offers over

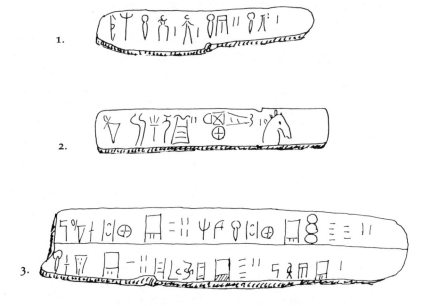

Linear B tablets: (1) Ag 88: a man, a woman, two girls and one boy; (2) Sc 103: horse, chariot and tunic; (3) Ld 587: different kinds of cloth. (After Chadwick 1976, 22.)

ninety-six square miles of highly fertile, arable land, almost completely isolated from the rest of the Peloponnese by extensive mountain ranges.

The sites of the royal residences within the plain were chosen with practical and strategic objectives in mind. Generally speaking, the majority of sites around a circular fertile plain in Greece would be situated on the foot of the south-facing slopes.[152] During times of intensive landuse, for instance the Classical period, farmsteads were often placed just outside the arable land at the bottom of the surrounding hills, using the solid bedrock as a foundation for the structure as well as the source of building stones. Such a site put the house in a slightly elevated position providing a view of a larger area and protection from rainwater runoff. Thus, not surprisingly, even one thousand years before Classical Greece, the Achaeans founded their residences in the Argive Plain on solid bedrock, mostly on the eastern side of the plain, near fertile soil. Hilltops on elevated positions were chosen because they provided a commanding view of a larger territory. Another important parameter for site choice was freshwater supply. But the hydrography of the upper western plain is determined by a lack of springs and the presence of a large ephemeral stream, the Inakhos, which still tends to inundate the suburbs of modern Argos every twenty-odd years. Before the recent overexploitation, however, the opposite (eastern) side of the plain, where most prehistoric settlements had been, was extremely rich in freshwater which kept welling out at the bottom of the alluvial fans.

Although the Achaean citadels in the Argive Plain appear to have been the residences of independent rulers, their distribution may also reflect a coordinated effort to protect the whole of the plain. In contrast to the Minoan civilization on Crete, defense seems to have been a fundamental desire of the Achaeans. The western side of the Argive Plain is guarded by mountain ranges up to almost six thousand feet high and several hundred miles wide and thus required fewer fortified citadels to protect it from potential intruders. The north and northeast passages into the plain, on the other hand, were covered by Mycenae itself; Tiryns protected the coast, and Asine, the southeastern entrance to the Argive Plain. As time went on and Achaean wealth expanded, the desire for protection escalated too. Around 1250 B.C. many Achaean citadels were reinforced to an extent far beyond military necessity. Tiryns was then surrounded by up to twenty-three-foot-thick walls made of huge limestone boulders; its fortified area was much enlarged, possibly to offer protection for more than just the highest echelons of the society. Both Mycenae and Tiryns had protected access to freshwater springs, and Tiryns obtained an innovative defense system of galleries and palisades. Architecture of this peak phase (LH IIIB) bears close resemblance at different sites: the great *tholos* tombs at Orchomenos and Mycenae are similar in measurement and technique, the Lion Gate at Mycenae is similar to the main gate of Tiryns in measurement and building stones, and the frescoes in Mycenae and Tiryns even appear to have been drawn by the same artist.[153] Hence, the latest palatial phase of construction might be conceived as a team effort by the individual rulers, who had engaged a league of engineers and architects, possibly including foreign advisers.[154] Not long after these reinforcements, Achaean culture collapsed, but one cannot be certain whether the citadels in the Argive Plain were ever used for defense against an attacker.

HEINRICH SCHLIEMANN

According to many ancient writers, most notably Homer, the Achaeans became involved in a war against the city of Troy (or Ilion) shortly before their demise. A long-lasting controversy among experts as to whether this war was a mythical invention or not almost came to an end when Heinrich Schliemann rediscovered Ilion on a hill called Hisarlık in northwest Turkey. The term "discovery" though, appears incorrect in this context, because Ilion's location had been analytically deduced from descriptions in ancient literature before by people such as Charles MacLaren and Frank Calvert. Schliemann was literally guided to Hisarlık and had to be convinced by others that it was the most likely location of Troy.[155] Schliemann made history, however, because he had the courage and the capital to launch an excavation. But the term "excavation" again seems inappropriate, because he mainly *removed* most of the remains which Bronze Age and Roman destruction had left.

Today's conventional wisdom characterizes Schliemann as an innovative amateur who was unable to conduct proper scientific research. Most of these deductions are wrong. Although he was innovative, he made much use of other people's ideas and skills without always acknowledging them properly.[156] He did not *discover* Troy because Troy had already been rediscovered by Charles MacLaren in the year that Schliemann was born. Nor did Schliemann discover Mycenae or Tiryns: both sites were sitting there waiting to be excavated—the Lion Gate had always been half exposed. Schliemann was not a complete amateur either; he held a doctoral degree in philology—obtained with the lowest possible grade, though, and apparently with some influential help from his father.[157] One of Schliemann's most valuable skills was the ability to assemble a team of experts from various disciplines at a time when teamwork was anything but customary. Schliemann stands out as an enormously hard worker with an unrivaled speed of publication. His admirably simple, nevertheless convincing and extremely successful approach to science contributed significantly to the formation of a new discipline. Above all, however, Heinrich Schliemann possessed an unusual skill for publicity. He deliberately concealed his forerunners' achievements and made us believe, even today, that he had been striving to discover Troy since childhood. In truth, he was nothing but a wealthy man, willing to work frantically but anxious not to perish without immortality.

THE END OF THE BRONZE AGE

Most Mediterranean prehistorians now accept the existence of a Trojan War; only its extent in terms of time and significance remains disputed. At the end of the Bronze Age Troy had been destroyed twice within a few decades. According to Carl Blegen, excavator of Ilion in 1932–1938, the site was first demolished by an earthquake between 1300 and 1275 B.C., but other authors assume this destruction to have occurred a few decades later.[158] One of the huge defense walls collapsed during the earthquake, staircases broke and foundations were shifted.[159] Nevertheless, some doubt remains whether the destruction of Troy VI was really caused by an earthquake,[160] because most of the defense walls remained completely undamaged. Blegen had also ascribed the collapse of some buildings to the suspected earthquake although they were seriously burned.

The Trojans rebuilt their fortress with a new design in mind: the layout within the reinforced defense systems changed from a princely fashion with expansive megarons and ample open space to smaller buildings with hardly any alleys in between. Very large storage jars were sunk into the floors with their rims only slightly protruding over the previous surface. Wooden beams or flat rock slabs covered these reservoirs. At the same time, imports from Mycenae, which had been abundant from 1400 to 1250 B.C., ceased totally: only one shard is known from the period of the final Achaean palace constructions, LH IIIB2.[161] Within one generation after the redesigned Troy VIIa was finished—with a layout that has been interpreted as a preparation for siege[162]—the city was sacked. This second destruction by cataclysmic fires is generally attributed to the Greeks. Unfortunately, to the present day, scientists have not been able to establish the absolute date of Troy's fall; thus the field has to rely on the potentially subjective experiences of accomplished scholars.[163]

Shortly after the destruction of Troy VIIa the Achaean states collapsed too. Within a decade the great citadels on the mainland suffered demolition, and many of them were abandoned. On a

From *Cartoon History of the Universe* by Larry Gonick. (Copyright © 1990 by Larry Gonick. Used by permission of Doubleday, a division of Bantam Doubleday Dell Publishing Group, Inc.)

much reduced level Achaean culture lingered on for as much as 150 years, but by 1100 B.C. or 1000 B.C., at the latest, it had completely vanished. Refugees fled to marginal lands away from the Achaean centers, such as Cyprus, while the Greek mainland became desolated. The population rate fell to a fraction of its previous level; and for the next 300 years literacy vanished from the Greek landscape, thus leading to the popular conception of a "dark age".

Achaean wealth had depended on a combination of a meticulously organized, highly specialized society and reliable long-distance trade connections, since both the raw materials and the finished products must have been carried by sea. Either upheavals at home or interruptions in sea trade could have triggered a domino effect, with dramatic consequences for the whole Achaean economy. A shortage of metals, and thus an indication that sea trade had been disturbed, is indicated by one interpretation of a Linear B tablet from Pylos, which dates to the last few months before the conflagration of the palace. According to the tablet, bronze objects were being collected, possibly in preparation for defense against an attacker.[164]

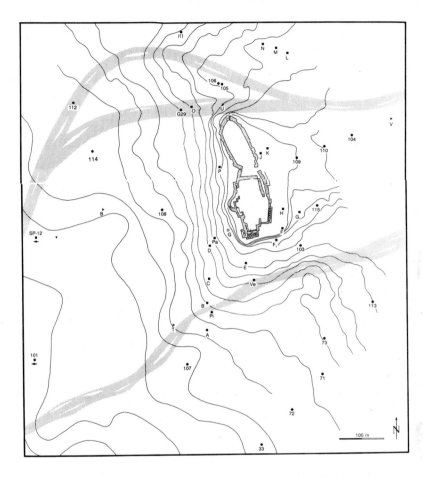

Map of the area around the citadel of Tiryns showing locations
of cores taken during the geoarchaeological investigation (dots
and triangles) and excavations taken into account (squares).
(After Zangger 1991a.)

THE TIRYNS PROJECT (2)

Today, Mediterranean prehistory still lacks a comprehensive
explanation for the end of the Bronze Age. For a long time the
invasion of northern tribes was held responsible for the Achaean
downfall. When excavation seemed to challenge such an idea,

81

natural catastrophes, in particular sudden climatic changes, were considered as possible causes.[165] In order to prove or disprove these suppositions, I conducted a landscape reconstruction of the Achaean center in the Argolid including the sites of Mycenae and Tiryns. This study led to the conclusion that the Achaean environment did not differ significantly from the present one. The most radical landscape changes had occurred between 4000 and 3000 B.C., when dense forests were rapidly reduced by human deforestation, soils were eroded from the hill slopes and the coastline was pushed seaward by redeposited alluvium. At the end of the Bronze Age the landscape had regained equilibrium. Thus, there were no geological indications at all that long-term environmental changes caused the Achaean collapse.

Nevertheless, in the fourth year of fieldwork in the Argolid, I made a surprise discovery. Some auger cores east of Tiryns revealed an unstratified floodplain deposit several feet thick. Sediments of this type occur during ephemeral stream floods, but usually these layers are only a few inches thick. At Tiryns, however, the lack of stratification indicated deposition in one event. Accordingly, a catastrophic flood must have occurred at Tiryns which probably buried the eastern parts of the lower town under several feet of mud. In some of the cores, this deposit, up to sixteen feet thick, produced an abundance of quite well-preserved pottery fragments including rare pieces. Most of these shards dated to the end of the palatial period, thus indicating that the flood must have occurred at that time (LH IIIB2).

In addition to the flood, the excavations at Mycenae and Tiryns have also revealed hints pointing at earthquakes during this period, though the interpretation of these findings is controversial. At some point in the LH IIIB period heavy burning occurred in some parts of the settlement at Mycenae. At the same time a few houses collapsed, crushing at least one occupant in a doorway.[166] Other extremely fragile constructions, however, such as the early *tholos* tomb of Aegisthus (c. 1450 B.C.) and much superb masonry escaped undamaged. Tiryns has produced clues for several earthquakes including one at the LH IIIB2/C transition,[167] i.e., after the proposed earthquake at Mycenae. After this destruction the people of Tiryns lived in simple makeshift dwellings before they started a totally new rebuilding program for their city.[168] The flood therefore falls into a chronological period when the Argolid may have been earthquake prone, just before the onset of the Achaean

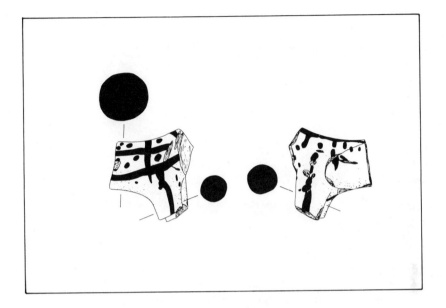

The first auger core which hit the sixteen-foot-thick flash-flood deposits at Tiryns yielded this fragment of a Mycenaean animal figurine.

demise. At that time not only the citadel of Tiryns itself but also the lower town around it may have suffered severely from natural catastrophes.

The flash flood at Tiryns was not triggered by a tidal wave, or *tsunami*, which sometimes accompanies earthquakes and sea-quakes, because the mud was transported downhill by a stream emanating from the slopes east of the citadel. Such torrential floods frequently occur as a consequence of earthquakes, since collapsing riverbanks tend to dam and redirect the streams away from their usual courses. The same happened at Tiryns: the flash flood occurred because the stream was forced to abandon the millennia-old bed south of the citadel. The preceding final phase of palace constructions may have been accompanied by the deci-mation of the remaining forests in the hinterland of Tiryns. After the removal of the trees, the soil had become unstable; all that was needed to wash it down the hill was an earthquake during a rainy season. The earthquake could have caused a landslide and, once unstable and in motion, the mud was picked up by the stream

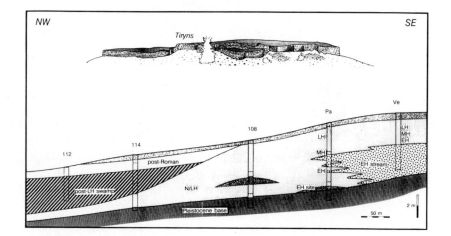

Aligning the sequences found in auger cores and archaeological excavations produces a cross-section like this one which shows the deposits southwest of Tiryns. An Early Bronze Age site (EH site) was found at sixteen-to-twenty-foot depth in excavation Pa. Further ancient remains may well be covered by the thick alluvial deposits. The gravel in the southeast stems from the stream which passed south of Tiryns from the Neolithic to the Late Bronze Age.

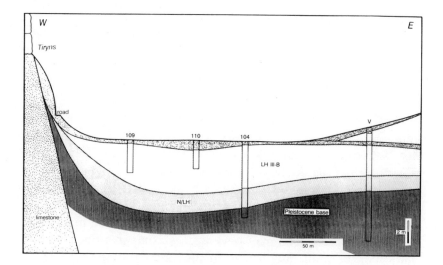

This cross-section through the area east of the citadel shows the extent of the flash-flood deposits (LH IIIB). Once again, nobody can tell how much there is to be found beneath this up-to-sixteen-foot-thick unit.

and dumped at the first obstacle, the limestone knoll of Tiryns.

After this disastrous flood the people at Tiryns decided to redirect the entire river in order to prevent a future recurrence of such a catastrophe. They erected a thirty-three-foot-high barrier across the stream bed a few miles east of the citadel and protected the lower face of this barrier with a Cyclopean wall. A one-mile-long channel was dug, beginning at the dam, to direct the water into an adjacent natural streambed. After the river had been diverted, the lower town of Tiryns was safe from further flash floods. Thus, the foundations of the next phase of habitation (LH IIIC), which had been built on top of the alluvial deposits, are still near the surface, and the Achaean dam is still effective—3,200 years after its construction.[169]

The catastrophic flood at Tiryns, in combination with the earthquakes in the Argolid, may have contributed to the onset of the Achaean demise in this particular area. By themselves, however, such local events are extremely unlikely to result in a regional effect or in the collapse of a civilization. The Achaean communities had clearly passed their cultural and political peak when these catastrophes occurred at c. 1200 B.C.—and there are no indications for cataclysmic events at the end of the Bronze Age in general, apart from the recent discovery of unusual tree-ring patterns around 1159 B.C. But, however trifling the immediate consequences of the events in the Argive Plain may have been on a regional scale, they are likely to have found their way into an oral tradition.

THE POST-ACHAEAN ERA

Achaean trade began to drop at the end of LH IIIB1 at c. 1250 B.C., long before the incidents at Tiryns. Until then prosperity and stability in the eastern Mediterranean was ensured by the balanced powers of Egypt, Hittite Anatolia and Achaean Greece. With the death of Pharaoh Rameses II at 1224 B.C. and of the last powerful Hittite king, Tudhaliyas IV, shortly thereafter, this equilibrium came to an end. The Egyptian influence in the Levant ceased, the Hittite Empire in Anatolia fell in ruins and widespread destruction of cities occurred in mainland Greece, in the Levant and on Cyprus.[170] The Achaean demise must be viewed within this general instability of the Late Bronze Age eastern Mediterranean,

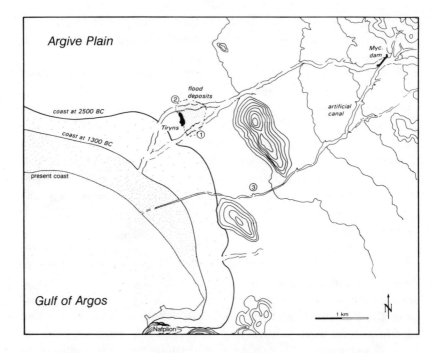

Tiryns was an important settlement around 2500 B.C. when the coastline was close to the site. By the time of the palatial Late Bronze Age (1300 B.C.), sedimentation in the shallow Gulf of Argos had forced the shore about half a mile seaward. The map shows the original course of the stream (1) south of the citadel and its new bed after the catastrophic flash flood (2). To prevent such floods, the people of Tiryns erected the dam (upper right corner) and an artificial canal, thereby redirecting the stream into another bed (3).

which represented a system collapse that might indeed be compared to a chain reaction.

The decline was accompanied by a dispersion of the Achaean population toward marginal lands. Many large centers, such as Pylos, Gla, Midea, Prosymna and Berbati, were almost totally abandoned, while other settlements, such as Iolkos, were apparently safe for a few more generations. Such an intermittent succession of disasters may indicate the consequences of civil war, which, according to several ancient authors, ravaged Greece after the sack of Troy.[171] When their homes were in danger, the inhabitants of the mainland states flew to areas of greater security, especially on the islands and toward the margins of the Achaean sphere of influence. As a consequence, the population density on the Greek mainland dropped dramatically. On the Cycladic islands, however, people continued to dwell on the same level, and other areas such as eastern Attica, Euboea and Cyprus even saw a peak in late Achaean activity. While Mycenaean pottery had thus far been astonishingly uniform throughout the Aegean, in LH IIIC it was being manufactured in regional styles of lesser quality.

Within a century the era of stability and prosperity, of superb craftsmanship and long-distance trading, was replaced by isolation and decline. Many cultural and technological achievements of the Late Bronze Age vanished, central political control broke down, the elaborate administration disintegrated and the art of writing disappeared.[172] This collapse was accompanied by the movements of the Sea Peoples, a name used in Egyptian records to describe thirteenth- and twelfth-century onslaughts. These attackers (not all came by sea) were not a united people; the Egyptian hieroglyphs report many groups building different coalitions at different times. Their assaults certainly aggravated the political situation, but by themselves they, too, are unlikely to have caused the political downfall. As states were collapsing, displaced people may have engaged in piracy, too, thereby escalating the unrest further.

In Greece, late in the eleventh century B.C., when the dust had settled, nothing was left of the glamorous Achaean civilization apart from a few Cyclopic ruins. A lifeless spirit, termed sub-Mycenaean, had taken over Greece. Building skills had sunk abysmally from the Achaean heyday, as is recorded by the few remains of pathetically constructed houses which have survived. A diminished population dragged on for several generations, producing only most essential household tools and dull wares.[173] This culture, generally described as a dark age, characteristically recorded itself mostly in the form of graves.

Yet, the end of the Achaeans also marked the beginning of a new era. Already during the time of turmoil steps were taken toward the formation of a new political and cultural society, which was going to evolve slowly but steadily to culminate in Classical Attika. At least one royal Achaean palace, on the Acropolis in Athens, appears to have escaped the widespread destruction at the end of the Bronze Age. A rare record of continuous inhabitation lasting from the late Helladic IIIC until the Classical period was discovered in the Kerameikos cemetery near the Acropolis. Later Athenian generations were aware and proud of their uninterrupted occupation of Athens after the Achaean demise.[174] The findings in Kerameikos and elsewhere, especially in the Argolid, document a clear continuity of artistic styles with roots in the Achaean and earlier ages. Art and craftsmanship steadily evolved and regained momentum until a new, consolidated Hellenic culture emerged in the eighth century B.C. when writing was re-established, Homer composed the *Iliad* and the *Odyssey*, and the first Olympic games were held.

At that time the western and eastern shores of the Aegean, including the islands in between, had become a cultural unit which served as the base for the Greek expansion in the Archaic era. During the century from 750 B.C. to 650 B.C. an intricate political and economic system developed in Greece, linking the country again to the eastern Mediterranean and opening it to Near Eastern influences. Greece's political organization developed gradually from kingships to city states, which continued to consolidate under aristocratic authority. Trade expanded exponentially; the Greeks established colonies on the shores of the eastern Mediterranean and reached for the western Mediterranean and the Black Sea.

Toward the end of the seventh century a major class strife arose in Athens, where the poorer people felt increasingly suppressed by the wealthy aristocrats. Many impoverished citizens became unable to pay debts to their aristocratic creditors and were consequently enslaved. In order to settle the escalating conflict, the rival groups agreed (in 594 B.C.) to appoint a man called Solon as a mediator with extraordinary powers. Solon (c. 640–560 B.C.) came from a wealthy, aristocratic, Athenian family; he was a successful military leader who had won the island of Salamis for Athens from Megara. During his archonship Solon ordered the cancellation of all land debts and the release of indebted slaves, and reorganized measurements, weights and various laws. Furthermore he introduced new governmental institutions, including a parliament and a people's court where all citizens were treated as equals. His constitution laid the foundation not only for the political system of Classical Greece but for modern democracies in general. According to Herodotus, Solon left Athens just after his archonship for a period of ten years '*in order to avoid having the necessity of repealing any of the laws he had made*'.[175] Several ancient authors describe his travels, which began with a visit to Egypt.[176]

Egypt had held close contacts with Greece since the Late Bronze

Age. The country survived the depression much better than Greece and Anatolia and was successfully defended against the raids of the Sea Peoples. After the death of Rameses III in 1153 B.C., however, a political and economic downturn was inescapable. Marginal areas such as Nubia and Palestine were lost, and Egypt itself fell under foreign rulership, causing the division of the country into petty kingdoms. But internal uprisings in the seventh century B.C. eventually toppled the foreign control. The new theocratic rulers in Saïs, the Egyptian capital of that time in the western Nile delta, gradually developed a centralized national government leading to the last long period of independence and stability in Egypt (Saïtian Period: 624–525 B.C.). The leader, Psamtik the First (664–610 B.C.), intended to counteract the rising Babylonian force by installing an Egyptian/Greek military and economic coalition. He encouraged permanent Greek military colonies in Egypt and founded his rule over Egypt by combining Egyptian forces with Carian and Ionian mercenaries. As a result Greeks from Miletos established the colony of Naucratis in the western Nile delta. This city played a significant role in sea-borne trade and possibly even held a monopoly as the only port of entry for foreign goods.[177] The ties between Greece and Egypt were further enforced under Amasis (569–526 B.C.), who even married a Greek woman.

Although Solon's visit to Egypt comes close to being an historical fact, its date remains disputed. The visit may have taken place just after Solon's archonship around 593/2 B.C.[178] Herodotus, however, stated clearly that King Amasis reigned at the time of Solon's visit, in which case it must have been between 569 and 526 B.C. Diogenes Laërtius,[179] too, claimed that Solon was in Egypt toward the end of his life when Peisistratus was coming into power. Therefore an alternative date around 560 B.C. would appear plausible, too, especially considering Plutarch's statement that Solon had become too old to turn his travel notes from Egypt into epic poetry.[180] Nevertheless, in 590 B.C. and 560 B.C. the political and economic situation in Egypt was similar; at that time both Greece and Egypt enjoyed unusual prosperity and an extremely close friendship. The Greek colonial port of Naucratis was flourishing throughout the sixth century, and considering that Solon made his livelihood from land ownership and commerce, nothing would have been more natural for him than to visit this Greek colony and trading center. In fact, one of the few preserved fragments of Solon's poems describes the Canopic mouth of the Nile,[181] where Naucratis was located, at a distance of only ten miles from the capital in Saïs.[182]

Solon's position as the most distinguished person of the closest ally to Egypt must have made a prolonged visit to the capital compulsory. Moreover, the economic prosperity had ensured increasing opportunities in the development of natural sciences in both countries. Considering Solon's breadth of interests and qualifications, he must have been curious to discuss the most recent scientific achievements with people of equally outstanding reputation but different background. According to Plato, it was during these relaxed conversations between Solon and the episcopal leaders in Saïs that the story of Atlantis originated. The theme of these conversations was history—precisely the history which we have just recapitulated. If there is any framework in which Atlantis might be placed, it would have to be the eastern Mediterranean world before 560 B.C. Let us now listen to Critias once again, as he recalls the legendary conversation between Solon and the priests.

CHAPTER FIVE

DECIPHERING A LEGEND

TIMAEUS 21E–25D: THE ACHAEANS

"In the Delta of Egypt," said Critias, "where, at its head, the stream of the Nile parts in two, there is a certain district called Saitic. The chief city in this district is Saïs—the home of King Amasis,—the founder of which, they say, is a goddess whose Egyptian name is Neïth, and in Greek, as they assert, Athena. These people profess to be great lovers of Athens and in a measure akin to our people here. And Solon said that when he travelled there he was held in great esteem amongst them; moreover, when he was questioning such of their priests as were most versed in ancient lore about their early history, he discovered that neither he himself nor any other Greek knew anything at all, one might say, about such matters. And on one occasion, when he wished to draw them on to discourse on ancient history, he attempted to tell them the most ancient of our traditions, concerning Phoroneus, who was said to be the first man, and Niobe; and he went on to tell the legend about Deucalion and Pyrrha after the Flood, and how they survived it, and to give the genealogy of their descendants; and by recounting the number of years occupied by the events mentioned he tried to calculate the periods of time."

In his introduction Critias draws a vivid picture of Solon's visit to Saïs. Solon is received with great honor and is now conversing with the most knowledgeable priests in an amicable atmosphere. The men who govern Egypt are spending a few days exchanging their views with the Greek general, politician and merchant, and their main discussions most likely revolved around political and trade issues. Everybody present is considered to be a *"great lover of Athens,"* a fact that may have influenced parts of the conversation. Solon enjoys his time with these wise men and on one occasion deliberately draws them into a discourse on the most ancient history. As it turns out, the Greek view of history consists only of fairy tales and vague visions of the past. Soon Solon discovers that neither he himself nor any other Greek knows "anything at all" about history.

> "Whereupon one of the priests, a prodigiously old man, said, 'O Solon, Solon, you Greeks are always children: there is not such a thing as an old Greek.' And on hearing this he asked, 'What mean you by this saying?' And the priest replied, 'You are young in soul, every one of you. For therein you possess not a single belief that is ancient and derived from old tradition, nor yet one science that is hoary with age.'"

One has to be a *"prodigiously old man"* to venture confronting Solon with the truth. In comparison to the Egyptian people, the Greeks are like children *"young in soul"* and without ancient traditions, says the priest. The venerable man will now dominate the discourse, limiting it to a dialogue between men who might be considered the two most accomplished veterans in the western world: Solon who has been called *"the wisest of the Seven Sages"* (20E), the "father of democracy," the "noblest of all poets" (21C), meets an exceptionally veteran member of those *"most versed in ancient lore"* of the episcopal government of Egypt. Part of this man's expertise is the knowledge of a legendary high culture which once existed on Greek soil, but of which Solon seems to be completely oblivious. Naturally, the old man would like to tell Solon about his famous ancestors, but because his story is so wondrous and to increase everybody's curiosity, he wisely chooses a prolonged introduction during which his mixed feelings will become apparent. His speech is dominated by pride in his country's achievements and traditions. He correctly ranks Egypt's competence in history much higher than Greece's. The priest escapes offending Solon, but he does reveal a certain indignation toward his visitor's ignorance. In his introduction, the old man first compares the histories of Egypt and Greece: Egypt had seen constant cultural progress for a few thousand years, and soon after writing became established during the third millennium, the Egyptians began to keep continuous records of the events in the Mediterranean. The Greek people, having just emerged from a dark age, are in comparison *"young in soul,"* meaning that the historical records of the Greek world do not go back to a distant period.[183] In fact, while writing was known in Egypt over two thousand years before this conversation, it had only been reintroduced to Greece within the preceding two centuries.

> "And this is the cause thereof: There have been and there will be many and diverse destructions of mankind, of which the greatest are by fire and water, and lesser ones by countless other means."

Apparently, the Greeks lost their knowledge of history during the *"many and diverse destructions"* that have taken place. According to the priest, the greatest catastrophes are caused by fire and floods, but there are many other possibilities for destruction. The priest has now come close to the essence of his narrative, the destruction of a legendary Greek culture by a devastating flood. He may feel he has reached this point too early and therefore takes another loop in the introduction. By choosing to mention some recent discoveries in Egyptian astronomy, he grants extra authority to his country's scientific achievements, although he is still trying to explain recurring catastrophes.

> "For in truth the story that is told in your country as well as in ours, how once upon a time Phaethon, son of Helios, yoked his father's chariot, and, because he was unable to drive it along the course taken by his father, burnt up all that was upon the earth and himself perished by a thunderbolt—that story, as it is told, has the fashion of a legend, but the truth of it lies in the occurrence of a shifting of the bodies in the heavens which move round the earth, and a destruction of the things on the earth by fierce fire, which recurs at long intervals. At such times all they that dwell on the mountains and in high and dry places suffer destruction more than those who dwell near the sea; and in our case the Nile, our Saviour in other ways, saves us also at such times from this calamity by rising high."

Although the catastrophes on earth are unrelated to the shifts of celestial bodies, both phenomena do occur and their existence has been proven by Egyptians. The priest thinks the legend of Phaeton may seek to link these two occurrences. By itself, this allegory seems inappropriate and not well chosen in the context. Based on this prologue, however, the priest draws a picture of recurring catastrophes and the environmental differences between Greece and Egypt. Turning his attention first to *"fierce fires,"* he remarks that:

- people on the mountains and in high and dry places suffer more than people near the sea
- the Nile is the Saviour of Egypt in many ways
- the Nile saves the Egyptians from such calamity by rising high

"And when, on the other hand, the Gods purge the earth with a flood of waters, all the herdsmen and shepherds that are in the mountains are saved, but those in the cities of your land are swept into the sea by the streams."

Contrary to the *"fierce fires"* which occur at long intervals there are also catastrophes caused by an excess of water when:

- the Gods purge the earth with a flood of waters
- herdsmen and shepherds in the mountains are saved
- Greeks living in the cities are swept into the sea by streams

In both cases, fierce fires and floods, Egypt provides advantageous living conditions, because the annual rising of the Nile ensures sufficient water to counteract droughts while at the same time it is so regular that people can adapt to them, for instance in choosing settlement locations. In Greece, however, floods are unusual; they occur so rarely that the people are not able to plan and prepare for them, thus these floods cause maximum damage.

Correlating the priest's narrative with the archaeological knowledge of the eastern Mediterranean requires the details that will be provided by the story at a later stage: a federal organization of Greece with a united army, royal citadels, bronze weapons, horse-drawn chariots, a large navy, shipyards and horse-racecourses, all of which help to fix an archaeological date. These achievements correspond to the last centuries of the Bronze Age, 1400–1150 B.C., Homer's heroic age. At that time, the principal settlements were in unusual positions on hilltops while the seashore, riverbanks, lowlands and mountains were usually avoided. Such an uncommon place for cities, one that had not been used before, may have sparked concern and curiosity abroad. Moreover, the auger cores in Tiryns record a flood that was most likely caused by heavy rainfall, possibly a catastrophic downpour, which destroyed parts of the city and "swept it into the sea." Perhaps the story attempted to link these two unusual phenomena, the peculiar site choice and the devastating flash flood, to a causal chain, but the argument is not at all convincing. Nonetheless, from the priest's perspective the distinction between catastrophic floods in Greece and salvaging floods in Egypt makes sense: one describes disastrous downpours, the other slow, annual river rises.

The end of the Bronze Age was accompanied by a selective disappearance of the city populations consisting of the leading classes, aristocrats and officers, while the bulk of the people lived on.[184] The priest emphasized a similar phenomenon, the survival of *"herdsmen and shepherds"* after the catastrophes in Greece. The peak phase of the Achaean civilizations was characterized by aristocratic rule, but the post-Achaean era was clearly a time of plebeians. Homer, too, dramatically emphasized this sudden change in his poems. The protagonists of the *Iliad*, which relates the culmination of the Trojan War, were exclusively nobles; while the *Odyssey*, describing the aftermath of the Trojan War, assigned a leading role to herdsmen and shepherds. Thus, there are some distant parallels between the end of the Bronze Age, Homer's heroic age and the Atlantis account, but so far the evidence is anything but convincing.

> "whereas in our country neither then nor at any other time does the water pour down over our fields from above, on the contrary it all tends naturally to well up from below. Hence it is, for these reasons, that what is here preserved is reckoned to be the most ancient; the truth being that in every place where there is no excessive heat or cold to prevent it there always exists some human stock, now more, now less in number."

The priest continues explaining the differences between floods in Greece and in Egypt: In Greece, the water *"pours down over the fields from above"* thereby causing catastrophes; while in Egypt the water *"tends to naturally well up from below."* Since the Nile has no tributaries within Egypt, its floods, caused by the annual snowmelt in the south, are predictable, safe for the Egyptian farmer and beneficial for the winter crops due to the deposition of fertile silt over the floodplain. Because of the perennial occurrence of these floods, the Egyptian culture was able to develop steadily over a long time.[185]

Thus, the Nile is considered to be the great unifying force in Egyptian history,[186] which is why Herodotus called the country *"the gift of the river."* The fact that the catastrophe in Greece was caused by water coming down from above should exclude the possibility of a tidal wave caused by earthquakes, as was suggested when Atlantis was sought in context with the eruption of Thera.[187]

Although the priest considers Egypt the most propitious country to live in, he realizes that people will occupy any place on earth apart from the most extreme deserts and cold regions.

> "And if any event has occurred that is noble or great or in any way conspicuous, whether it be in your country or in ours or in some other place of which we know by report, all such events are recorded from of old and preserved here in our temples."

Solon now learns from the priest that the Egyptian officials have long used their millennia-old knowledge of writing to keep records of all remarkable events that have occurred in any country known to Egypt, including Greece, of course. Egyptian inscriptions, however, do not generally consist of detailed technical depictions of foreign countries; hence, on first sight, it would be highly unlikely to find a detailed account like the story of Atlantis on a hieroglyphic column. It was not the scribes' concern or duty to present an objective view of the past;[188] on the contrary, their hieroglyphic writing concentrated on praising pharaoh.[189] In two significant periods, however, under the rule of pharaoh Merenptah (1224–1204 B.C.) and of Rameses III (1181–1153 B.C.),[190] foreign affairs were indeed noted in much detail. This was also the time, immediately after the Trojan War, when long-distance trade collapsed and the Sea People raided the eastern Mediterranean. Egypt, like any other country bordering the eastern Mediterranean, was directly affected by these political events. Much of our knowledge about the end of the thirteenth century is derived from these Egyptian records.[191] They also tell us how closely related the different eastern Mediterranean countries were in trade and politics. If the hieroglyphic text recollected by the priest originated shortly after the Trojan War, its composition would fall precisely into the short era of more pragmatic inscriptions.

Naturally, those ancient texts which can be examined by historians today have only survived by chance; most Egyptian writings were lost, for example, during Caesar's, and later, burning of the libraries in Alexandria.[192]

"whereas your people and the others are but newly equipped, every time, with letters and all such arts as civilized states require; and when, after the usual interval of years, like a plague, the flood from heaven comes sweeping down afresh upon your people, it leaves none of you but the unlettered and uncultured, so that you become young as ever, with no knowledge of all that happened in old times in this land or in your own."

Returning to Greece and its disasters, the priest provides the following details:

- the knowledge of writing was lost during catastrophes
- all other arts which characterize a civilized state were lost
- the flood came down from heaven
- the catastrophe resulted in a selective genocide of the lettered and cultured people
- all historic knowledge was lost

Once again, the priest emphasizes that the floods came down from heaven, not from the sea, and that it selectively eliminated the more cultivated echelons of the society, leaving only *"the unlettered and uncultured."* Solon is now explicitly told that the knowledge of writing once existed in Greece but that it was lost during the catastrophe, like all other qualities required by civilized states. Today, most scholars agree on four essential prerequisites for "civilization": subsistence by agriculture, the existence of cities, advanced social organization and the use of writing.[193] Writing, especially, was held in the highest regard in the ancient world, and its origin or invention was associated with gods and heroes.[194] However, the only written documents that have survived from the Aegean world date to the Minoan and Achaean civilization of the second millennium: the Linear A and Linear B clay tablets from Crete, the Linear B tablets from Greece and the "Cypro-Minoan" inscriptions from Cyprus.[195] The people of Archaic and Classical Greece, including Solon and Plato, were unaware of their predecessors' knowledge of writing. Rhys Carpenter, a renowned archaeologist, therefore declared that the entirely exact statement in the Atlantis account about the loss of writing in ancient Greece should convince the most skeptical scholars of the genuineness of Solon's conversation with the Saïtian priests, because Plato could not have known about his predecessors' literacy.[196] Homer, who composed his poems just after writing was reestablished, recalled a heroic age when literacy was known. The description of a letter in the form of a wooden, folding tablet consigned to a wayfarer, appeared to the poet himself as something exotic and almost magical (VI.169).[197] Yet the excavation of the Ulu Burun shipwreck has brought to light precisely the kind of folding tablet depicted by Homer.

The account conforms to our current archaeological knowledge of the Late Bronze Age. Looking back from the sixth century B.C., the Achaean era was the only time when civilizations in control of writing dominated the Aegean. Many of their crafts and abilities were later lost (in the priest's opinion due to the catastrophe he is describing) and the sixth century B.C. inhabitants of Greece must have been unaware of their own resourceful forefathers. The destructive processes described by the priest—earthquakes, floods and fires—all occurred virtually simultaneously around 1200 B.C. when most Achaean residences were devastated: Tiryns was destroyed by earthquakes and floods, Mycenae and Midea by fires and possibly by earthquakes and Pylos by conflagration.

> "Certainly the genealogies which you related just now, Solon, concerning the people of your country, are little better than children's tales; for, in the first place, you remember but one deluge, though many had occurred previously; and next, you are ignorant of the fact that the noblest and most perfect race amongst men were born in the land where you now dwell, and from them both you yourself are sprung and the whole of your existing city, out of some little seed that chanced to be left over; but this has escaped your notice because for many generations the survivors died with no power to express themselves in writing."

Critias said in the introduction how Solon soon realized his inability to match the wisdom of his hosts, which rested on millennia-old records. Solon had reiterated the ubiquitous story of a great deluge, but even in this regard, the priest's knowledge exceeded his. One must realize that the flood around which the priest's story revolves was different from the legendary deluges mentioned in the Bible and in traditional accounts of civilization all around the world. Moreover, the priest thought that Solon was unaware *"that the noblest and most perfect race of man were born in the land where you now dwell."* But the priest was mistaken. No doubt,

Solon knew Homer's heroic age, the Trojan War and the famous deeds of Achaean heroes like Odysseus and Agamemnon; after all, the remains of their citadels were visible in several places, including Athens. During the conversation in Saïs, however, Solon concentrated on discussing the very ancient past and old oral traditions, without including the more recent accounts of the Greek heroic age. Atlantis and the 2,500 years of search for it might never have come to life if Solon had realized at this point that the priest's story was not all that original.[198] The exciting atmosphere of the visit and the Egyptians' efforts to impress their guest, especially those of the principal priest, succeeded in confusing Solon so much that he was unable to realize that Atlantis had its place in Homer's heroic age. Once he was persuaded that the Egyptians held the patent for historical knowledge, he had entered a track which was going to carry him farther and farther away from reality.

According to the priest, Solon's famous ancestors were *"born in the land"* where Solon now resides, and from them *"the whole of your existing city"* has sprung. This phrase represents a key problem to the understanding of the legend. Where precisely did these acclaimed predecessors live? Other translators avoid the word "city" in this context; for instance, Desmond Lee rendered *"You and your fellow citizens are descended from the few survivors that remained,"*[199] while the standard German edition of Plato uses the word for state or country.[200] Hence, the phrase appears to lack sufficient exactness to be applied to "Athens," "Attika" or "the Athenian city state" only, as it has traditionally been done. It rather seems to allude to the Greek territory in general, *"the land where you now dwell."*

Solon's entire generation is said to derive from *"some little seed that chanced to be left over"* after the catastrophe; which would be applicable to the end of the Bronze Age when, after the collapse of the Achaean states, the population density in Greece plummeted dramatically. Athens did play an unusual role at that time, because it was the only city which escaped the disruption. Therefore, only Athenian traditions reached back into the Bronze Age.[201]

The priest assumes that the reason for the Greek's ignorance of history lies in the fact that *"for many generations the survivors died with no power to express themselves in writing."* Although the knowledge of writing was indeed lost after the Achaean demise, this view is slightly mistaken, because it does not consider the possibility of oral transmission. Through Homer's poems, the Greeks had acquired a faint idea about the *"noblest and most perfect race of man"* which had preceded them on Greek soil.

> "For verily at one time, Solon, before the greatest destruction by water, what is now the Athenian State was the bravest in war and supremely well organized also in all other respects. It is said that it possessed the most splendid works of art and the noblest polity of any nation under heaven of which we have heard tell."

Once again, the account stresses the *"greatest destruction by water"* which lead to the collapse of the ancient Greek civilization. Now, the priest specifically names the *"Athenian State"* as a successor of this civilization. He might have chosen this term to avoid reusing the phrase *"the land where you now dwell"* or in order to please Solon, for, as was said initially, all people present were *"great lovers of Athens."* Or perhaps the priest might not have used the term the *"Athenian State"* at all; Solon may have introduced it into the narrative. Greece at Solon's time was still a disorganized collection of petty states, and a unified nation might have been beyond Solon's imagination.[202]

The Achaean realm included Attika, of course, but had its center in the adjacent Argolid. The other characteristics mentioned in this paragraph, however, are quite applicable to the Achaean era: an outstanding military power, a well-organized state, noble polity and splendid works of art. There is no doubt that the Achaeans were well prepared for warfare. Their readiness for military conflict is obvious from the Linear B tablets, which devote much detail to armaments. Lord William Taylour said of the Achaeans: *"It would almost seem as if they loved strife for its own sake."*[203] They had installed themselves in dominating positions for strategic purposes, while the preceding Minoans on Crete had chosen merely pleasant and convenient sites, without being concerned about strategic importance.[204] Thus the description of an ancient Greek military power seems far more applicable to the Achaeans than, for instance, to the Minoans.

During Solon's life span, Greek civilization still lingered on at a comparatively low level: houses were constructed mainly of wood and mud-brick; precious materials were scarce and the arts of painting and sculpture were limited.[205] Therefore this chronological period has been termed "Archaic." Since Schliemann's excavations of the Late Bronze Age citadels in Greece, we know of an earlier civilized populace, the Achaeans, masters in arts, crafts, engineering and warfare. The people of this era and particularly their products reached distant shores. Fine Achaean pottery was known and appreciated in Egypt and all around the eastern Mediterranean, and many themes depicted in Achaean art seem to reveal impressions gained abroad.[206] Thus if any Greek high culture was known in distant places, it would have been the Achaean.

> "Upon hearing this, Solon said, that he marvelled, and with the utmost eagerness requested the priest to recount for him in order and exactly all the facts about those citizens of old. The priest then said: "I begrudged you not the story, Solon; nay, I will tell it, both for your own sake and that of your city, and most of all for the sake of the Goddess who has adopted for her own both your land and this of ours, and has nurtured and trained them—yours first by the space of a thousand years, when she had received the seeds of you from Gê and Hephaestus, and after that ours. And the duration of our civilization as set down in our sacred writings is 8000 years. Of the citizens, then, who lived 9000 years ago, I will declare to you briefly certain of their laws and the noblest of the deeds they performed: the full account in precise order and detail we shall go through later at our leisure, taking the actual writings."

The long introduction has fulfilled its purpose, the intimidated Solon requests with *"utmost eagerness"* to hear the full account of his ancestors! The Greek high culture existed nine thousand years ago, i.e. nine thousand years before Solon's visit to Saïs. As was said before, the story will provide many particulars (individual states or kingdoms in Greece, a united Greek army, citadels, bronze weapons, chariots, a large navy fleet, shipyards and horse-racecourses) which should help to fix an archaeological date: to assume such a level of achievement at c. 10,000 B.C. is absurd,[207] but it does correspond to the last centuries of the Bronze Age, 1400–1150 B.C., and to no other time in Mediterranean prehistory.[208]

A possible explanation for the discrepancy between the archaeological dating and the one given in the legend might be derived from Diodorus Siculus' (first century B.C.) remark, that *"in early times . . . it was customary to reckon the year by the lunar cycle."*[209] While Babylonia and Greece employed lunar (or lunisolar) calendars,[210] Egypt was using three calendars simultaneously (two lunar and religious, one civil) since 2500 B.C. Considering that the 8,000 years may have been lunar years, which need to be converted by division by 12.37 (the number of moons per year in a Metonic Cycle of eight years), the actual time of the event would have been around 1207 B.C.[211]—i.e., if Solon's visit in Egypt was in 560 B.C. The discrepancies between lunar and solar calendars could also explain the very large dates (17,000 years) which Herodotus received from the Egyptians for the age of their deities.[212] The biblical longevity of exceptionally old men such as Adam (930 years), Seth (912), Enos (905), Methusaleh (969), Lamech (777) and Noah (950), too, appears plausible if their life spans were measured in lunar years.[213] Converted into our modern solar calendar, their lives would have lasted between sixty-two and seventy-eight years. Furthermore, the Egyptian historians Manetho, Syncellus and Eusebius claimed that the time span between the first Dynasty (about 3100 B.C.) and the end of the thirtieth (332 B.C.) was 36,525 years;[214] divided by 12.37 this figure decreases to 2,952 years and thus comes close to the roughly 2,800 years provided by today's (disputed) archaeological chronology for Egypt.

Such juggling with dates, however tempting, should be carried out with extreme care. Ancient accounts are full of absolute numbers which, from our present-day perspective, make no sense at all. The story of Atlantis is a good example, because the description of the city contains several absolute measurements. Some of these appear plausible, for instance the half-mile diameter of the city center, but others do not make sense at all: the plain around the city, for instance, was said to be 335 by 223 miles, thus completely disproportionate to the size of the town. There have always been problems with absolute measurements from antiquity, and even the numbers provided by much later authors like Pausanias (second century A.D.) are not readily transferable to modern times. These discrepancies may have been due to the lack of absolute standards. In Classical times the weight "talent" had different meanings,[215] just as the distance "mile" or the measure "gallon" still have today. As a consequence, it will be best to disregard absolute dimensions whenever possible.

According to the priest the events recollected by the hieroglyphs 8,000 years ago coincide with the age of Saïtian civilization. If this really corresponds to c. 1200 B.C., Saïs could have been established in the aftermath of the Trojan War. Katherine Folliot considers this a plausible link, because many Greek ships ended at Egyptian shores when they returned from Troy. Homer relates that some of the Greek heroes including Menelaus stayed in Egypt for several years; others may have remained in the country for the rest of their lives.[216] If Saïs was indeed settled by such a Greek contingent, it would explain the introductory remark that the people there *"profess to be great lovers of Athens and in a measure akin to our people here."*

In the last sentence the priest indicates that he is recalling the inscriptions without looking at the actual writings. Since Solon asks for *"all the facts"* about his legendary ancestors, the priest agrees to describe first *"certain of their laws and the noblest deeds they performed"* from his memory, then he will provide Solon with the complete account, *"taking the actual writings."* This twofold structure is mirrored in Plato's report of the legend. Plato gives a general description, concentrating on the Greek high culture, in *Timaeus* first; later, in *Critias*, he renders the full account of Atlantis with all its technical details. After having received the general introduction into the subject, Solon may have been led to the inscribed pillar to receive a full translation of the whole legend. He may have taken notes, which would then have been handed down in his family for a few generations. Since Plato was a descendant of Solon, the original manuscript could well have been in Plato's hands. In that case, an oral stage may never have been necessary for the transmission, a fact which could explain the enormous detail of the narrative.

> "To get a view of their laws, look at the laws here; for you will find existing here at the present time your city. You see, first, how the priestly class is separated off from the rest; next, the class of craftsmen, of which each sort works by itself without mixing with any other; then the classes of shepherds, hunters, and farmers, each distinct and separate. Moreover the military class here, as no doubt you have noticed, is kept apart from all the other classes, being enjoined by the law to devote itself solely to the work of training for war."

The priest describes the legendary Greek culture as being divided into professions: priests, shepherds, hunters, farmers, military and craftsmen, subdivided by their occupation, formed individual groups which did not mingle. Such a social stratification is one of the most remarkable characteristics of the Achaean society.[217] The Linear B tablets describe a hierarchical system, with the *Wanax* as the king and foremost leader, followed by the *Lawagetas*, the so-called leader of the people. A group of *hequetai* or "followers," constituting the nobility, escorted the king.[218] These aristocrats presumably acted as officers—they held estates and owned slaves, wore a distinctive form of dress and had their own chariots.[219] The artisans were further divided by their craft; among them, the bronzesmiths enjoyed a special status and were entitled to extra benefits. Other trades mentioned in the tablets are those of masons, woodcutters, shipbuilders, cabinetmakers, tailors, hunters, saddlers, planters, bakers, perfumers, bath attendants and physicians,[220] a discipline which the priest will soon mention too. Twenty-six professions have been distinguished from the Linear B tablets of which twenty-three were also known to Homer.[221] Some of these professions became evident in the excavations, too, for instance "the house of the oil merchant," "the house of the potter," the archive room of the scribe etc. The priest compares the specialized classes of the ancient Greek civilization with the Egyptian society of his time, which included at least six separate classes: priests, craftsmen, shepherds, hunters, farmers and military. A very similar division of Egyptian society was reported by Herodotus (fifth century B.C.): *"The Egyptians are divided into seven classes: priests, warriors, cowherds, swineherds, tradesmen, interpreters, and pilots."*[222]

> "A further feature is the character of their equipment with shields and spears; for we were the first of the peoples of Asia to adopt these weapons, it being the Goddess who instructed us, even as she instructed you first of all the dwellers in yonder lands."

According to the priest, shields and spears were first adopted by Egyptians and Greeks. Indeed, such armaments distinguished the Achaean mainlanders sharply from their Minoan precursors—one reason why the priest's account cannot be applied to the Middle Bronze Age Minoans.

> "Again, with regard to wisdom, you perceive, no doubt, the law here—how much attention it has devoted from the very beginning to the Cosmic Order, by discovering all the effects which the divine causes produce upon human life, down to divination and the art of medicine which aims at health, and by its mastery also of all the other subsidiary studies."

The Linear B tablets unfortunately only bear the record of commerce and tax transactions, thus, we lack knowledge of the level of scientific achievement—*"wisdom,"* as the priest calls it—that was reached in Late Bronze Age Greece. The engineering feats of the Achaeans, however, their impressive citadels, embraced by walls several feet thick, their roads and bridges, the dam and canal near Tiryns and the Lake Kopais drainage system yield a faint impression of the level of technical achievement at that time.[223]

> "So when, at that time, the Goddess had furnished you, before all others, with all this orderly and regular system, she established your State, choosing the spot wherein you were born since she perceived therein a climate duly blended, and how that it would bring forth men of supreme wisdom. So it was that the Goddess, being herself both a lover of war and a lover of wisdom, chose the spot which was likely to bring forth men most like unto herself, and this first she established. Wherefore you lived under the rule of such laws as these— yea, and laws still better—and you surpassed all men in every virtue, as became those who were offspring and nurslings of gods. Many, in truth, and great are the achievements of your State, which are a marvel to men as they are here recorded."

The famous high culture described in the Egyptian story was able to form on Greek soil because the Goddess considered its climate advantageous. The priest emphasizes the quality and importance of the laws and declares that the Greeks were *"offspring and nurslings of the gods."* The ubiquitous presence of gods and their close affinity to the Achaean heroes provided the basis for Greek mythology and played an important role in the Homeric epics.[224] The account alludes to Greek mythology as well as the many deeds of the legendary Achaean heroes like Jason, Odysseus and Agamemnon, whose fame apparently reached foreign lands across the Mediterranean. The Achaeans can also be said to have *"surpassed all men in every virtue"* at least with regard to their craftsmanship. Achaean artists were expected to strive for the highest possible mastery (XI.784): *"Let your motto be* I lead. *Strive to the best,"* said Homer (VI.207). This excellence may have been at least encouraged if not demanded by the higher echelons of the society, since the lack of natural resources in Greece forced the economy to thrive on the quality not the quantity of its products.

To summarize the interpretation of the Atlantis legend up to this point: when compared with the information from excavations, the study of the Linear B tablets and the interpretation of Homer's epics, the hieroglyphic inscriptions, recollected by the priest, seem to be reasonably applicable to life in Greece during the fourteenth and thirteenth centuries B.C. At that time an extremely well stratified society in possession of the knowledge of writing developed a meticulously organized administration which achieved a high level of technical and artistic expertise. Moreover, the protagonists of this civilization were esteemed as *"nurslings of gods"* and their *"achievements were a marvel to men,"* just like the legendary feats of the Homeric heroes, who were also descendants of the gods. At this point, the premise seems to be sufficiently supported to allow for further steps and deductions. One should, of course, seek to verify this working hypothesis as more details become available.

> "But there is one which stands out above all both for magnitude and for nobleness. For it is related in our records how once upon a time your State stayed the course of a mighty host, which, starting from a distant point in the Atlantic ocean, was insolently advancing to attack the whole of Europe, and Asia to boot. For the ocean there was at that time navigable; for in front of the mouth which you Greeks call, as you say, 'the pillars of Heracles,' there lay an island which was larger than Libya and Asia together; and it was possible, for the travellers of that time to cross from it to the other islands, and from the islands to the whole of the continent over against them which encompasses that veritable ocean. For all that we have here, lying within the mouth of which we speak, is evidently a haven having a narrow entrance; but that yonder is a real ocean, and the land surrounding it may most rightly be called, in the fullest and truest sense, a continent."

In addition to all the legendary achievements of Solon's ancestors *"there is one which stands out above all both for magnitude and for nobleness,"* says the priest. They *"stayed the course of a mighty host"* which, as the priest will soon reveal, was decisively overthrown by the Greeks. If the Greek high culture describes the Late Bronze Age, one would, of course, expect this conflict to have been the Trojan War.[225] The priest provides some detailed information regarding the geographic location of the enemy's land; he says that it was:

- an island
- in the Atlantic Ocean
- larger than Libya and Asia together
- inside a strait
- with difficult navigability

The first three of these characteristics are not applicable to Troy, but the latter two might be. In order to clarify the myth the priest's geographic description should be examined more closely from a sixth-century B.C. perspective. First of all, one must realize that, if our interpretation is correct, he translated the account from over 500-year-old hieroglyphic inscriptions into a foreign language, Greek. Although he could probably cope with Greek, he may have encountered the same problem with the foreign names in the hieroglyphic inscription that still today restricts their translation:

> Egyptian hieroglyphic documents suffer greatly in value from the imperfect system of vocalization used in them in transcribing foreign names.[226]

The foreign names mentioned in the Atlantis account are largely responsible for preventing its decipherment. The word "island," for example, could not be more clearly defined today. In the Late Bronze Age, however, the situation was quite different. For the Egyptians, most foreigners came from islands: *"as for the foreign countries, they made a conspiracy in their islands,"*[227] or: *"Now the northern countries which were in their islands were quivering in their bodies."*[228] Rhys Carpenter provided a straightforward explanation for this misinterpretation:

> Because there were virtually no islands in Egypt there was no specific ancient Egyptian word for such features. The hieroglyphic sign often rendered in translation as "island" properly denotes a sandy tract or shore, and is widely used as a determinative symbol for foreign lands or regions beyond the Nile valley.[229]

Today, the Egyptians speak of an "Island of Meroë," which lies well inland, and the Maghrib, too, is still called "Gizereh el Maghrib" or "the island of the West."[230] The term "island" seems to be much more clearly defined now than it was three thousand years ago. For example, Agamemnon, the commander-in-chief of the united Greek forces in the Trojan War, was considered the ruler *"of many*

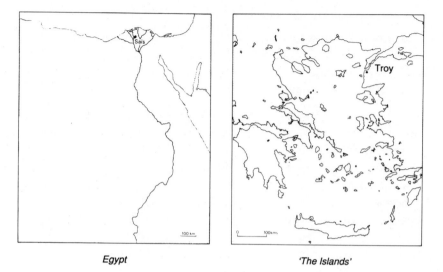

Egypt
     'The Islands'

A comparison of the land/sea distribution in Egypt and in the
Aegean shows why the latter was referred to as "The Islands."

islands and all the Argive lands" (11.108), although his personal kingdom only included the country between the northern Argive Plain
and Corinthia.[231] *"To the islands"* appears also as a common phrase
in Hittite texts from the thirteenth century B.C.,[232] in particular
when they refer to *Ahhiyawa*, which is generally identified with
Achaea or Achaean Greece. During the Mycenaean dominion of
the Aegean the Egyptian records frequently used the expression
"the islands of the Great Green "[233] and most historians agree that this
idiom describes the Aegean ‚slands under Achaean control, including the shores of mainland Greece.[234] Thus, during the Late Bronze
Age the lands in and around the Aegean seem to have been called
"the islands"—comparing maps of Egypt and the Aegean shows
why this could have been so.

Perhaps Solon helped the priest's translation by providing what
he thought were the correct place-names. Plato mentions in *Critias*
(113A–B) that Solon later even changed some of the original names
back to what he considered to be their Greek equivalent. Looking
from a maritime perspective, the text states that the country in
question lay *"in front of the mouth which you Greeks call, as you say, 'the
pillars of Heracles,'"* meaning: in front of a narrow water passage.
By using the phrase *"which you Greeks call, as you say,"* the priest

reveals some uncertainty whether the inscriptions and Solon's interpretation really relate to the same passage. The "pillars of Heracles" are today generally identified with the Straits of Gibraltar, which were in fact outside the range of Achaean ships; but the term first appeared in the *Odyssey* (1.53–54), and Homer most probably had not heard of the Straits of Gibraltar![235] Even in Strabo's time (63 B.C.–A.D. 26) there was still confusion on what precisely the phrase meant.[236] Richard Hennig, a German geographer who investigated the root of the term "the pillars of Heracles" decided that it was not initially applied to the Straits of Gibraltar but to another locality at the end of the Greek sphere of influence.[237] This ambivalence was also expressed in ancient literature, and Servius (*c.* A.D. 400) provided a hint where the original pillars of Heracles might have been:

> *Columnas Herculis legimus et in Ponto et in Hispania*[238]
> (We pass through the pillars of Heracles in the Black Sea as well as in Spain)

The Mediterranean includes two narrow waterways leading to distant seas: the Straits of Gibraltar (to the Atlantic Ocean) and the Dardanelles/Bosporus (to the Black Sea). According to Servius, both passages were called "the pillars of Heracles," but only one of them lay in the range of Achaean ships: the one to the Black Sea. Hennig concluded that the phrase was applied to the Straits of Gibraltar only after 500 B.C.[239] Thus the conversation between Solon and the priest falls into the transitional period when the idiom changed its meaning. Solon's possible confusion of the Black Sea and Atlantic passages may become understandable in the light of contemporary history. Just a few years before his visit to Egypt, the Greek colony of Massilia (Marseilles) was founded in southern France, which had put the Straits of Gibraltar for the first time within the reach of Greek ships.[240] Traditionally, the pillars of Heracles marked the end of the known world[241]—to venture beyond them was a symbol for going beyond the limits of man.[242] In the Late Bronze Age, however, the principal Greek world ended at the Bosporus, while in Solon's time it extended to Gibraltar. When the Greeks' geographic sphere expanded, this mythological place was apparently moved to the new edges of the known world.[243] Thus, when Solon heard about the narrow waterway in a distant place, he naturally thought of the passage into the Atlantic. By using a contemporary perspective he committed the same

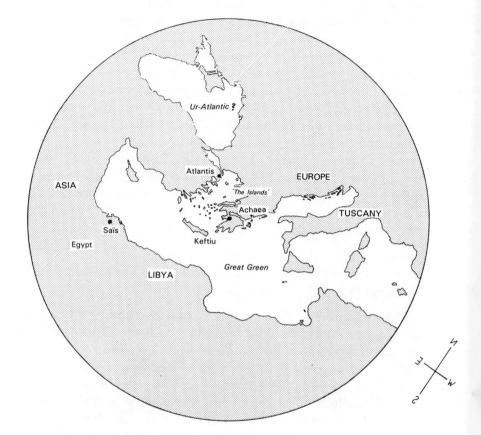

To imagine the thirteenth-century B.C. world as described by the Atlantis account, we must disregard modern preconceptions. This familiar map has been "alienated" to allow us to see it with new eyes. Although looking strange, the mirror image is completely accurate and provides the same information as a regular map of the Mediterranean. In the thirteenth century B.C. the Egyptians called the Mediterranean Sea the "Great Green"; Crete was named Keftiu, and the many Aegean islands and mainland shores were just "The Islands." ("Achaea" is the name used by Homer for the Greece of the heroic age.) The "island" of Atlantis was described as being "in front of a mouth" which leads to a "veritable ocean . . . encompassed by the whole of the continent." There is only one passage and one ocean within the Mycenaean world that qualifies as a candidate for this description: the Dardanelles leading to the Black Sea (labeled Ur-Atlantis).

mistake that would characterize the study of the Atlantis account for the next two and a half millennia.[244]

The term "Atlantic Ocean" occurs in Plato's original writing just before the mention of the "pillars of Heracles." Whether Solon or Plato introduced the expression into the text cannot be determined. It first occurred in documents written by Herodotus (c.480–425 BC),[245] about one century before Plato wrote *Timaeus*, but more than a century after Solon's visit to Saïs. Herodotus mentions the name Atlantic in conjunction with a mountain range called "Atlas," but the Greeks knew of several different ranges bearing this name; these lay in today's Crete, the Peloponnese, Turkey, Sicily, Saudi Arabia, Ethiopia and in the Sahara.[246] Since all these mountains received their names relatively late, certainly after the Atlantis account had been composed, the original name Atlantic may be more likely derived from *antlos* or *antl-ant*, meaning "strong, splashing current."[247]

There is no evidence that the ocean which we today call the Atlantic was reached by eastern Mediterranean people during the Bronze Age. Because it was apparently not known in the Aegean world, there was no need to have a word for it either. Between 1470 B.C. and the middle of the twelfth century B.C. Egyptian records often referred to an ocean called the "Great Green," especially in connection with the "islands of the Great Green" as mentioned above. One island, called "Keftiu," generally identified with Crete, is said to lie "in the middle of the Great Green"[248] which thus clearly delineates the Mediterranean Sea. The term "Great Green" may imply the existence of at least one other ocean of smaller size and different color, and a map of the Achaean world shows a candidate matching these requirements: the Black Sea.

The ancients knew of a dark and mysterious sea, described by Becher as *"the infamous mare coagulatum,"* the coagulated sea.[249] Humboldt, too, recounts the existence of such an ancient *"muddy, shallow, dark, and misty sea,"* calling it *mare tenebrosum*, and both authors identify it with the Atlantic Ocean. Aristotle[250] described the waters outside the pillars of Heracles as *"shallow owing to the mud, but calm, for it lies in a hollow."* If the Atlantic Ocean, however, was not reached by prehistoric people from the eastern Mediterranean but the Black Sea was, how can there be so many references to the former and none to the latter? Moreover, why are attributes of the Black Sea used to describe the Atlantic Ocean when they do not fit?

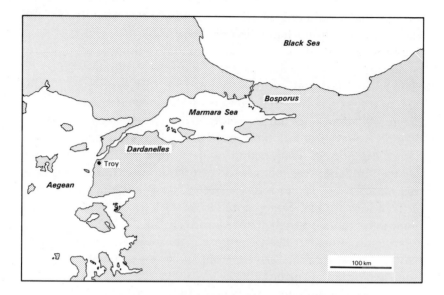

A map of northwest Anatolia shows Troy's strategic location at the Dardanelles (called Hellespont in ancient Greece), the entrance to the Marmara Sea (Propontis), the Bosporus and the Black Sea. For 2,000 years Troy was able to take advantage of this favorable geographic position. Later, the city of Byzantium thrived at the Bosporus for another millennium on the same geographic advantages.

Both oceans came within the reach of Greek ships during the seventh century B.C.—the Atlantic Ocean for the first time, the Black Sea for the second time, because the Bosporus passage had not been possible for a few centuries during the Dark Age. Apparently, some dim memory of a dark and misty sea continued to be expressed, for instance, in Homer's poems and in oral traditions. When the long-distance shipping routes opened up, the Atlantic Ocean was the more remote and mystical sea of the two, and the ancient knowledge of a perilous, coagulated sea may have become applied to the wrong one.

The foreign land is said to have lain *"in front of a mouth,"* and it provided *"a haven having a narrow entrance."* This characterization, too, seems more applicable to the entrance to the Black Sea than to the Straits of Gibraltar. The original Greek text emphasized the difference between the "ocean" (*pelágos*) on this side of the straits, the "passage" (*stóma*) and the "sea" (*póntos*) on the other side.

Póntos, of course, is also a synonym for the Black Sea (*Póntos Euxínus*). One translator therefore interpreted Plato's text as follows:

> The traveler came from the open ocean to an inland sea, the *póntos*—as *Póntos Euxínus*, Black Sea, this name for a particular inland sea survived to the present day.[251]

Like the Black Sea, the *Póntos* beyond the passage was surrounded by a continent in the fullest sense (meaning an endless landmass). Unlike the Atlantic Ocean and the American continents, the Black Sea was in the range of Achaean ships. According to Greek mythology, Jason left the Achaean port of Iolkos for Colchis on the Black Sea shore of Georgia in quest of the Golden Fleece. Mycenaean artifacts have been found at various places around the Black Sea: nine swords, a dagger, potsherds and a few other objects were recovered from fourteen different prehistoric sites in Romania. Mycenaean pottery was retrieved from the seabed off the Bulgarian coast and from the northern Hittite city of Maşat, while a number of swords were found in Georgia.[252] Homer, too, may allude to the Black Sea several times when he speaks of fast ships heading toward the Dark Sea.[253] In conclusion, the entrance to the Black Sea passage, where Troy is located, seems to suit the geographic description of Atlantis better than a locality near the Straits of Gibraltar.

Regarding the size of the mysterious "island," most translations state that it *"was larger than Libya and Asia together"*; the Greek text, however, does not use an adjective in this context; instead it uses the adverbial idiom "to be of greater significance."[254] One of the translators therefore maintains categorically that Plato uses the expression "the sphere of influence" of the kings of Atlantis, rather than "their territory."[255] Besides, Libya and Asia were differently defined at that time: Asia probably characterized the Near East including Egypt, while Libya described the then known Africa. The first known appearance of the term "Libya" again dates to the time of Merneptah at 1227 B.C.[256]

The account states that *"the ocean there was at that time navigable,"* thus emphasizing that the knowledge to navigate this passage once existed but was later lost, a fact that is fully applicable to the Dardanelles and Bosporus. Today, few archaeologists will doubt that the Achaeans at least occasionally navigated into the Black Sea,[257] but not long ago it was assumed that the strong currents in the Bosporus prevented this voyage until the invention of the Ionic pentakonter, c. 680 B.C.[258] There are no finds indicating exchange across the Bosporus from the tenth to eighth century B.C.,[259] thus the impression given by the account, that the straits used to be negotiable in the past, but that this potential was lost (for a few centuries) appears correct.

> "Now in this island of Atlantis there existed a confederation of kings, of great and marvellous power, which held sway over all the island, and over many other islands also and parts of the continent; and, moreover, of the lands here within the Straits they ruled over Libya as far as Egypt, and over Europe as far as Tuscany."

For the first time, the name of the foreign nation is mentioned: Atlantis. The term is an adjective derived from "Atlas."[260] Luce calls it a *patronymikón*, a word which describes a father/daughter relation; literally translated Atlantis would mean "Atlas's daughter." As it happens, Atlas is the source of the Trojan lineage; his mortal daughter Electra conceived children from Zeus, who became the inhabitants of Troy. According to Apollodorus (3.12.1) and Homer (xx.215), the complete genealogy of Troy until the Trojan War consisted of:[261]

1. Atlas
2. Electra
3. Dardanus
4. Erichthonius
5. Tros
6. Ilus
7. Laomedon
8. Priam

Priam was the leader of the Greeks' opponents in the war. Laomedon, his father, was the erector of the fortress's walls. Trojans, Ilians and Dardanians are the names of the peoples fighting the Greeks. Thus, the names of five progenitors (out of eight) were actively used in the Homeric vocabulary. It would not seem implausible if there were even older traditions going back to the very first forefather, Atlas, or his daughter "Atlantis."

There are indeed some indications that the name of Atlantis and its inhabitants, the Atlanteans, was used to describe the people of Troy. In 1776, Jacob Bryant published a six-volume encyclopedia entitled *Analysis of Ancient Mythology* (bearing the intriguing sub-title: *Wherein an Attempt is made to divest Tradition of Fable; and to reduce the Truth to its Original Purity*). Bryant, an expert on Homeric Troy,[262] derived the Trojans from Meropians (11.830), whom he described as people of great ingenuity and pride, who claimed to be descendants *"of the earth-born giant brood."* These Meropians or Meropida are also named *"Atlantians the supposed off-spring of Atlas"*:

> The Trojans were also of this family and the poet speaking of the foundations of Troy, mentions it as a city of the Meropes. Their history is comprised in that of Dardanus . . . the founder of Ilium or Troy. The common opinion is, that the city was built by Ilus, the son of Dardanus who must consequently have been of the same family, a Merop-Atlantian.[263]

According to Bryant, these Merop-Atlantians settled in the far west as well as in the far east: *"thus we find, that whether we inquire in Mauritania, or at the Indus, the same names occur."* Such traditional knowledge of Atlanteans west and east of Egypt may have contributed to the confusion of directions in the story. Bryant arrives at the conclusion that the people of Troy, *"the Dardanians, were Atlantians, being the reputed children of Electra."* If this was indeed a very ancient name for the Trojans, it would not be surprising to find it used in Egypt, the native land of the Atlantis legend, because the Egyptians had a tendency to apply outdated names to new populations occupying the same area.[264] The subsequent discussion will show that both the Trojans and the Atlanteans, were extremely *"skilled in the sciences,"* as Bryant said, and that they both claimed to be *"allied to the gods and heroes."*[265]

Atlantis was governed by a confederation of kings, like the Achaean realm.[266] They *"held sway"* over all of the straits (Bosporus and Dardanelles?) and parts of the continent (Asia Minor?), but they also *"ruled"* over a much larger territory: Europe as far as Tyrrhenia and Libya as far as Egypt. The ancient meaning of these geographic names is not well established, and they may have been mistranslated too. Nevertheless, if Atlantis was near the Straits of Gibraltar, its territorial influence in Europe would have ended in the Tyrrhenian Sea without overlapping with the Greek dominion! If the dispute, however, recounts the Trojan War, Atlantis/Troy's territorial claim would have covered the whole eastern Mediterranean, touching the Achaean, Hittite and Egyptian states. Once again, one must distinguish between the relatively small territory which was under direct control of Atlantis, and the very large region over which it had an influence, possibly through trading.

The names of the Aegean people ("*Drdny*") who fought Egypt in the battle of Qadesh in 1300 B.C., as allies of the Hittite empire and as recorded by Egyptian inscriptions, coincide with the inhabitants of Troy as named in the Homeric poems ("*Dardanians*"),[267] perhaps hinting at a coalition between the Trojans and Hittites during the thirteenth-century wars against Egypt.[268] The expression "*to hold sway*" may point to direct attacks of the "Atlanteans," possibly indicating an active involvement of Trojan troops in the early raids of the Sea People. It might be considered more likely, however, that Atlantis/Troy exerted an indirect dominion over the eastern Mediterranean, for instance by controlling the export/import routes through the Dardanelles. Professor Manfred Korfmann, the current excavator of Ilion, declares: "I might not be wrong should I describe Troy as a pirate fortress which exercised control over the straits."[269]

> "So this host, being all gathered together, made an attempt one time to enslave by one single onslaught both your country and ours and the whole of the territory within the Straits. And then it was, Solon, that the manhood of your State showed itself conspicuous for valour and might in the sight of all that world. For it stood pre-eminent above all in gallantry and all warlike arts, and acting partly as leader of the Greeks, and partly standing alone by itself when deserted by all others, after encountering the deadliest perils, it defeated the invaders and reared a trophy; whereby it saved from slavery such as were not as yet enslaved, and all the rest of us who dwell within the bounds of Heracles it ungrudgingly set free."

The priest finally turns to the most remarkable deed of Solon's predecessors: their defeat of the mighty host of Atlantis by one single onslaught which freed all the people who lived on this side of the straits.

Unfortunately, the archaeology provides no evidence for the historicity of the Trojan War.[270] There is an archaeological site which qualifies as the locality of the dispute and there are two destruction layers at about the time when the war would have taken place, but that is all we have in terms of scientific proof. All the other information rests on ancient texts, primarily on Homer, although many other authors referred to the war, too, often

The Argive Plain in the background of this photograph stretches over 15 km from west (left) to east and over 20 km from north to south. Nauplion is visible in the foreground, while the city of Argos lies on the western side of the plain in the background.

The view of Argos is dominated by the steep mountain cone called Larisa, the location of another Late Bronze Age fortress. This photograph was taken in March 1934. (Courtesy of Deutsches Archäologisches Institut Athen, Neg. Nr. 84/998).

The citadel of Mycenae, the residence of the legendary commander-in-chief Agamemnon, is strategically located on a knoll at the northern end of the Argive Plain.

Late Bronze Age masonry, as on the walls at the entrance to Mycenae, is famous for its large boulders. The ancient Greeks thought that these blocks could have been moved by giants only, which is why this masonry is called 'Cyclopean'.

The famous Lion's Gate at Mycenae was not discovered by Heinrich Schliemann, as most people think – it has always been half-exposed.

But Schliemann did discover this grave circle just inside the citadel walls of Mycenae. Much of the Mycenaean gold – including the famous death mask of Agamemnon – was retrieved from these graves.

The citadel of Tiryns, another Mycenaean stronghold in the Argive Plain, sits on a 17 m high limestone knoll and is surrounded by fertile, arable land. (View of Tiryns from southeast taken in 1913. Courtesy of Deutsches Archäologisches Institut, Athen, Neg. Nr. TIR. 417).

Another view of Tiryns and the surrounding alluvial plain as they look today.

This photograph of the western side of Tiryns' walls shows how the boulders were placed on exposed limestone bedrock. The cleanly cut faces of the bedrock foundation below the masonry provide evidence of human quarrying. Clearly, the builders of the royal residence took most of their material from the construction site itself.

Above: This 1899 view from Tiryns toward Nauplion (south) shows how the coastal zone of the Argive Plain looked 100 years ago. Around 2500 BC the shore was 300 metres from the site; by the end of the Bronze Age it had moved back 1 km, or two-thirds of the way to its present position. (Courtesy of Deutsches Archäologisches Institut, Athen, Neg. Nr. TIR. 34).

Inset: Some of the deposits in the Argive Plain are so consolidated that they cannot be penetrated with a hand coring device. In such cases we used a power drill. To gain undisturbed samples, auger cores were taken inside the power hole.

About 200 m east of Tiryns is an old tree shown dominating the centre of this 1926 photograph. The first auger core, revealing an almost 5 m thick, unstratified layer containing much Mycenaean pottery, was taken just below this tree. (Courtesy of Deutsches Archäologisches Institut, Athen, Neg. Nr. TIR. 755).

After the flood at Tiryns, the inhabitants of the city erected the impressive wall shown here to redirect the stream that caused the catastrophe. It was about 10 m high and its lower parts were protected by Cyclopean masonry, visible under the tree and near the scale. (Courtesy of Deutsches Archäologisches Institut, Neg. Nr. TIR. 681).

The crown of the artificial dam east of Tiryns dissects the original river bed which lies to the left and right.

An aerial photograph of the area east of Tiryns (1) shows the original path of the stream (2), the Mycenaean dam (3) and the artificial canal (4).

In some remote areas on the central Peloponnese thick limestone soils have remained intact and are able to support a dense, mixed vegetation. The coexistence of fertile soils on mountains and thick forests can no longer be found in the densely inhabited areas of Greece.

After the soil has been washed from the mountains only thin pine forests and maquis are able to grow on the barren slopes.

The Skourta Plain is on the northern slopes of the Parness mountains, about 550 m above sea level. Just behind these peaks lies Athens. The Greek landscape may have looked similar during the Neolithic era when farming was limited to the fertile plains while soils and vegetation on slopes were left undisturbed.

Early on the Greeks realized the devastating impact of agriculture on unprotected slopes. Old terrace walls marked by parallel stripes of brush occur even on abandoned fields like these near Mycenae. These terraces were erected in or before Classical times; that is, they were in place when Plato wrote his commentary on soil erosion.

A close-up of the ancient terraces below left shows the large size of the boulders, which were too big to have been handled by individuals. Terraces made of big boulders occur at various places in southern Greece, perhaps indicating a period of centrally-organized soil protection efforts.

Many modern terrace walls protect what little is left of arable soil after the early Bronze Age erosion.

The Parthenon on the Acropolis in Athens was erected in 447-406 BC, at about the time when Plato was born (427 BC). In *Critias*, Plato states that the Acropolis used to look very different in the past. Archaeologists have found the Cyclopean walls of a Late Bronze Age citadel here.

The Atlantis account describes the city as sitting on a 'mountain low on all sides'. This photograph shows the mount of Hisarlık where Ilion is located. The view is from the north, Ilion lies at the end of the ridge just right of the centre.

The artificial canal through the coastal ridge at Sigeum has never been thoroughly investigated. Cook (1973) thought that it was never completed because the ground rises relatively high above the sea. All of this material, however, could postdate the abandonment of the construction.

This photograph shows the width of the artificial canal near Sigeum. The road running diagonally through the photo follows the bottom of the cut.

The walls of Troy VI near the eastern gate of the city show the beautiful, characteristic masonry.

Another view of the eastern wall of Troy VI and Tower VIh.

Mysterious sand heaps occur at many places in the Trojan Plain, especially near abandoned stream channels. They consist of the same river sand as the rest of the plain, but there are no natural processes that could explain their origin. Today, the sand is being used by the local people.

Mount Ida is still an important source for timber.

One of the pedestals just left of the main entrance to the sixth city of Troy. The excavators Dörpfeld and Blegen considered these pedestals to have played a role in the Trojan cults.

Another view of the pedestal at the South or Scaean Gate.

providing details lacking in the *Iliad*. Thus, there must have been a popular tradition recounting such a conflict, and it is generally assumed that Homer only used a small portion of this tradition as the theme of his poetry.

In the above paragraph, the priest reveals that Atlantis was the initial aggressor, a circumstance that, when applied to Troy, would contradict conventional beliefs. The Atlantis account attributes more power to Troy than is generally acknowledged by archaeological scholarship; but Troy must have been unusually strong, if it really required 100,000 men, 1200 ships and ten years of combat to overthrow it.

In both the *Iliad* and the Atlantis legend, the Greek contingent consisted of a united army representing the interests, and apparently embodying the troops, of various Mediterranean countries; the Greeks, however, led the alliance. The *Iliad* commences with *"an evil pestilence, and the folk were perishing"* (1.10, Murray), while the Atlantis account reports *"the deadliest perils"* from the Greek camp. Yet, in both legends the Greeks ascended as the mighty host, and although they were at times *"deserted by all the others,"* they overthrew the opponent and gained a magnificent victory.

> "But at a later time there occurred portentous earthquakes and floods, and one grievous day and night befell them, when the whole body of your warriors was swallowed up by the earth, and the island of Atlantis in like manner was swallowed up by the sea and vanished; wherefore also the ocean at that spot has now become impassable and unsearchable, being blocked up by the shoal mud which the island created as it settled down."

Conventional wisdom believes that Atlantis was destroyed by a single catastrophe and subsequently drowned in the sea. Plato's original text, however, speaks of the ancient Greek civilization, *"the whole of your warriors,"* being *"swallowed up by the earth"* during *"portentous earthquakes and floods."* This tragedy occurred during one single *"grievous day and night"* after the warriors had returned from their successful combat at Atlantis. The earthquake at Tiryns coincides with the later LH IIIB period between 1250 and 1200 B.C. Hence the destruction occurred only a few years or decades after the Trojan War (*"but at a later time"*). The earthquake was accompanied by a devastating flood, which literally *"swallowed up"* parts of

the lower town. All these events, earthquakes, floods and chronological boundary coincide with the abrupt commencement of the
Achaean decline. The natural catastrophes are clearly attributed to
Greece,[271] although Atlantis is said to have disappeared *"in like
manner."* Again, this statement corresponds to the events in the
Argolid and in the Troad: parts of Tiryns's lower town were buried
very rapidly during the flash flood, just as any Trojan building in
the plain would have been buried by alluvium after the war.

There is one further consequence, however: *"the ocean at that spot
has now become impassable and unsearchable."* This phrase may reveal
how the knowledge to navigate the Dardanelles and Bosporus was
lost after Trojan pilot services were no longer available. The interpretation that the sea was *"being blocked up by the shoal mud which the
island created as it settled down"* seems to be another attempt to
develop a causal chain from two independent phenomena, similar
to the explanations for Phaeton's blunder and the shift of celestial
bodies, or the odd site choice during the Achaean era and the
destruction by floods. Here, Atlantis's disappearance may provide
an excuse for the loss of ability to navigate the Dardanelles. Myths
frequently entail such interlocked chains where A causes B, B
impels C and so on.[272] While the description of static stages and
phenomena (A, B, C) may contain a memory of historic events and
places, their supposed causal relationship usually rests on vis-
ionary attempts to rationalize mythical lore.

The first part of the Atlantis legend, a general introduction
possibly given to Solon before he actually saw the inscriptions,
concludes here. Critias, the speaker, continues:

> "I am ready to tell my tale, not in summary outline only but in
> full detail, . . . [but] consider now, Socrates, the order of the
> feast as we have arranged it. Seeing that Timaeus is our best
> astronomer and has made it his special task to learn about the
> nature of the Universe, it seemed good to us that he should
> speak first, beginning with the origin of the Cosmos and
> ending with the generation of mankind. After him I will
> follow, taking over from him mankind, already as it were
> created by his speech."

The rest of the volume consists of a monologue by Timaeus on the
origin of the earth and the constitution of life. In the second part of
the trilogy, Critias takes up the conversation again. He first summarizes his introduction to the Atlantis account, then continues to

describe ancient Attika in some detail. The source for the information on Attika is clearly not Solon's manuscript, as Critias will indicate later. His description of Attika, although fully comprehensible, because of its context has often been associated with the Atlantis legend itself, reducing its believability. It appears like a 2,300-year-old introduction to the principles of geoarchaeology in Greece and also alludes to the soil erosion which played an important role in the fate of Tiryns.

CRITIAS 108E–112E: ATTIKA

"Now first of all we must recall the fact that 9000 is the sum of years since the war occurred, as is recorded, between the dwellers beyond the pillars of Heracles and all that dwelt within them; which war we have now to relate in detail. It was stated that this city of ours was in command of the one side and fought through the whole of the war, and in command of the other side were the kings of the island of Atlantis, which we said was an island larger than Libya and Asia once upon a time, but now lies sunk by earthquakes and has created a barrier of impassable mud which prevents those who are sailing out from here to the ocean beyond from proceeding further."

Plato summarizes how he saw the events described in *Timaeus*; without leaving leeway for different interpretations, he recapitulates that Atlantis was:

– an island
– outside the "pillars of Heracles"
– larger than Libya and Asia combined
– at war 9,000 years ago
– opposed by a host under the command of "Athens"
– sunk by earthquakes
– and that it has produced a barrier of impassable mud

As was demonstrated above, the more detailed account in *Timaeus* allows different conclusions. In particular, it was not before said that Atlantis was sunk by earthquakes. Furthermore, in *Timaeus*, Plato wrote of "the land where Solon lives" or even "Greece," while here, the whole legend of the mythical Greek culture is applied to *"this city of ours,"* and thus to Athens only. Earlier, Plato said that the ancient Greek culture originated nine thousand years ago; now he claims that the war between it and Atlantis took place nine thousand years ago. These discrepancies reveal that Plato himself misinterpreted Solon's notes.

> "Now as regards the numerous barbaric tribes and all the Hellenic nations that then existed, the sequel of our story, when it is, as it were, unrolled, will disclose what happened in each locality, but the facts about the Athenians of that age and the enemies with whom they fought we must necessarily describe first, at the outset—the military power, that is to say, of each and their forms of government. And of these two we must give the priority in our account to the state of Athens."

Although the previous paragraph stated that Athens was in command of the one side during the war, here Plato notes that numerous Hellenic nations existed in Greece at that time. Plato's speaker, Critias, outlines the structure of his contribution: he will unveil what happened at each locality, starting with Attika itself, then continuing with the description of its opponents abroad. Unfortunately, since Plato terminated the book after the description of Atlantis, he never disclosed what happened at the other places. The remainder of the account consists of a description of Attika from local traditions and then a very detailed description of Atlantis based on Solon's report.

> "Once upon a time the gods were taking over by lot the whole earth according to its regions—not according to the results of strife: for it would not be reasonable to suppose that the gods were ignorant of their own several rights, nor yet that they attempted to obtain for themselves by means of strife a possession to which others, as they knew, had a better claim. So by just allotments they received each one his own, and they settled their countries, and when they had settled them, they reared us up, even as herdsmen rear their flocks, to be their cattles and nurslings; only it was not our bodies that they constrained by bodily force, like shepherds guiding their flocks with stroke of staff, but they directed from the stern where the living creature is easiest to turn about, laying hold on the soul by persuasion, as by a rudder, according to their

own disposition; and thus they drove and steered all the mortal kind. Now in other regions others of the gods had their allotments and ordered the affairs, but inasmuch as Hephaestus and Athena were a like nature, being born of the same father, and agreeing, moreover, in their love of wisdom and of craftsmanship, they both took for their joint portion this land of ours as being naturally congenial and adapted for virtue and for wisdom, and therein they planted as native to the soil men of virtue and ordained to their mind the mode of government."

Critias summarizes in very general terms how the Greeks thought their country was initially settled. Once again, these are local Greek traditions and completely unrelated to Solon's report from Egypt.

"And of these citizens the names are preserved, but their works have vanished owing to the repeated destruction of their successors and the length of the intervening periods. For, as was said before, the stock that survived on each occasion was a remnant of unlettered mountaineers which had heard the names only of the rulers, and but little besides of their works. So though they gladly passed on these names to their descendants, concerning the mighty deeds and the laws of their predecessors they had no knowledge, save for some invariably obscure reports; and since, moreover, they and their children for many generations were themselves in want of the necessaries of life, their attention was given to their own needs and all their talk was about them, and in consequence they paid no regard to the happenings of bygone ages. For legendary lore and the investigation of antiquity are visitants that come to cities in company with leisure, when they see that men are already furnished with the necessaries of life, and not before."

It is very important to realize that these are Plato's words, not those of Solon or the Egyptian priest. Plato is using and evaluating oral traditions from ancient Greece in general and from Attika in particular. He nevertheless applies the knowledge brought home by Solon to these Greek traditions, thereby fully accepting the Egyptian account of *"unlettered mountaineers"* who inhabited Greece during much of prehistory. During such times only *"invariably obscure reports"* were transmitted from generation to generation. Plato uses this as a justification that so little can be said about Greek prehistory. However, he is confusing two different periods when *"unlettered mountaineers"* prevailed in Greece, because both of these periods were connected with flood legends. The first flood was the one of Deucalion, the Greek equivalent to the biblical great deluge; it was followed by the earliest inhabitants of Greece. The other flood was the catastrophe in the Argolid, which was succeeded by a dark age. Plato's confusion of these two events and the periods of primeval culture that followed them is even more obvious in his next and final book, the *Laws*.[273] His willingness to accept Solon's narrative of Atlantis may have rested partially on recognition of the parallels between the flood/dark-age association in the Egyptian and Greek legends—although both traditions were talking about different events at different times.

Plato continues to draw an exceptionally poetic, but nevertheless faithful portrait of the minimal requirements for intellectual progress. *"Legendary lore and the investigation of antiquity are visitants that come to the city with leisure."* For Plato *muthologia* and the investigation of the remote past were comparable, indicating that he considered the study of old traditions a serious and important task. Moreover, by labelling much of the ancient legends as *"invariably obscure report"* he elevated the correctness of Solon's Atlantis report. In Plato's eyes, cities are needed, where *"men are furnished with the necessaries of life"*; but for many thousands of years, these premises were not met in Greece, because the people were in want *"for the necessaries of life."* Thus, there is very little historic knowledge in Greece; only the names of the rulers and those *"obscure reports"* have been preserved.

> "In this way, then, the names of ancients, without their works, have been preserved. And for evidence of what I say I point to the statement of Solon, that the Egyptian priests, in describing the war of that period, mentioned most of those names—such as those of Cecrops and Erechtheus and Erichthonius and Erysichthon and most of the other names which are recorded of the various heroes before Theseus—and in like manner also the names of the women. Moreover, the habit and figure of the goddess indicate that in the case of all animals, male and female, that herd together, every species is naturally capable of practising as a whole and in common its own proper excellence."

Plato emphasizes the parallels between the Egyptian account and the Greek oral tradition which are, to him, mutually endorsing each other.

> "Now at that time there dwelt in this country not only the other classes of the citizens who were occupied in the handicrafts and in the raising of food from the soil, but also the military class, which had been separated off at the commencement by divine heroes and dwelt apart. It was supplied with all that was required for its sustenance and training, and none of its members possessed any private property; and from the rest of the citizens they claimed to receive nothing beyond a sufficiency of sustenance; and they practised all those pursuits which were mentioned yesterday, in the description of our proposed Guardians.'"

This information on the military class once again reflects a parallel between the oral reports of Attika and Egypt describing the situation in the Late Bronze Age. This, however, does not mean that all details revealed below apply to the Late Bronze Age. It is quite clear that Plato had no concept of chronology.

> "Moreover, what was related about our country was plausible and true, namely, that, in the first place, it had its boundaries at that time marked off by the Isthmus, and on the inland side reaching to the heights of Cithaeron and Parnes; and that the boundaries ran down with Oropia on the right, and on the seaward side they shut off the Asopus on the left; and that all other lands were surpassed by ours in goodness of soil, so that it was actually able at that period to support a large host which was exempt from the labours of husbandry. And of its goodness a strong proof is this: what is now left of our soil rivals any other in being all-productive and abundant in crops and rich in pasturage for all kinds of cattle; and at that period, in addition to their fine quality it produced these things in vast quantity. How, then, is this statement plausible, and what residue of the land then existing serves to confirm the truth?"

The boundaries outlined above extend beyond the territory of Classical Attika at the time of Plato, possibly to accentuate a political claim.[274] Current archaeological research has attempted to reconstruct the boundaries of Bronze Age states; Plato's statement indicates that such boundaries existed. Plato moves from political

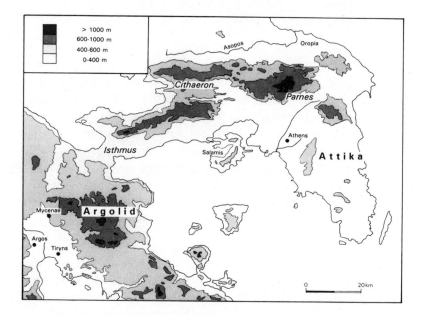

Plato describes ancient Attika as stretching as far as the Isthmus (of Corinth) and the Cithaeron and Parnes mountains, with the Asopos River being the northern boundary. He applies the information given by the Egyptian priest only to ancient Attika, though it now seems more likely that the flood and earthquake occurred in the adjacent Argolid, an area that played a far more important role in pre-Classical Greece.

organization (military class, boundaries) to the subject of environmental changes. His intelligible description of changes in soil quality may represent yet another oral tradition interwoven in his recollection of history. The existence of superior soils in prehistoric Attika can today be considered as much of a fact as the existence of Achaeans in Athens.

"The whole of the land lies like a promontory jutting out from the rest of the continent far into the sea; and all the cup of the sea round about it is, as it happens, of a great depth. Consequently, since many great convulsions took place during the 9000 years—for such was the number of years from that time to this—the soil which has kept breaking away from the high lands during these ages and these disasters, forms no pile of

124

sediment worth mentioning, as in other regions, but keeps sliding away ceaselessly and disappearing in the deep."

Plato's examination of the environmental changes in ancient Greece parallels that of modern field archaeology. Today's archaeologists are well aware that human habitation and cultural progress are interrelated with the environmental evolution,[275] therefore the past landscape must be reconstructed and its historic changes understood before the human land-use can be interpreted. Like a contemporary geoarchaeologist, Plato starts out by illustrating the physiography of ancient Greece before he describes the bathymetry of the sea around it. The *"promontory jutting out from the rest of the continent"* has been assumed to represent the Peloponnese, the center of the Achaean civilization, although on a smaller scale, it would also fit the promontory of southern Attika. Around the Peloponnese are the greatest depths in the Mediterranean Sea; in the Hellenic Trough on its western side the depth reaches as much as three miles.[276] Although there were no means of sounding such depths in antiquity, Plato knew that *"the sea round about it is, as it happens, of a great depth."*

Plato accurately described the process of soil erosion during which topsoil and weathered bedrock are washed away and the underlying bedrock becomes exposed.[277] The review of the Aegean man-landscape interrelations in chapter three has shown that soil erosion was the most disastrous environmental destruction ever to have occurred in Greece. Plato, too, considered it the most important factor of environmental change in ancient Greece, stressing the awareness of people in the Classical period toward their environmental impact. The long time which elapsed since occupation began, and the *"many great convulsions"* that have taken place, resulted in a *"ceaseless"* loss of soil.

Archaeological knowledge of prehistoric Greece lends credence to Plato's descriptions of the great convulsions that have occurred since human occupation began: the first inhabitation of Greece by Middle Paleolithic Neanderthals was followed by total abandonment. The second phase of inhabitation by Final Paleolithic cavedwellers was apparently also followed by total abandonment. At the end of the Early Helladic II period and then again at the end of the Mycenaean era were times of widespread destruction combined with significant drops in population density and a rehabitation by merging indigenous and foreign peoples. The recent deposits of the Argive Plain show that these two latter *"convul-sions"* especially were accompanied by unprecedented soil erosion, just as Plato described it.

Both physiography and bathymetry have important consequences for soil erosion. Attika's high subaerial and submarine relief prevented the eroded soil from forming a *"pile of sediment worth mentioning"*; instead the suspended load of the rivers was carried to the sea, where it disappeared in the depths. In other parts of Greece, where the topography is less pronounced, soil erosion resulted in redeposition and accumulation of sediment piles. Many coastal plains accumulated up to thirty-three feet of silt over the last 10,000 years, which caused their shorelines to regress gradually. The profundity of Plato's observation and the confident elegance of his sketch verify his comprehension of these processes. This is the first description of geologic processes in ancient literature, and Plato therefore rightly deserves the credit for the first distinct enunciation of a most important geological doctrine.[278]

> "And, just as happens in small islands, what now remains compared with what then existed is like the skeleton of a sick man, all the fat and soft earth having wasted away, and only the bare framework of the land being left."

No modern geoarchaeologist has equaled the unerringness of Plato's comparison between soil erosion and the skeleton of a sick man. I gave this passage to a colleague to elicit a second opinion, and he said, "It makes you wonder how little we have learned in the past 2,300 years."

Unlike most other visitors to Greece, I have never seen much of the islands. Most of them are small and their hills steep, thus the soil is eroded quickly without leaving traces in the form of recent sediments which I could examine. Plato was fully aware of these interrelations (*"just as it happens in small islands"*) and so was Homer: *"None of the islands that slope down to the sea are rich in meadows and the kind of place where you can drive horses"* (4.608).

> "But at that epoch the country was unimpaired, and for its mountains it had high arable hills, and in place of the 'moorlands,' as they are now called, it contained plains full of rich soil;"

The climatic improvement after the last ice age was initially accompanied by a dramatic increase in vegetation density and a virtual abandonment of human habitation. The drastic climatic changes therefore did not result in soil instability; on the contrary, the landscape surface was stable, and a rich, fertile soil was able to form on it.[279] Plato calls this stage of natural equilibrium "unimpaired" and notes the subsequent change from arable hills to moorland. A similar remark was later made by Aristotle (*Meteorologica* 1.14); describing the plain of Argos, he said:

> At the time of the Trojan war the land of Argos was marshy, and could only support few inhabitants; the land of Mycenae, on the contrary, was good and highly esteemed. Now, however, the opposite is the case, for the land of Mycenae is dried up, and therefore lies idle; while the land of Argos, which was a marsh, is now good arable land.

Clearly, the Greeks were aware of environmental changes and their consequences, and they also knew that the landscape's fate is largely dependent on human use and abuse. Plato continues:

> "and it had much forest-land in its mountains, of which there are visible signs even to this day; for there are some mountains which now have nothing but food for bees, but they had trees no very long time ago, and the rafters from those felled there to roof the largest buildings are still sound. And besides, there were many lofty trees of cultivated species; and it produced boundless pasturage for flocks."

The disappearance of the natural Mediterranean forest cover, assumed to have occupied up to ninety-five percent of the surface,[280] is largely attributed to human deforestation. Plato highlights the fact that some *"visible signs"* of these forests are still left in his days, and indeed, Broneer found beams of full ship-mast size set into the Achaean siege-fountain below the Acropolis.[281] Even today's pine-woods in northern Attika, at the boundary with Boeotia, appear to be a remnant of Classical times.

> "Moreover, it was enriched by the yearly rains from Zeus, which were not lost to it, as now, by flowing from the bare land into the sea; but the soil it had was deep, and therein it received the water, storing it up in the retentive loamy soil; and by drawing off into the hollows from the heights the water that was there absorbed, it provided all the various districts with abundant supplies of springwaters and streams,

whereof the shrines which still remain even now, at the spots where the fountains formerly existed, are signs which testify that our present description of the land is true.'

Plato's thorough comprehension of landscape changes does not stop at the interrelation between human land-use and forest cover: here he continues to describe the links between ephemeral and perennial streams on one side, and vegetation cover, surface soils and water retention on the other. He correctly remarks that bare soils allow surface water to run into the sea unimpeded, whereas a *"deep, retentive, loamy"* soil will draw the rain into its *"hollows,"* thereby absorbing and saving it for a long time. The retained water is only gradually released to form perennial springs and streams. Zdeněk Kukal, perhaps the most scientific investigator and "disbeliever" of Atlantis's historicity, wrote about this statement, *"even a professional hydrologist would not be ashamed of such a description."*[282] In Attika of Plato's time, former springs and fountains were still marked with shrines, though the streams themselves had run dry.

Plato has described a remarkable causal chain revealing how loss in vegetation will ultimately cause a loss of soil and of surface-water retention. The accuracy of his deductions are in sharp contrast to the causal chains we have heard before. These discrepancies indicate a different source and transmission for this part of the account and perhaps some personal interest and observations on Plato's side. Today's landscapes of Classical Attika[283] and other parts of Greece[284] reveal how the people of ancient Greece put their insights regarding soil preservation into practice: wherever the land surface was not completely flat, terraces were built, even in the remotest places. Many of these terraces are still effective today; they represent a prime target for archaeological research. During one such survey in the Berbati Valley just behind Mycenae we found two distinct generations of terraces: one dated to the last two hundred years and was still maintained; the other one was more extensive and densely overgrown; it dated at least to the Archaic/Classical era. At that time and in this area, *all* surfaces which were not barren bedrock had been stabilized with terraces.

"Such, then, was the natural condition of the rest of the country, and it was ornamented as you would expect from genuine husbandmen who made husbandry their sole task, and who were also men of taste and of native talent, and

128

possessed of most excellent land and a great abundance of water, and also, above the land, a climate of most happily tempered seasons."

Plato's final remark on *"natural conditions"* in prehistoric Greece summarizes how climate, soil and water used to be favorable and unspoiled while the country was inhabited by fewer people, *"genuine husbandmen."*

Despite Plato's thorough understanding of man-landscape interrelations, he had no notion of the chronology of events. In the above paragraphs he seems to be confusing, firstly, an "Eden-like" condition of lush vegetation with no human interference as could have existed in Mesolithic to Early Neolithic times; secondly, a period of widespread but still modest land-use such as occurred during the later Neolithic; and, thirdly, times of a highly organized society with a separate military class, such as existed in the Late Bronze Age. Plato should be excused, though, since the chronologies of most pioneering thinking in historical sciences, whether geological or archaeological, has always been a far cry from reality.

"And as to the city, this is the way in which it was laid out at that time. In the first place, the Acropolis, as it existed then, was different from what it is now. For as it is now, the action of a single night of extraordinary rain has crumbled it away and made it bare of soil, when earthquakes occurred simultaneously with the third of the disastrous floods which preceded the destructive deluge in the time of Deucalion."

Plato assures his audience that the Acropolis existed in the past, too, but it looked naturally very different. He applies the events described by the Saïtian priest to the Acropolis, because, following Solon's resolute Athenian perspective, Plato considered ancient Attika to have been the subject of the Egyptian narrative. As discussed above, the Egyptian priest was more likely to have talked about mainland Greece in general than about Attika only. Although the Acropolis bore an Achaean citadel, the flood and earthquake described in the Atlantis account occurred in the Argolid which at that time played a more significant role than Attika. Since those natural disasters are said to have occurred 9,000 years ago, Plato placed them even before the "great deluge" of Deucalion, once again exposing his lack of a correct chronological framework.

"But in its former extent, at an earlier period, it went down towards the Eridanus and the Ilissus, and embraced within it the Pnyx, and had the Lycabettus as its boundary over against the Pnyx; and it was all rich in soil and, save for a small space, level on the top. And its outer parts, under its slopes, were inhabited by the craftsmen and by such of the husbandmen as had their farms close by; but on the topmost part only the military class by itself had its dwelling round about the temple of Athene and Hephaestus, surrounding themselves with a single ring-fence, which formed, as it were, the enclosure of a single dwelling. On the northward side of it they had established their public dwellings and winter messrooms, and all the arrangements in the way of buildings which were required for the community life of themselves and the priests; but all was devoid of gold or silver, of which they made no use anywhere; on the contrary, they aimed at the mean between luxurious display and meanness, and built themselves tasteful houses, wherein they and their children's children grew old and handed them on in succession unaltered to others like themselves. As for the southward parts, when they vacated their gardens and gymnasia and messrooms as was natural in summer, they used them for these purposes. And near the place of the present Acropolis there was one spring—which was choked up by the earthquakes so that but small tricklings of it are now left round about; but to the men of that time it afforded a plentiful stream for them all, being well tempered both for winter and summer. In this fashion, then, they dwelt, acting as guardians of their own citizens and as leaders, by their own consent, of the rest of the Greeks; and they watched carefully that their own numbers, of both men and women, who were neither too young nor too old to fight, should remain for all time as nearly as possible the same, namely, about 20,000.

"So it was that these men, being themselves of the character described and always justly administering in some such fashion both their own land and Hellas, were famous throughout all Europe and Asia both for their bodily beauty and for the perfection of their moral excellence, and were of all men then living the most renowned. And now, if we have not lost recollection of what we heard when we were still children, we will frankly impart to you all, as friends, our story of the men who warred against our Athenians, what their state was and how it originally came about."

The Athenians were about the only Achaean community who survived the eleventh century B.C. more or less intact. Even in Classical times they were aware of this inheritance, and it seems only natural that some tradition of the handing down of oral accounts existed. The role of the Athenians themselves was bound to become exaggerated during such transmissions, thus Plato believed they have once been "*administering*" Hellas, a role which certainly exceeded the powers of Late Bronze Age Attika.

CRITIAS 113A–121C: ATLANTIS

"But before I begin my account, there is still a small point which I ought to explain, lest you should be surprised at frequently hearing Greek names given to barbarians. The reason of this you shall now learn. Since Solon was planning to make use of the story for his own poetry, he had found, on investigating the meaning of the names, that those Egyptians who had first written them down had translated them into their own tongue. So he himself in turn recovered the original sense of each name and, rendering it into our tongue, wrote it down so. And these very writings were in the possession of my grandfather and are actually now in mine, and when I was a child I learnt them all by heart. Therefore if the names you hear are just like our local names, do not be at all astonished; for now you know the reason for them. The story then told was a long one, and it began something like this."

Plato has finished the description of ancient Attika from local traditional sources and turns to the Atlantis legend again. His prelude to the story is of great significance for its interpretation. Plato's own voice resounds here in Critias' words for almost the last time; once, in the middle of the narrative, he will add that some dimensions sound unbelievable. He is clearly treating Solon's story as a precious, historical source not meant to be interfered with. Plato's high esteem for ancient tradition materializes in Critias' remark that, first of all, he has known the whole story by heart since his childhood, but in addition to that, he actually possesses Solon's manuscript. Plato again hints at the importance of "story-telling" in the past; above all, however, he furnishes yet another indication for the historicity of the account.

Plato literally dives into the telling of the legend (*"it began something like this"*) stressing the fact that it had remained an unaltered entirety. Being aware that, once he has embarked on telling the legend, he will be unable to add his own opinion, Plato uses the preamble (*"but before I begin my account"*) to explain what he apparently considered the only changes that have been made to the legend, the translation of the names of the local *"barbarians."* As it turns out, the names were changed twice, first by the Egyptians, then by Solon. Perhaps the true meaning of the legend would have been revealed much earlier if Solon had not retranslated the locals' names. In any case, a decipherment of the account based on the linguistic sources of place- and people-names would have become impossible after this distortion. But Solon's interpretation of local names was not uncommon in ancient Greece. In Homer's *Iliad* the Trojans, too, bear Achaean names, and the alternative name of the Trojan prince Paris, Alexandros, is thought by some philologists to be a Greek corruption of the Anatolian name Alaksandus.[285]

But how could Plato know about Solon's interference with the story? Was where a remark added by Solon to the manuscript or an oral report which accompanied Solon's notes? Or did Plato detect Solon's changes himself; in which case there may have been many more changes which escaped Plato's attention.

> "Like as we previously stated concerning the allotments of the Gods, that they portioned out the whole earth, here into larger allotments and there into smaller, and provided for themselves shrines and sacrifices, even so Poseidon took for his allotment the island of Atlantis and settled therein the children whom he had begotten of a mortal woman in a region of the island of the following description."

Very appropriately Atlantis's divine creator was Poseidon, the god of the sea, of earthquakes and of horses. Later, the legend will furnish a detailed description of the stunning Poseidon temple in the center of Atlantis. According to the legend, Poseidon's children, begotten of a mortal woman, settled in Atlantis. In Troy's mythology, the offspring of Zeus and the mortal woman Electra were the first inhabitants of the place. Electra herself was a daughter of Atlas. Yet, Poseidon was also the patron of Troy and the erector of its walls. The *Iliad* describes how Poseidon cheated Heracles in a horse trade (v.650)—an event that is generally related to the actual trade between the two sites Troy and Tiryns, represented by these gods.[286] The *Iliad* also relates how Poseidon followed a battle during the Trojan War from the 4,600-foot-high Fegari Mountains on Samothrace, forty miles away from the Hellespont (XIII.10).[287]

These parallels by themselves, of course, provide no evidence for the identification of Troy as Atlantis. Poseidon was, for instance, also the most important god in Pylos;[288] however, they confirm rather than contradict a general impression of coincidence.

> "Bordering on the sea and extending through the centre of the whole island there was a plain, which is said to have been the fairest of all plains and highly fertile; and, moreover, near the plain, over against its centre, at a distance of about 50 stades, there stood a mountain that was low on all sides."

This is pretty much how one would describe the location of Troy looking at it from the ridge at the Aegean shore. *"Novum Ilium [Troy] was situated on a low height in the plain; that is to say, nearly in its centre,"* wrote Schliemann.[289] It is enclosed by a fertile alluvial plain on its southern, western and northern sides. The plain is *"bordered on the sea"* by a narrow strip of low mountains which drop steeply into the sea on one side. Hisarlık itself, the mount on which Ilion rests, lies *"near the plain, over against its centre"* forming a mount *"low on all sides"*. "At a distance of about 50 stades" applies to the span between Atlantis and the sea, as will later be specified. Fifty stades, or five and one-half miles, is the distance between Troy and Beşik Bay, today the nearest natural harbor for Troy.

> "Thereon dwelt one of the natives originally sprung from the earth, Evenor by name, with his wife Leucippe; and they had for off-spring an only-begotten daughter, Cleito. And when this damsel was now come to marriageable age, her mother died and also her father; and Poseidon, being smitten with desire for her, wedded her; and to make the hill whereon she dwelt impregnable he broke it off all round about; and he made circular belts of sea and land enclosing one another alternately, some greater, some smaller, two being of land and

A fish-eye panorama of the plain of Troy after William Gell (1804): *The Topography of Troy and Its Vicinity* (Plate 19). Hisarlık, the mount on which Ilion rests, is marked by an arrow, with the plain in front of it.

three of sea, which he carved as it were out of the midst of the island; and these belts were at even distances on all sides, so as to be impassable for man; for at that time neither ships nor sailing were as yet in existence."

Poseidon, having created the settlement, generated three *"circular belts of sea and water,"* channels in other words, around the low hill. Because perennial streams are the most important blessing of fertile alluvial plains, their oldest mythological histories usually begin with such a parable of the river and its divine creator.[290] Plato's description implies a natural origin for the circular belts in the distant past, before ships were invented. Their location, a few miles inland from the shore, may point to the channels of a braided or meandering stream. Because they were of natural origin, these channels can have been neither complete circles nor perfectly concentric. The plain of Troy is indeed dominated by such meandering rivers and abandoned streambeds.[291]

"And Poseidon himself set in order with ease, as a god would, the central island, bringing up from beneath the earth two springs of waters, the one flowing warm from its source, the other cold, and producing out of the earth all kind of food in plenty."

A pair of hot and cold springs as a blessing of a principal city is mentioned in only two ancient texts, the Atlantis legend and Homer's *Iliad*.[292] In both, the authors emphasized the uniqueness and the significance of these springs. Later in the Atlantis legend, Plato will again refer to the springs:

"The springs they made use of one kind being of cold, another of warm water, were of abundant volume, and each kind was wonderfully well adapted for use because of the neutral taste and excellence of its waters."

Homer's description of the hot and cold springs in the *Iliad* sounds very similar:

[Achilles and Hektor] came to the two lovely springs that are the sources of Scamander's eddying stream. In one of these the water comes up hot; steam rises from it and hangs about like smoke above a blazing fire. But the other, even in summer, gushes up as cold as hail or freezing snow or water that has turned to ice. (XXII.147–156)

Despite innumerable attempts ancient travelers and modern archaeologists have not been able to locate this pair of springs at Troy. They may have ceased to be active already in antiquity, because the Roman city at Troy, Novum Ilium, had to be supplied with water from far away, directed to the city via an aqueduct across the Kimar-Su.[293]

"And he begat five pairs of twin sons and reared them up; and when he had divided all the island of Atlantis into ten portions, he assigned to the first-born of the eldest sons his mother's dwelling and the allotment surrounding it, which was the largest and best; and him he appointed to be king over the rest, and the others to be rulers, granting to each the rule over many men and a large tract of country. And to all of them he gave names, giving to him that was eldest and king the name after which the whole island was called and the sea spoken of as the Atlantic, because the first king who then reigned had the name of Atlas. And the name of his younger twin-brother, who had for his portion the extremity of the island near the pillars of Heracles up to the part of the country now called Gadeira after the name of that region, was Eumelus in Greek, but in the native tongue Gadeirus—which fact may have given its title to the country. And of the pair that were born next he called the one Ampheres and the other Evaemon; and of the third pair the elder was named Mneseus and the younger Autochthon; and of the fourth pair, he called the first Elasippus and the second Mestor; and of the fifth pair, Azaes was the name given to the elder, and

135

Diaprepes to the second. So all these, themselves and their descendants, dwelt for many generations bearing rule over many other islands throughout the sea, and holding sway besides, as was previously stated, over the Mediterranean peoples as far as Egypt and Tuscany."

This paragraph contains a large number of personal names which were probably translated by Solon. The account states, however, that there had been a confederation of altogether ten related rulers; one of them, the principal of Atlantis, also served as the king of the whole territory. Such a divided dynasty coincides with Homer's description of the Trojan realm in the *Iliad*, which has been extensively discussed in both ancient[294] and modern literature.[295] The number of rulers varied between eight and ten, but virtually nothing is known about the political system of Troy.[296]

In Atlantis, the eldest son inherited the central residence; others were less fortunate: one of his brothers received *"the extremity of the island near the pillars of Heracles."* According to the account this area is now called Gadeira. A landscape of this name really exists in southern Spain near the Straits of Gibraltar, but the name is Punic and therefore postdates the Phoenicians' colonization of the area during the eighth century.[297] Hence, this particular term provides strong evidence for Solon's insertion of contemporary names which fitted his interpretation of the story. If the "pillars of Heracles" had been misinterpreted, the name of Gadeira, too, could have been introduced erroneously at the same time. Applied to the setting of Troy the geographic description would correspond to the peninsula of Yenişehir at the Dardanelles only three miles from Troy. Accordingly, distances between the residences of the rulers may have been very short and thus similar to the distances between the Achaean kingdoms in the Argolid. Although the catalog of the Trojan allies in the *Iliad* covers western Asia Minor from the Propontis to Lycia and parts of the European side of the Hellespont, these territories were probably not under direct control from Troy. If there was indeed a confederation of kings at Troy, as is indicated by the large number of *megara* in Troy VI, their realm may have been limited to the immediate surroundings of the Trojan Plain.[298]

"Now a large family of distinguished sons sprang from Atlas; but it was the eldest, who, as king, always passed on the sceptre to the eldest of his sons, and thus they preserved the sovereignty for many generations; and the wealth they possessed was so immense that the like had never been seen before in any royal house nor will ever easily be seen again."

While Atlantis ranks as the best-known legendary place in the world, Ilion might be considered the most famous, *real* archaeological site. Troy's reputation rests mostly on Homer's fame and on Schliemann's extraordinary publicity campaign. In addition, the Late Bronze Age Troy VI stands out, because of its wealth.[299]

The *Iliad* portrays the Greek perspective of only fifty-one days of the Trojan War and therefore contains no mention of the peacetime relations between the opponents. It also concludes before the sack of the city and thus lacks a description of the opulence waiting for the Greeks behind the gates. Homer only characterized Troy as "well built" (XXI.433, 516), "flourishing" (XXIII.380), "great" (II.332, 803), "beetling" (XXII.410, 411), "with broad streets" (II.141) and "pleasant or elegant" (V.210). Other ancient authors, however, have tried to fill the gaps left by the *Iliad*, attempting to put oral traditions such as "The Sack of Troy" and "The Homecomings" into writing. Quintus of Smyrna (3rd/4th century A.D.), for instance, recounted the Trojan War from the conclusion of the *Iliad* to the departure of the Greeks. His book was subtitled *"What Homer Didn't Tell."* He has an observer watching the sack of Troy from the sea, saying, *"The strong-minded Greeks have done a deed beyond telling, all Troy, vastly rich before, is now being consumed with fire."*[300] Later he adds that the Greeks took special delight in loading their ships with the booty from Troy, *"because the amount of it was so vast."*[301]

"and they were provided with everything of which provision was needed either in the city or throughout the rest of the country. For because of their headship they had a large supply of imports from abroad, and the island itself furnished most of the requirements of daily life—metals, to begin with, both the hard kind and the fusible kind, which are extracted by mining, and also that kind which is now known only by name but was more than a name then, there being mines of it in many places of the island—I mean 'orichalcum,' which was the most precious of the metals then known, except gold."

The Atlantean earth produced *"all kind of food in plenty."* This statement is here reemphasized twice: *"the island itself furnished most of the requirements of daily life"* and *"they were provided with everything of which provision was needed."* The Troad contains good agricultural land, described by Homer as *"deep rich soil,"* and also allows superb tuna-fishing in the Propontis.[302] Troy's wealth rested on such outstanding local resources, especially for agriculture and metal production, combined with trade and traffic control. The position of the site is unique, because it dominates the link between two continents, Europe and Asia, and two seas, the Aegean and the Black Sea. Troy was able to *"hold sway"* over these passages through and across the Dardanelles for two thousand years and may well have exacted levies for safe passages, pilot services or harbor use.[303] After its demise, a new city, Byzantium, arose on the nearby Bosporus; thriving on the same geographic advantages, Byzantium became the center of a Eurasian empire for another millennium.[304] It has been argued that the strength and the wealth of Troy vi and vii implies a command of both the Hellespont and the Bosporus.[305] From this intercontinental focal point land and sea trade routes radiate to the lower Danube basin, to central Greece via the Thracian coast, to the southern Aegean and Cyprus along the Asiatic coast, and to the Hittite empire in central Asia Minor.

Due to its role as an international market and port, Troy was rich in imports from foreign cultures.[306] Since the Early Bronze Age it received obsidian, marble idols, vessels and bone tubes from the Cycladic Islands.[307] Much Achaean pottery (LHI–LHIIIB) reached Troy from the Greek mainland, while other products came from Cyprus, Crete and central Anatolia.[308]

Metals were among the highest ranking and therefore in Atlantis either the most important or most abundant native resources for *"the requirements of daily life."* The account distinguishes a hard and a fusible kind, translated by some to describe solid materials like building stone and marble from *"fusible substances,"* i.e. metals.[309] Troy, the Troad and Turkey in general are unusually rich in metal.[310] Several hundred sites with lead, copper, zinc, arsenic, mercury, antimony, gold and iron have been registered by the Turkish geological survey MTA, and archaeometallurgists have been able to detect the remains of ancient mining at many of these sites.[311] Tin bronze first occurred in the Aegean in this area and on the islands off the northwestern Anatolian coast. Despite the fact that much of the copper and tin for the bronze had been imported, Troy represents one of the most important centers for bronze production and trade in the eastern Mediterranean. H. Frankfort described it as the *"world market"* where the raw material and finished products were sold.[312] William Gell recollected the mythological context of the Trojans (whom he also calls Atlantians) and their history of mining:

> *The son of Batieia, Ericthonius, was a rich and powerful monarch, and is said to have discovered the mines of precious metals, with which the country abounded, and of which the traces are yet visible in the vicinity of Skepsis.*[313]

In the first century B.C. Strabo reported Demetrius of Skepsis' observations in the Troad, describing gold mines near Astyra, silver from Alybe and copper from Kithene and Tmolos.[314]

The Loeb translation has a footnote attached to the precious and enigmatic metal "orichalkos": "i.e. *'mountain-copper'*; a *'sparkling' metal (116c) hard to identify*." Indeed, many Atlantologists have attempted in vain to identify this metal. According to the narrative orichalkos was:

– only known as a name in Solon's or Plato's time
– mined and therefore not an artificial alloy
– extremely valuable, almost as precious as gold

Later the account will add that orichalkos was:

– sparkling like fire
– used to cover walls
– used for inscriptions on *stelae*

The mysterious metal still has its place in the modern Greek vocabulary—today, it is the word for brass, an alloy of copper and zinc. Zinc itself, however, was not a known metal in antiquity, although many of the metals named in the account (iron, gold, silver, copper and tin) occur together in hydrothermal dykes of lead-zinc ores which are worldwide the most abundant ore bodies and also most frequent among the mineral resources of the Troad. Even though zinc was not recognized as a metal, brass was nevertheless produced using zinc ore, mainly smithonite.[315]

> There is a stone in the neighborhood of Andeira which, when burned, becomes iron, and then, when heated in a furnace

with a certain earth, distills mock-silver [i.e. zinc]; and this, with the addition of copper, makes the "mixture," as it is called, which by some is called "ὀρείχαλκον."[316]

In the above quotation Strabo describes the process of brass production using copper and *"a certain earth"* (smithonite)—the final compound is called orichalkos. The report implies that ore, process, product and name are unusual. Although the name "orichalkos" appeared elsewhere in the ancient literature,[317] its production seems to have been limited to the very area from where Strabo reported it: the Troad.[318] Andeira lay east of Edremit,[319] about fifty miles southeast of Troy. The readiness of the Trojans to experiment with the smelting of metals and to invent alloys is evident from their early production of tin bronze and from electrum objects found in the excavations. Electrum is a compound consisting of four parts of gold and one part of silver.[320] But in the Atlantis account orichalkos was said to have been mined and not smelted; it is thus likely to have been, at least initially, the natural alloy of copper and zinc.[321] This ore was rare but not unknown in ancient times. Aristotle said it was used for *stelae*.[322] Today, it is called "aurichalcit."

> "It brought forth also in abundance all the timbers that a forest provides for the labours of carpenters; and of animals it produced a sufficiency, both tame and wild. Moreover, it contained a very large stock of elephants; for there was an ample food-supply not only for all the other animals which haunt the marshes and lakes and rivers, or the mountains or the plains, but likewise also for this animal, which of its nature is the largest and most voracious."

Neither a lush vegetation nor a diversified wildlife sounds improbable for the prehistoric Troad. Its back country has mostly been sparsely inhabited by people, leaving fauna and flora undisturbed for a long time. Homer had described Mount Ida as "the mother of wild beasts" (XIV.283). Its dense forests were inhabited by bears, wolves, and jackals—even lions were still found in Asia Minor in the sixteenth century A.D. Among the domesticated or *"tame"* animals, horses were most common in the Troad, but asses, mules, oxen, goats, camels and sheep were and still are almost equally plentiful.[323] The archaeological excavations of Troy have unveiled bones from bovines, sheep, goats, wild boar, deer and some poultry.

In addition to this affluence of wildlife and working animals, Atlantis also contained elephants and not just a small drove but *"a very large stock."* Elephants in Troy? Well, who can tell?

> "And in addition to all this, it produced and brought to perfection all those sweet-scented stuffs which the earth produces now, whether made of roots or herbs or trees, or of liquid gums derived from flowers or fruits. The cultivated fruit also, and the dry, which serves us for nutriment, and all the other kinds that we use for our meals—the various species of which are comprehended under the name 'vegetables'—and all the produce of trees which affords liquid and solid food and unguents, and the fruit of the orchard trees, so hard to store, which is grown for the sake of amusement and pleasure, and all the after-dinner fruits that we serve up as welcome remedies for the sufferer from repletion—all these that hallowed island, as it lay then beneath the sun, produced in marvellous beauty and endless abundance. And thus, receiving from the earth all these products, they furnished forth their temples and royal dwellings, their harbours and their docks, and all the rest of their country, ordering all in the fashion following."

The products described here have been translated in footnotes of the Loeb edition as vine, corn, olive or cocopalm, pomegranate or apple and citron.[324] All that have been found in Troy by excavations published so far are: barley, rye, fine-grained wheat, various pulses (peas, beans) and two types of corn.

> "First of all they bridged over the circles of sea which surrounded the ancient metropolis, making thereby a road towards and from the royal palace. And they had built the palace at the very beginning where the settlement was first made by their God and their ancestors; and as each king received it from his predecessors, he added to its adornment and did all he could to surpass the king before him, until finally they made of it an abode amazing to behold for the magnitude and beauty of the workmanship."

The account now turns to the description of the remarkable architecture and landscape management of Atlantis. At first the people bridged over the channels around the acropolis, so that they could get to all parts of the plain. There is nothing in this paragraph that would be unusual for a Late Bronze Age city:

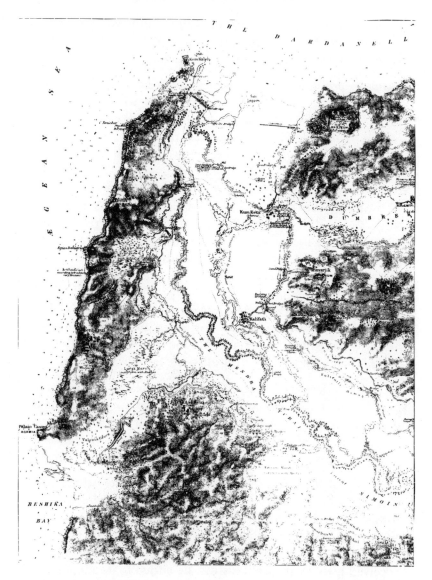

Thomas Spratt's map of "The Plain of Troy," here in an edition of 1877, remains unsurpassed with respect to its topographical detail. It shows that the plain of Troy is full of abandoned river channels, mysterious marshes and inexplicable sand heaps.

- the palace of Atlantis stood still at the same place *"where the settlement was first made"*
- in the distant past the whole Atlantean settlement used to be at this central spot, but now it only hosted the royal palace
- the settlement *"was first made by their God"* and by the ancestors of the current inhabitants
- the rule over the city was handed down through many generations
- many generations lived at Atlantis in prosperity, using their resources to gradually enhance the architecture of the city itself and the control of the landscape around it
- at the end of this process the residence had become truly *"amazing to behold for the magnitude and beauty of the workmanship"*
- the royal palace was surrounded by water
- the people of Atlantis constructed a bridge over the waterway integrating it into *"a road towards and from the royal palace"*

At Troy, too, the same spot had been used for over two thousand years, and the settlement gradually evolved and became more and more prosperous.[325] While the settlement grew, its central part became too small for the whole city and was only used for the fortified residences of the royal family (Troy vi). Although the current knowledge of Ilion is limited by the many destructions it suffered, it would probably still qualify as *"amazing to behold for the magnitude and beauty of the workmanship."*

According to the reconstructions of the river Scamander's former streambeds by Forchhammer, Virchow and Schliemann, one of its branches used to pass directly below the acropolis.[326] Surrounded by steep slopes on the northern and western sides, the citadel had a more gradual descent to the south. Ilion's main access, a relatively broad street ascended from this slope to the principal entrance of the fortress, the Skaean Gate.[327] Hence, a bridge at the bottom of the hill would have been imperative to connect the palace with the plain.

> "For, beginning at the sea, they bored a channel right through the outermost circle, which was three plethra in breadth, one hundred feet in depth, and fifty stades in length; and thus they made the entrance to it from the sea like that to a harbour by opening out a mouth large enough for the greatest ships to sail through."

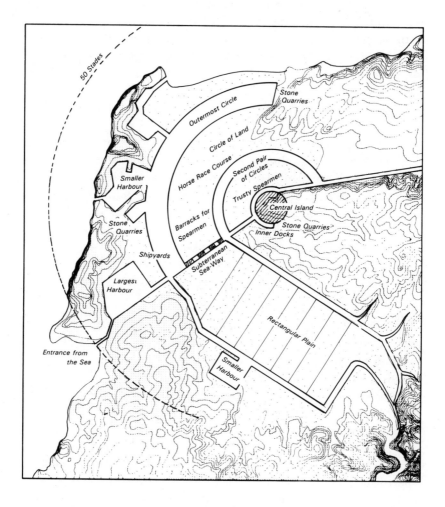

The strictly geometric information about the topography of Atlantis fits the Plain of Troy reasonably well. The city is said to have been surrounded by circular belts of water that were entered by ships through a narrow canal whose opening was 50 stades (5½ miles) from the citadel. To the south of the central island was a rectilinear plain with a trench dug around it. This trench received the streams coming from the mountains. The alluvial plain at Troy, however, extends almost 8 square miles whereas the one at Atlantis is said to have covered almost 88,000 square miles.

The Plain of Troy may have seen more geographical and geomorphological descriptions than any other place in the world; Cook
estimated their number to be around two hundred.[328] Yet, the
various reconstructions of the ancient topography are as fiercely
debated today as they have ever been. Despite all the research that
has been carried out at Ilion, its prehistoric harbor has never been
found.[329] The absence of a harbor curiously coincides with the
existence of numerous, still recognizable, artificial trenches and
other interferences with the natural environment of the plain.
Topographic maps of the Trojan Plain are full of ancient canals and
unexplained sand heaps, but nobody has so far attempted to
combine these individual constructions to determine the system
behind them.

The people of Atlantis are said to have *bored* a canal from the sea
to the outermost natural circle of water which surrounded the city.
This canal was *"one hundred feet in depth"* and *"fifty stades in length"*
(c. 5½ miles). An artificial channel that fits this description is
known from the Plain of Troy and appears on every topographic
map of the area. The entrance to the canal at Beşik Bay lies at a
distance of 5½ miles from the citadel of Ilion. The canal was not
just dug through the plain, but *bored* through thick layers of bedrock.[330] Its direction points toward the palace of Ilion. Determining
the date of the construction has never been seriously attempted,
although Schliemann argued plausibly that the canal must have
been very ancient, because it had accumulated a beach at its mouth
in Beşik Bay, 1½ square miles in size, and it could not have done so
in just a few centuries.[331] Schliemann also listed several phases of
rebuilding and reusing of the canal and quoted Mauduit,[332] who
said that, despite restorations at various times,[333] the canal already
existed in the time of Xerxes (fifth century B.C.), and that at the
time of Demetrius of Skepsis it led off all the water of the Scamander into the Aegean.[334] Pliny (first century A.D.) spoke of a
navigable Scamander,[335] and many scholars applied this comment
to the artificial canal at Beşik Bay.[336] Such an ancient redirection of
an entire stream may have found its way into the mythology too:
Heracles was said to have dug a course for the Scamander, whose
name, σκάμμα ἀνδρός, literally translated means "man made
foam."[337] If the canal at Troy was indeed constructed to redirect
the entire Scamander toward Beşik Bay, the accumulation of large
amounts of sediment at its mouth would have been the direct effect
of it. These sediments now form the sandy beach of Beşik Bay.

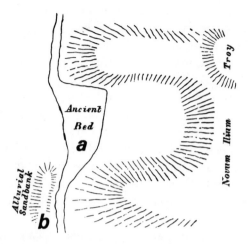

Schliemann's small sketch of the interface between Ilion and
the Trojan Plain highlights the ancient course of the Scamander as well as one of the mysterious alluvial sandbanks next
to it. Without knowing it, Schliemann may have reconstructed
a small port basin for royal vessels (a) and the foundations of a
bridge (b) leading to the main entrance of the citadel, the
Scaean Gate.

They filled the canal itself, too, but the inhabitants were able and
willing to maintain or reuse it on a minimal level for other than its
original purpose, for example to drain the swamps or to drive a
watermill.

Although this argument does not yet rest on any scientific
evidence, it serves quite well as a hypothesis, one that can easily be
tested by excavating a trench across the canal. In such an exposure
it should be possible to identify the original size of the construction
and the various phases of reuse, for which dates might even be
obtainable with the help of radiocarbon determinations on wood or
other organic material bound to be buried in the bed.

Artificial canals were not at all unusual in antiquity. The irri-
gation systems of Mesopotamia, described for instance by
Herodotus, contributed to the sudden rise of civilization. In order
to connect the Nile and the Red Sea, the Egyptians, too, dug, a
canal as early as the fourteenth century B.C.,[338] while the
Achaeans excavated the channel at Tiryns, drained Lake Kopais in
Boeotia and constructed water-control systems at many places in
Greece.[339]

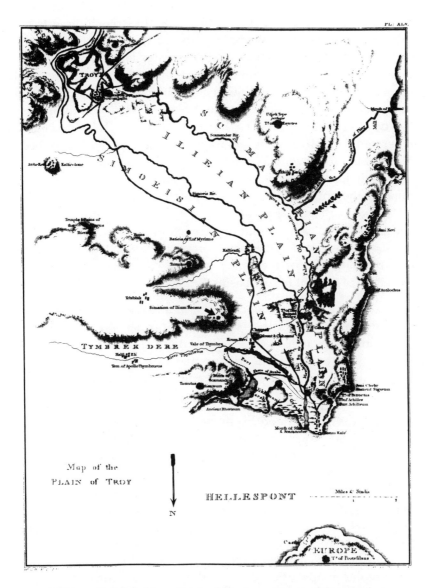

William Gell (1804) emphasized the importance of the canal at Beşik Bay in this map of the Trojan Plain (he placed north upside down). Since Chevalier's (1791) publication *Description of the Plain of Troy*, the ancient city was believed to have been at Pinarbasi near the upper edge of this map. Schliemann, however, located it on Hisarlık (arrow). The canal from Beşik Bay, described by Pliny (first century A.D.) to be navigable, points directly toward Ilion.

Another channel runs parallel to the one at Beşik Bay but three miles farther north. Just like the first one, this trench dissects the ridge to the Aegean. Schliemann assumed the construction of the second canal to have required even greater labor than the first, because it is much wider and deeper.[340] Forchhammer provided the measurements: its depth was more than one hundred feet and its upper width about one hundred feet.[341] What was the size of the canals at Atlantis? *"One hundred feet in depth."* Schliemann reiterated Forchhammer's assumption that the canal had been made to drain the waters from the plain, but it would be unnecessarily wide for that purpose. Solon's account implied the use of the canal as the entrance to a harbor by stating that it was made *"like that to a harbor"* with *"a mouth large enough for the greatest ships to sail through."*[342] The canal is said to have led to the outermost circle of water, which served as the main port of the city. Extensive swamps at the inland end of the canals at Troy could indeed qualify as remnants of ancient harbor basins.[343]

> "Moreover, through the circles of land, which divided those of sea, over against the bridges they opened out a channel leading from circle to circle, large enough to give passage to a single trireme; and this they roofed over above so that the sea-way was subterranean; for the lips of the land circles were raised sufficient height above the level of the sea."

Atlantis was surrounded by three natural channels of water. In order to connect these streams, the people produced another artificial canal *"leading from circle to circle."* The account describes a single conduit as having linked the natural rings, not many, as is often depicted in illustrations of Atlantis. This canal, still *"large enough to give passage to a single trireme,"* was the direct continuation of the first, the breakthrough from the sea. It began on its landward side *"over against the bridges."* Since only one bridge has been described so far, it must have begun at the royal palace. Again, topographic maps from the Troad show the course of a canal beginning below the citadel of Hisarlık and extending toward the artificial cut at Beşik Bay.

The people of Atlantis may have dug their canals below sea level in order to have them filled with seawater. This would have resulted in steep and high banks—asking to be bridged over with wooden planks. The sand from the excavations, too, was probably dumped next to them to minimize transport and to further raise

The eighteenth-century scholars who visited the Trojan Plain emphasized the different abandoned stream channels of the Scamander River. In this map by Henry Acland (1849), the connection between the artificial canal at Beşik Bay and Ilion is highlighted (arrows). This channel would have linked the citadel with the Aegean Sea at Beşik Bay.

the embankments. Such elevated levees could have been used, for instance, as the foundation for a road running parallel to the canal and connecting the palace with the ports and the sea.

"The greatest of the circles into which a boring was made for

149

the sea was three stades in breadth, and the circle of land next to it was of equal breadth; and of the second pair of circles that of water was two stades in breadth and that of dry land equal again to the preceding one of the water; and the circle which ran round the central island itself was of a stade's breadth. And this island, wherein stood the royal palace, was of five stades in diameter."

The measurements given by the account appear reasonable for the width of the three streams in the Trojan Plain, though the land circles in between would have been a bit wider. The five-stade diameter for the center of the city including the royal palace fits Ilion perfectly (one stade equals about 590 feet).[344]

"Now the island and the circles and the bridge, which was a plethrum in breadth, they encompassed round about, on this side and on that, with a wall of stone; and upon the bridges on each side, over against the passages for the sea, they erected towers and gates. And the stone they quarried beneath the central island all round, and from beneath the outer and inner circles, some of it being white, some black, and some red; and while quarrying it they constructed two inner docks, hollowed out and roofed over by the native rock."

The description of the quarrying *"beneath the central island all round"* characterizes the most common ancient construction technique involving natural stones. These were usually taken from the nearest possible source, and since citadels were generally placed on outcropping bedrock, the building material was often derived from the foot of the citadel itself. By removing the outermost circumference of the bedrock base and piling the stones up on top of the hill, the slope became much steeper, thereby reinforcing the citadel further. The north and northwestern sides, especially, of the hillock on which Ilion was erected, are so steep that they could be artificially amplified.[345] The story mentions three colors for the building stones. which could be explained by fresh (white), weathered and lichen-overgrown (black) and iron oxide-rich (red) limestone, a common rock all around the Aegean that also served as the building stone for Ilion.[346]

Leaf emphasized that the Trojan Plain offered the three most important building materials—timber, stone and clay.[347] As the account stated earlier, the people *"were provided with everything of which provision was needed."* According to Leaf, the available lime-stone can easily be quarried around the citadel. The Atlanteans turned the destructive process of quarrying into a constructive one: by leaving a roof of natural rock over the hollow, they produced large artificial caves. The equivalent of these have been found at Troy as Schliemann reports:

> At a distance scarcely 328 yards from my house, on the south side . . . I have now discovered the stone quarry, whence all those colossal masses of shelly limestone were obtained. The entrance to the quarry which is called by the native Greeks and Turks *lagum* (from the Arabic word for "mine" or "tunnel"), is filled with rubbish, but, as I am assured by all the people here, it was still open only twenty years ago, and, as my excavations have proved, it was very large.[348]

The Atlantis report describes the former quarry to have been converted into a shipyard. Coincidentally, the nearest village to the quarry, three miles distant from the coast, is today called Kalifatli, the Turkish word for shipyard (while Hisarlik means palace).

> "And of the buildings some they framed of one simple colour, in others they wove a pattern of many colours by blending the stones for the sake of ornament so as to confer upon the buildings a natural charm."

Of most houses in Ilion only the foundations have remained for the excavators, so we do not know whether ornaments were used on house walls. The preserved masonry of the citadel walls, however, is of very fine quality. The base of the large square tower on the east side consists of *"beautifully fitted limestone blocks."*[349] Homer, too, described the masonry as *"well-fitted," "well-dressed"* and of *"smoothly worked blocks,"*[350] while Blegen described the walls as *"built in a sophisticated style of neatly, not to say elegantly, worked blocks . . . fitted together with great care."*[351] Special effects were achieved by inserting vertical offsets which divided the fortification wall into segments.

> "And they covered with brass, as though with plaster, all the circumference of the wall which surrounded the outermost circle; and that of the inner one they coated with tin; and that which encompassed the acropolis itself with orichalcum which sparkled like fire."

Walls covered with metals appear bizarre today but are not uncommon in the ancient literature. Hesiod tells of *"a wall of bronze"* which runs around Tartarus,[352] and of Poseidon who *"set bronze gates upon the place, and all around it runs the wall."*[353] In *Works and Days*, Hesiod pictured *"houses of bronze"* at a time when *"black iron was not known."*[354] Odysseus reported *"an unbroken wall of bronze"* around the island of Aeolia (10.3), while Herodotus described ancient Ecbatana in western Iran as being built on a hillock with seven concentric rings of walls around it, each a different color and the two innermost ones plated with silver and gold.[355] He also spoke of Babylon and its bronze gates with bronze uprights and lintels.[356] The Colossus of Rhodes (third century B.C.), too, was sheathed in bronze.

If these metal veneers really existed, they would almost certainly have vanished through plundering or reuse at a later time. In the case of a conflagration, however, precious metals would be lost to the fire without the possibility of rescue. Schliemann described the possible result of such a devastation: *"a stratum of scoriae of melted lead and copper from 0.2 to 1.2 inches thick which extends nearly through the whole hill at a depth of 29–29½ ft."*[357] This layer of molten metal was associated with the remains of Troy II, but its existence was not confirmed during subsequent excavations.

> "The royal palace within the acropolis was arranged in this manner. In the centre there stood a temple sacred to Cleito and Poseidon, which was reserved as holy ground, and encircled with a wall of gold; this being the very spot where at the beginning they had generated and brought to birth the family of the ten royal lines. Thither also they brought year by year from all the ten allotments their seasonable offerings to do sacrifice to each of those princes. And the temple of Poseidon himself was a stade in length, three plethra in breadth, and of a height which appeared symmetrical therewith; and there was something of the barbaric in its appearance. All the exterior of the temple they coated with silver, save only the pinnacles, and these they coated with gold. As to the interior, they made the roof all of ivory in appearance, variegated with gold and silver and orichalcum, and all the rest of the walls and pillars and floors they covered with orichalcum. And they placed therein golden statues, one being that of the God standing on a chariot and driving six

winged steeds, his own figure so tall as to touch the ridge of the roof, and round about him a hundred Nereids on dolphins (for that was the number of them as men then believed); and it contained also many other images, the votive offerings of private men. And outside, round about the temple, there stood images in gold of all the princes, both themselves and their wives, as many as were descended from the ten kings, together with many other votive offerings both of the kings and of private persons not only from the State itself but also from all the foreign peoples over whom they ruled. And the altar, in respect of its size and its workmanship, harmonized with its surroundings; and the royal palace likewise was such as befitted the greatness of the kingdom, and equally befitted the splendour of the temples."

Unfortunately, the central section of the acropolis of Troy vi was completely destroyed by leveling in Roman times.[358] Homer speaks only occasionally about the interior of Ilion, describing a temple of Apollo (v.446) and Priam's palace at the highest spot of the citadel, which was called Pergamos (xxiv.700). These buildings were surrounded by the grand residences of Hector and Paris (vi.317). The latter had engaged the best craftsmen in the country for the construction of his house (vi.314).

Once again, the narrative refers to *"votive offerings . . . from all the foreign peoples over whom they ruled."* Such excises, voluntary or compulsory, fit Troy's geographical position and cultural character quite well. So, too, do the *"images in gold of all the princes,"* because many pedestals have been excavated at Ilion; unfortunately none of these bears a statue anymore.

One of the excavators of Troy, Carl Blegen, once produced a general summary of his impression of Troy which is very reminiscent of the picture provided by the Atlantis account:

Throughout its long existence Troy vi was obviously a royal stronghold where the ruler of the surrounding district had his seat. At the summit of the hill, within the fortified circuit, which was apparently twice remodeled, we may conclude, stood a substantial palace, and around it on descending terraces perhaps a score or more of large houses in which the members of the ruler's family and his immediate subordinates lived. At least four gateways provided access to the citadel, and from these entrances roadways led up to the central area. The whole establishment bears the impress of vigor and power, and the ambitious program of construction that was carried out implies a state of economic prosperity. Its basis was no doubt in large part agricultural, and the bulk of the working population presumably lived in small communities spread about the district. But another source of revenue may have been provided by control of the sea passage through the Dardanelles and the land route that led from the western coastal areas of Asia Minor to a crossing of the straits.[359]

The temple of Poseidon as described in the Atlantis account (590 by 295 feet in size) would cover half of the total area of Ilion (c. 590 by 525 feet); therefore these dimensions definitely do not fit the acropolis of Ilion. They cannot be accurate anyway. Even the Parthenon on the Acropolis in Athens, built roughly one thousand years later, covers only 220 by 77 feet. On the other hand, the description of a *"golden statue . . . of the god . . . so tall as to touch the ridge of the roof"* which was "ivory in appearance," is reminiscent of a similar golden and ivory statue of Zeus, which nearly touched the roof of the temple in Classical Olympia.[360] The Parthenon on the Acropolis, too, contained a golden and ivory sculpture of Athene. Both of these were created by Pheidias, a celebrated sculptor of Classical Greece. A group similar to the one described in the text with Poseidon surrounded by Nereids had also been created by Scopas, a contemporary of Plato.[361]

> "The springs they made use of one kind being of cold, another of warm water, were of abundant volume, and each kind was wonderfully well adapted for use because of the neutral taste and excellence of its waters; and these they surrounded with buildings and with plantations of trees such as suited the waters; and, moreover, they set reservoirs round about, some under the open sky, and others under cover to supply hot baths in the winter; they put separate baths for the kings and for the private citizens, besides others for women, and others again for horses and all other beasts of burden, fitting out each in an appropriate manner. And the outflowing water they conducted to the sacred grove of Poseidon, which contained trees of all kinds that were of marvellous beauty and height because of the richness of the soil; and by means of channels they led the water to the outer circles over against the bridges."

The narrative describes hot and cold springs from the area outside the citadel walls. These springs were surrounded by *'reservoirs'* used for bathing. As was discussed earlier, a pair of hot and cold springs was one of the most remarkable blessings of Troy mentioned in the *Iliad*. Homer continued his description of the place around the spring by saying,

> Close beside them, wide and beautiful, stand the troughs of stone where the wives and lovely daughters of the Trojans used to wash their glossy clothes. (XXII.153)

In Atlantis, *"they set reservoirs round about, some under the open sky."* Furthermore, the city contained a system of water conduits leading from the springs and tubs to a sacred grove and beyond to the navigable channels. Relics of such a system have been found at Troy in the form of an underground drain which was covered with heavy slabstones.[362] Such elaborate drainage systems, however, were common among Late Bronze Age palaces.

> "And there they had constructed many temples for gods, and many gardens and many exercising grounds, some for men and some set apart for horses, in each of the circular belts of island; and besides the rest they had in the centre of the large island a race course laid out for horses, which was a stade in width, while as to length, a strip which ran round the whole circumference was reserved for equestrian contests. And round about it, on this side and on that, were barracks for the greater part of the spearmen; but the guard-house of the more trusty of them was posted in the smaller circle, which was nearer the acropolis; while those who were the most trustworthy of all had dwellings granted to them within the acropolis round about the persons of the kings."

The outer city of Atlantis was dominated by gardens, exercising grounds and barracks for the spearmen. Although Troy, too, must have extended considerably beyond the citadel walls, neither the *Iliad* nor archaeological excavations have furnished much information about the lower town. The citadel itself was only the seat of a ruler and his entourage,[363] but at one point the excavators estimated the whole fortress to have served as many as 50,000[364] or even 100,000[365] citizens, who may have lived in small dwellings in a lower town outside the walls and in villages and hamlets scattered about the surrounding countryside. However, since the activities described by Homer occurred after nine years of war during which all of Troy outside the fortification walls may have been obliterated, the lack of references to a lower town is not surprising.

The mythological history of Troy describes how the city spread with time:

> In the reign of Ericthonius, the city of the Trojans was either in another situation, or covered only the upper part of the hill . . . but when Tros, his son, ascended the throne, the people were so multiplied that they began to overspread the declivity, and the additional town was called Troy, in honour of that prince.[366]

Accordingly, Ilion would seem to have been the name for the initial settlement on the acropolis, while the name Troy was introduced later to describe the whole settlement including its extensive lower town. Since this town has not yet been found, the excavated citadel should perhaps be called Ilion. Its excavators generally considered the lower town to have laid on the shallower part of the Hisarlık hill, south of the citadel, but so far mainly post–Bronze Age monuments have been found in that area. There is no reason why the major parts of the city would not have been laid in the alluvial plain itself. In fact, slight elevations within the plain often contain prehistoric remains,[367] which may represent a relict of outer city districts, because the topographically lower areas would have been buried deeply by alluvium—just like Tiryns's lower town.

Until now, the alluvial plain has never seen substantial excavations. Although many geoarchaeological surveys were carried out, the stratigraphy examined was either small scale (about 3 feet)[368] or very large scale (about 325 feet).[369] The Trojan Plain, however, combines many of the characteristics of Greek alluvial plains[370] which commonly experienced post–Bronze Age deposition on a scale of 16–40 feet.[371] This might therefore be the most likely depth to look for the remains of the lower town of Troy.

The Atlantis legend parallels the archaeological knowledge of the Late Bronze Age in its near total lack of information about plebeians and domestic houses. Today, Aegean prehistorians know more royal Achaean residences than farmsteads. The protagonists in Homer's *Iliad*, too, are nobles only, although, according to the poem, about 100,000 Greek warriors must have been fighting before Troy. Similarly, the Atlantis account describes dwellings for nobles and warriors, but accommodation for workers and farmers is neglected.

The account reports a ranking of the Atlantean spearmen into the greater part, the more trusty and the most trustworthy. Their position determined the location of their guardhouses and dwellings. A distant resemblance with this arrangement can be found in Quintus of Smyrna's description of *"The War at Troy."*[372] Quintus' report continued where the *Iliad* ended; when Paris received more troops from Eurypylus, these *"soldiers made their camp in front of the city, where the stout-hearted Trojan guards were."*

Exercising played an important role in both the city of Atlantis and the legendary history of Troy.[373] The account reports exercising grounds even for horses and a very large racecourse. The role of horses in Atlantis became apparent earlier on, when the narrative mentioned special baths for horses only. In the *Iliad*, too, the most common of all the sixteen epithets used for the Trojans is: *"tamers of good horses"* (used nineteen times) and *"having fine foals"* (v.551; 2.18). The possession of good horses and the skill to tame and train them must have been among the most renowned characteristics of the Trojans.[374] Horses were held in high esteem in Anatolia, from where the earliest written text describing the training of horses comes (sixteenth century B.C.).[375] A racecourse was also mentioned in Quintus of Smyrna's account of the Trojan War.[376] Archaeological excavations frequently revealed horse bones in Troy VI and VIIa (the strata contemporary with the Trojan War).[377]

> "And the shipyards were full of triremes and all the tackling that belongs to triremes, and they were all amply equipped. Such then was the state of things round about the abode of the kings. And after crossing the three outer harbours, one found a wall which began at the sea and ran round in a circle, at a uniform distance of fifty stades from the largest circle and harbour, and its ends converged at the seaward mouth of the channel. The whole of this wall had numerous houses built on to it set close together, while the sea-way and the largest harbour were filled with ships and merchants coming from all quarters, which by reason of their multitude caused clamour and tumult of every description and an unceasing din night and day."

Navigation of primitive ships through the Hellespont was difficult.[378] Making headway up the straits against a current running at two and a half knots and the prevailing northerly winds must have been strenuous but not impossible.[379] In order to pass through the Dardanelles into the Sea of Marmara, the ships were forced to cast anchor and wait for a favorable south wind, a procedure not at all uncommon for Bronze Age seafarers. Troy's wealth may well have rested on its ability to provide protected harbors, provisions and pilot services for long-distance trade vessels.[380] *The Black Sea Pilot* described what the situation in the Tenedos Channel, the former entrance to the Trojan harbor, looked like only one hundred years ago: *"it is not a rare occurrence to see 200 or 300 vessels in Tenedos channel or in the other anchorages, waiting for favourable and enduring breeze."*[381] In addition, Troy may have possessed a large fleet on its own which might have been used for pilot services, trade and defense.

> "Now as regards the city and environs of the ancient dwelling we have now wellnigh completed the description as it was originally given. We must endeavour next to repeat the account of the rest of the country, what its natural character was, and in what fashion it was ordered. In the first place, then, according to the account, the whole region rose sheer out of the sea to a great height, but the part about the city was all a smooth plain, enclosing it round about, and being itself encircled by mountains which stretched as far as to the sea; and this plain had a level surface and was a whole rectangular in shape, being 3000 stades long on either side and 2000 stades wide at its centre, reckoning upwards from the sea."

The report about the city of Atlantis concludes here. Turning to the *"rest of the country,"* the narrator states that *"the whole region rose sheer out of the sea to a great height."* Again this description fits the coast near Troy, which has been portrayed as steep and rugged with very steep promontories.[382] Atlantis was, just like Troy, placed in the center of a plain surrounded by hills bordering the sea on their other side. The plain is described as being *"rectangular in shape,"* which would again apply to the Trojan plain—but the one of Atlantis was about 330 by 220 miles, while the biggest extension of the Trojan Plain is just 7 miles. This appears to be the most drastic mismatch between the description of Atlantis and Troy's characteristics.

The error regarding the size of the plain did not even escape Plato's attention. Just a few sentences later in the story, when it is said that the plain was surrounded by artificial channels, he intervenes for the first and only time, stating that the combination of such a large territory and an artificial trench running all around it, is unbelievable:

> "Now, as regards the depth of this trench and its breadth and length, it seems incredible that it should be so large as the account states, considering that it was made by hand, and in addition to all the other operations, but none the less we must report what we heard."

Plato noticed that something must have been mistranslated here, but his loyalty to transmitting old traditions without changing them overcame his personal opinion.

> "And this region, all along the island, faced towards the south and was sheltered from the Northern blasts."

A 310-mile-wide plain can hardly be protected from winds; hence, this statement provides further clues that the dimensions of the plain were wrong. But more importantly there is only one place in the Mediterranean where *"Northern blasts"* are so extreme and persistent that they were worth mentioning in the ancient literature. Of all the places that Homer describes in the *Iliad*, only one is *"windy"*: Troy. Moreover, *"windy"* represents Homer's most frequently used epithet for Troy (VIII.499; XII.115; XIII.724; XVIII.174; XXIII.64, 297). Even in modern times the *"Northern blasts"* are a unique attribute of Troy. Schliemann reported from his excavations at Troy:

> One of my greatest troubles is the continuing high winds.[383]
>
> The continual hurricane from the north, which drives the dust into our eyes and blinds us, is exceedingly disturbing.[384]

The strong and nearly ceaseless winds at Troy blow mainly from north and northeast. In spring, however, the frequency of winds from southwestern directions is relatively high, while the average occurrence of storms is lower than in summer or autumn.[385] Thus, spring would have been the best time for Bronze Age ships to navigate through the straits.

> "And the mountains which surrounded it were at that time celebrated as surpassing all that now exist in number, magnitude and beauty; for they had upon them many rich villages of country folk, and streams and lakes and meadows which

furnished ample nutriment to all the animals both tame and wild, and timber of various sizes and descriptions, abundantly sufficient for the needs of all and every craft."

The report portrays the character of the rural surroundings of Atlantis: a rich natural environment, whose resources were utilized but not abused. The importance of *"abundantly sufficient"* timber is emphasized, implying that wood had become a precious and finite resource when this account was composed. It was said before that the earth of Atlantis produced *"all kind of food in plenty,"* that it *"furnished most of the requirements of daily life"* and the Atlanteans *"were provided with everything of which provision was needed."* The affluent and largely undisturbed natural environs of Atlantis assured the uninterrupted progress of this culture much in the same way in which Troy's culture evolved steadily from generation to generation without any sign of cultural break.[386]

"Now as the result of natural forces, together with the labours of many kings which extended over many ages, the condition of the plain was this. It was originally a quadrangle, rectilinear for the most part, and elongated; and what it lacked of this shape they made right by means of a trench dug round about it. Now, as regards the depth of this trench and its breadth and length, it seems incredible that it should be so large as the account states, considering that it was made by hand, and in addition to all the other operations, but none the less we must report what we heard: it was dug out to the depth of a plethrum and to a uniform breadth of a stade, and since it was dug round the whole plain its consequent length was 10,000 stades. It received the streams which came down from the mountains and after circling round the plain, and coming towards the city on this side and on that, it discharged them thereabouts into the sea. And on the inland side of the city the channels were cut in straight lines, of about 100 feet in width, across the plain, and these discharged themselves into the trench on the seaward side, the distance between each being 100 stades. It was in this way that they conveyed to the city the timber from the mountains and transported also on boats the seasons' products, by cutting transverse passages from one channel to the next and also to the city. And they cropped the land twice a year, making use of the rains from Heaven in the winter, and the waters that issue from the earth in summer, by conducting the streams from the trenches."

The above paragraph provides a wealth of specific information regarding the plain of Atlantis:

- its shape resembled an elongated quadrangle, although it was not perfectly geometric
- its final shape resulted from a combination of natural forces and human constructions
- the Atlanteans dug a channel around the plain, accentuating its rectilinear shape
- the channel was 590 feet wide and 100 feet deep
- Plato calculates that the total length of the channel would have been over 1,000 miles if the dimensions for the plain were correct (but he felt these proportions were wrong)
- the artificial channel received the water from natural streams which emanated from the mountains
- the water was then directed toward the city via channels on both sides of the plain; *"thereabouts"* it was discharged into the sea
- transverse channels were dug, 100 feet wide and about 10 miles apart; these discharged their water into the trench on the seaward side
- streams and channels were used for transporting timber and natural produce from the mountains to the city
- the land was harvested twice a year, thanks to the successful irrigation system

Once again, the dimensions appear exaggerated: 100 feet depth and 590 feet width are excessive for a drainage and shipping canal in an alluvial plain, and a spacing of 10 miles of such trenches would be too wide, since the territory in between would still need to be drained by natural streams. Apart from these caveats, the whole description of the landscape management of the city makes sense for a place blessed with quantities of natural produce and century-long periods of uninterrupted development.

In Troy, too, there are many indications for massive human interference with the natural environment. The stream that traverses the plain of Troy bears two names; its first name, *"used by the gods"* (xx.73), was Xanthus ("yellow river"). Later, however, the streambed is said to have been changed by man and it was called

"Skamma andros" ever since.[387] All geographers who have examined the Trojan Plain agree that the modern bed of the Scamander is not identical with the ancient one and that the whole plain is full of abandoned riverbeds and artificial channels.[388]

Some of the sharpest observations regarding these abandoned channels go back to the last century.[389] In 1839, Peter Wilhelm Forchhammer, a geography professor at the university of Kiel in Germany, carried out a survey of the Trojan Plain. He was accompanied by Thomas Spratt, then a mate in the Royal Navy, later vice-admiral. Their reconnaissance aimed at producing the first topographic map of the area. Forchhammer was concentrating on the geographical observations while Spratt was responsible for surveying and mapping. To the present day, Forchhammer's notes and Spratt's map might be considered the most comprehensive collection of observations ever to have been produced of the Plain of Troy. Forchhammer noted more archaeological monuments in the area than anybody before or after him. He also devoted substantial parts of his publications to the discussion of abandoned streambeds and artificial channels. According to Forchhammer, sizable streams existed on both sides of the plain, where only discontinuous wetlands are found today.[390] He assumed that the entire Scamander used a course on the far western side of the plain,[391] because the present creek in that area, the Pinarbaşi Su, is using a disproportionately wide and deep bed, which must have belonged to a much bigger river. Artificial watercourses were still noted in that area only forty years before Forchhammer's survey.[392] The Pinarbaşi Su, just like the Kalifatli Asmak, the abandoned stream on the opposite side of the plain, are almost perfectly straight, despite the fact that—until levees were built during a canalization project in 1956–65—the Scamander meandered freely across the whole plain.

In addition to these past river courses, Forchhammer's and Spratt's map also showed several discontinuous sand heaps which they found to be associated with the old streambeds. To Schliemann these sand heaps were one of the most remarkable characteristics of the plain:

> The ancient bed of the Scamander, which is identical with the Kalifatli Asmak, is characterized by . . . little hills of alluvial sand, while the new bed has no alluvial sand hills.[393]

> In many places especially on the left bank, are rows of sand hills, which must once have been formed by alluvium.[394]

Apart from dunes, no geological structure resembles such ridges. Alluvial floodplain deposits accumulate individual, extensive layers during ephemeral floods, but they cannot pile up a mound. Rivers tend to build up natural levees along their banks, but these are continuous and cannot be limited to such a short distance. Thus, the sand ridges near the paleo-streambeds are best classified as a relict of artificial excavations. The same is true for the abandoned channels on both sides of the plain: unless tectonic displacement has tilted an area, a natural stream would not run along the margins of an alluvial plain, because of the elevated topography; nor would it produce a perfectly straight bed. Thus the combination of narrow, vertically incised and now abandoned channels in elevated positions, and sand heaps (from excavations) is a strong hint toward man-made canals.

Forchhammer discovered more channels, smaller in size and running perpendicular to the former main stream;[395] he concluded that these traverses were made artificially and that their age could be considerable.[396] Remnants of such traverses through the plain were also indicated in the topographic map.

Two conclusions can be drawn from the presence of such large-scale interferences with the natural environment: firstly, the Trojans must have had a strong motivation to redirect the streams, probably to reduce the malaria risk[397] and to increase the amount of arable land. Secondly, the Trojans must have been an extremely well-organized society with unusual resources in terms of man-power and engineering skills.[398]

> "As regards their man-power, it was ordained that each allotment should furnish one man as leader of all men in the plain who were fit to bear arms; and the size of the allotment was about ten times ten stades, and the total number of all the allotments was 60,000; and the number of the men in the mountains and in the rest of the country was countless, according to the report, and according to their districts and villages they were all assigned to these allotments under their leaders. So it was ordained that each such leader should provide for war the sixth part of a war-chariot's equipment, so as to make up 10,000 chariots in all, together with two horses and mounted men; also a pair of horses without a car, and attached thereto a combatant with a small shield and for charioteer the rider who springs from horse to horse; and two

hoplites; and archers and slingers, two of each; and light-armed slingers and javelin-men, three of each; and four sailors towards the manning of twelve hundred ships. Such then were the military dispositions of the royal City; and those of the other nine varied in various ways, which it would take a long time to tell."

The military forces described by the account are of the same kind as the ones in the *Iliad*. Chariots, of which Atlantis is said to have had 10,000, were among the most common equipment of the Trojans. The *Iliad* also highlights archers (11.827; 11.848) and spearmen (11.819; 11.841) in the Trojan contingents. Even opponents of the idea that Homer's *Iliad* proves the historicity of the Trojan War tend to agree that his *"Catalogue of Ships,"* sent to fight at Troy, represents a highly accurate portrayal of the Late Achaean geography and political organization.[399] In this catalog Homer listed the number of ships provided by each kingdom, adding up to a total of 1,185, while Atlantis was said to have been in command of 1,200 ships.

"Of the magistracies and posts of honour the disposition, ever since the beginning, was this. Each of the ten kings ruled over the men and most of the laws in his own particular portion and throughout his own city, punishing and putting to death whomsoever he willed. But their authority over one another and their mutual relations were governed by the precepts of Poseidon, as handed down to them by the law and by the records inscribed by the first princes on a pillar of orichalcum, which was placed within the temple of Poseidon in the centre of the island."

The political system of Atlantis was simple and effective:

- Atlantis had a class society with magistracies and other posts of honor
- ten kings ruled over people and laws in their individual kingdoms
- these kings were allowed to punish and execute whomever they wished, with the exception of fellow kings
- these practices went back to the very beginning; the mutual relations between the kings were governed by the precepts of Poseidon
- the earliest forefather of the Atlantean nobles had inscribed

> the laws on a pillar of orichalcum, which stood in the very
> center of the palace

The report emphasizes the presence of a federal structure and makes clear that the rulers exerted virtually unlimited totalitarian rule. Only the relations between aristocrats themselves had to be regulated. For the first time, the account states that writing was known in Atlantis, implying that it has been practiced for a long time. The evidence for a written script in Troy, however, is limited to characters on vases and spindle whorls,[400] no documents have been found on the site.[401] But a clay disk from Phaestus on Crete, dating to the Minoan period, shows an undeciphered script not related to Linear A; according to Hammond it may insinuate a warlike seafaring race from the Aegean islands or the coastland of Anatolia,[402] for its characters include a ship, an Asiatic bow, a plumed headdress and a round shield. The habit of inscribing the laws on stone pillars, as depicted in the above quote, was common practice among the people living in the fertile parts of Anatolia in the late second millennium.[403] Many such inscribed *stelae* have been found in the Near East, including, for example, the famous lawcode of Hammurabi of Babylon.

> "... and thither they assembled every fifth year, and then alternately every sixth year—giving equal honour to both the even and the odd—and when thus assembled they took counsel about public affairs and inquired if any had in any way transgressed and gave judgement. And when they were about to give judgement they first gave pledges one to another of the following description. In the sacred precincts of Poseidon there were bulls at large; and the ten princes, being alone by themselves, after praying to the God that they might capture a victim wellpleasing unto him, hunted after the bulls with staves and nooses but with no weapon of iron; and whatsoever bull they captured they led up to the pillar and cut its throat over the top of the pillar, raining down blood on the inscription. And inscribed upon the pillar, besides the laws, was an oath which invoked mighty curses upon them that disobeyed."

The bull rituals are linked to an age-old Bull Cult in Anatolia.[404] The occasional mentioning of iron is reminiscent of the *Iliad*; both texts put the emphasis on bronze, although the existence of iron is

Great altar for sacrifices found in Ilion by Schliemann (1875, Fig. 188).

noted. Individual iron objects have occurred in the Aegean as early as the Early Bronze Age, but the technique of fabrication was developed in Anatolia at *c.* 1500 B.C. and apparently not utilized for a few centuries.[405]

> "When, then, they had done sacrifice according to their laws and were consecrating all the limbs of the bull, they mixed a bowl of wine and poured in on behalf of each one a gout of blood, and the rest they carried to the fire, when they had first purged the pillars round about. And after this they drew out from the bowl with golden ladles, and making libation over the fire swore to give judgement according to the laws upon the pillar and to punish whosoever had committed any previous transgression; and, moreover, that henceforth they would not transgress any of the writings willingly, nor govern nor submit to any governor's edict save in accordance with their father's laws."

The central part of Troy VI was destroyed during Roman reuse of the site so that the remains of the city look like a doughnut with a big hole in the center. Nevertheless, the cultic rituals described in the above paragraph are equivalent to archaeological observations made in the part of Troy VI which was preserved. During the excavations in 1933, Carl Blegen discovered a disproportionately long and narrow building (c. 15 x 55 feet), called Anta House (Squares G–H 9), just outside the entrance to the South Gate.[406] A burned stratum had once covered most of the floor inside the house, marking it as a place where fires were repeatedly lit. A trench was dug through 4.5 feet of stratum after stratum of burned debris, indicating a long continuity in the custom of burning fires. The fireplace was much too extensive for an ordinary hearth; moreover the lower part of the burned debris predated the building itself. The burned layers contained several nondescript fragments of bronze and a chunk of lead, a few fragments of pottery and many animal bones. Blegen arrived at the conclusion that the structure was a religious edifice that housed a cult which required burned offerings. He interpreted the area just outside the gateway as sacred ground and considered the presence of four or more stone pillars set up against the south face of Tower VII as significant in this connection, for *"they are surely the visible symbols of a cult."*[407]

In this instance the parallels between legend and archaeological record are perhaps more striking than in any other. The account said that the royal princes hunted the bulls *"in the sacred precincts of Poseidon"* which were outside the citadel. Once they had captured a bull, they had to lead it up to the pillar on which the laws were inscribed. In other words the pillar was at some distance from the grazing ground. In Troy VI the pillars were right next to the entrance to the city, a site which would have been particularly suitable for the law codes.[408] On the other side of the entrance, opposite the pillars, was the ritual burning place.

The story of Atlantis is getting toward its end; little or nothing can be contributed from archaeological knowledge regarding the customs which are summarized in the following part of the account, but it might be appreciated as a valuable source describing aristocratic life at the end of the Bronze Age.

"And when each of them had made this invocation both for himself and for his seed after him, he drank of the cup and offered it up as a gift in the temple of the God; and after spending the interval in supping and necessary business, when darkness came on and the sacrificial fire had died down,

all the princes robed themselves in most beautiful sable vestments, and sat on the ground beside the cinders of the sacramental victims throughout the night, extinguishing all the fire
that was round about the sanctuary; and there they gave and
received judgement, if any of them accused any of committing any transgression. And when they had given judgement,
they wrote the judgements, when it was light, upon a golden
tablet, and dedicated them together with their robes as memorials. And there were many other special laws concerning the
peculiar rights of the several princes, whereof the most
important were these: that they should never take up arms
against one another, and that, should anyone attempt to
overthrow in any city their royal house, they should all lend
aid, taking counsel in common, like their forerunners, concerning their policy in war and other matters, while conceding the leadership to the royal branch of Atlas; and that
the king had no authority to put to death any of his brother-
princes save with the consent of more than half of the ten.

"Such was the magnitude and character of the power
which existed in those regions at that time; and this power the
God set in array and brought against these regions of ours on
some such pretext as the following, according to the story. For
many generations, so long as the inherited nature of the God
remained strong in them, they were submissive to the laws
and kindly disposed to their divine kindred. For the intents of
their hearts were true and in all ways noble, and they showed
gentleness joined with wisdom in dealing with the changes
and chances of life and in their dealings with one another.
Consequently they thought scorn of everything save virtue
and lightly esteemed their rich possessions, bearing with ease
the burden, as it were, of the vast volume of their gold and
other goods; and thus their wealth did not make them drunk
with pride so that they lost control of themselves and went to
ruin; rather, in their soberness of mind they clearly saw that
all these good things are increased by general amity combined
with virtue, whereas the eager pursuit and worship of these
goods not only causes the goods themselves to diminish but
makes virtue also to perish with them. As a result, then, of
such reasoning and of the continuance of their divine nature
all their wealth had grown to such a greatness as we previously described."

Only three sentences remain before the account breaks off and the Atlanteans are still being praised at great length for their *"divine nature"* and *"gentleness joint with wisdom."* Where are the moral lessons to be learned which allegedly made Plato invent all this? Just one sentence (below) is devoted to the downfall of the Atlanteans, and there certainly is an uncomfortable haste about the way Plato introduces a moral dimension into the story, as Christopher Gill has noted.[409] Moreover, while the report has thus far been exceedingly precise and unambiguous, the following conclusion describing the moral decay of the Atlanteans is convoluted and nebulous.

> "But when the portion of divinity within them was now becoming faint and weak through being ofttimes blended with a large measure of mortality, whereas the human temper was becoming dominant, then at length they lost their comeliness, through being unable to bear the burden of their possessions, and became ugly to look upon, in the eyes of him who has the gift of sight; for they had lost the fairest of their goods from the most precious of their parts; but in the eyes of those who have no gift of perceiving what is the truly happy life, it was then above all that they appeared to be superlatively fair and blessed, filled as they were with lawless ambition and power.
>
> "And Zeus, the God of gods, who reigns by Law, inasmuch as he has the gift of perceiving such things, marked how this righteous race was in evil plight, and desired to inflict punishment upon them, to the end that when chastised they might strike a truer note. Wherefore he assembled together all the gods into that abode which they honour most, standing as it does at the centre of all the Universe, and beholding all things that partake of generation; and when he had assembled them, he spoke thus: . . ."

Suddenly, in the middle of a sentence, the account breaks off. Plato had known that he was entering shaky ground when he involved himself with Atlantis. Thus, his speaker, Critias, began with an elaborate plea for indulgence in which he described the incredible magnitude of his task. Critias did not exaggerate; his story was like a dance on a high wire, and what nobody expected happened: he fell.

Why was the story left unfinished? I believe that Plato finally realized the parallels between Solon's account and the Trojan War. Plato's *Critias* ends abruptly just where the *Iliad* begins, with Zeus calling a council of all the gods to confer about the fate of the Trojans and the Greeks. The notes before Plato may have continued at least a bit farther, making the coincidence even more apparent.

Most scholars agree that Plato intended to continue writing, but that the project turned out to be *"too ambitious."*[410] Perhaps we should briefly review the interests and involvements of each of the transmitters to determine whether the priest and Solon ceased telling the story here too. The Egyptian priest had promised Solon a report which would highlight the legendary deeds of Solon's ancestors. We have heard the narrative and must admit that the priest did not keep the promise. The account, as recollected in *Critias*, contains no information on the Greeks whatsoever! Although the people of Saïs admired the Athenians and even felt related to them, they knew surprisingly little about them, and all they knew was said before in *Timaeus*. On the other hand, they possessed a wealth of detailed information about the Greeks' opponent, Atlantis. Perhaps the priest mentioned the legendary Greek culture to raise Solon's interest. As it turns out, however, the Egyptians did not possess a detailed hieroglyphic report on the Greeks; all they knew was common traditional information similar to Homer's depiction of the heroic age. What the Egyptians did have was an exceedingly specific description of Atlantis/Troy. After this remarkable city was wiped out by a military operation of unprecedented scale, it would have been normal to write down in detail what Troy had looked like and how it functioned, for the Egyptians claimed to have taken records of all remarkable events in their sphere of influence. The purpose of the description of Troy was identical with the purpose of all other inscriptions: the provision of a permanent record of remarkable events for future generations. Such a description would, of course, aim at listing technical details as accurately as possible. Subjective conclusions of the kind found in *Timaeus* do not occur in *Critias*, i.e. up to *Critias* 120D, three paragraphs before Plato's story breaks off. Thus, I assume that *Critias* 113C–120D represents an Egyptian recollection of Troy possibly written after the eradication of the city, while *Timaeus* 21E–25D reflects general, Saïtian knowledge derived from oral traditions. The priest provides several clues in *Timaeus* which postdate the sack of Troy. He knows about the flood that occurred in Greece, about the Achaean demise and about the problem of navigating the straits near Atlantis (which in my opinion occurred because Troy could not provide guidance after it had been ruined). No such hints of the postTrojan War era are given in *Critias*, thus the hieroglyphic inscription on which the book is based may also have been composed before the conflict. During his visit to Saïs, Solon must have been able to copy the Atlantis account word for word. He planned to use this material for his own writings and he may have composed the third paragraph before the abrupt end, where the Atlanteans' attitude is summarized (*Critias* 120D–121A). But Solon abandoned the project, just as Plato was going to abandon it later. Solon may have been too old, as Plutarch said, or too preoccupied, as Plato thought; but he may also have realized the parallels with Troy and thus discontinued using the text.

Plato seems to have employed Solon's manuscript as it was, without reflecting much on it. Thus, *Critias* (113C–120D), although incomplete, appears in a final, polished form with no trace of the infelicities indicative of an unfinished work. If the text was initially composed by somebody else, it should be possible to detect stylistic variations between the *Critias* and other Plato scripts. Multivariate computer analysis of Plato's style has shown that, first of all, *Timaeus* and *Critias* are close to each other regarding technique of composition; secondly, they differ sufficiently from all other texts by Plato that, if considered his composition, they would have to be placed at the very end of his life,[411] a position that is already occupied by the *Laws*, said to have been *"in the wax"* when Plato died.[412]

At the end of Solon's text, Plato was forced to contemplate the transition to his next source of historic knowledge, which would have been either in front of him or in his mind. At this point, Plato finally realized what the story of Atlantis was all about. This unexpected discovery had several consequences: first of all, Plato realized that Solon's notes were not as accurate as Plato had assumed all along. The chronology was inappropriate, and directions and place-names were confusing, to say the least. Secondly, the description of Atlantis vindicated Homer's *Iliad* and possibly even the *Odyssey*. As a consequence, Plato's respect for Homer's poetry grew dramatically, whereas before, he had looked down on poetic *"imitations,"*[413] criticizing Homer as unfit for the education of the young[414] to an extent that made Heraklitos demand, *"Let Plato the parasite, the traducer of Homer, be banished."*[415]

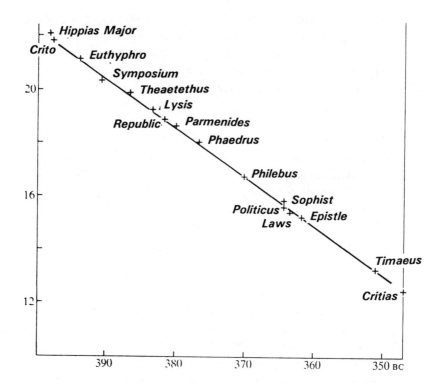

A multivariate computer analysis of Plato's style in which statistics are used to assign a relative date to each of Plato's books. The maximum (400 B.C.) and minimum (347 B.C.) values mark Plato's active period. On this basis, *Timaeus* and *Critias* are so different in composition technique that they would have to be placed at the very end of Plato's life, about fifteen to twenty years later than the preceding volumes. According to Diogenes Laërtius (3.37), however, Plato's *Laws* was still unfinished in the wax when he died. The stylistic differences, therefore, support the argument that *Timaeus* and *Critias* may have been composed by Solon and not by Plato. (After Ledger 1989, Fig. 9.1.)

Plato had already invested much time and hard work in the trilogy; almost half of the whole project was finished, and he was not immediately convinced that he had to abandon it altogether. First of all, he tried to save the story by introducing some nebulous, moral dimensions (*Critias* 121A–121B). Then, after Homer had been vindicated for Plato, he considered using Homeric techniques to get out of the Atlantis muddle and thus came up with Zeus' call for a council of the gods, in the same manner in which Homer had begun the *Iliad* and the *Odyssey*. But his desperate attempt to save the trilogy only made the story more paradoxical: while the Egyptian priest had described the demise of Atlantis and Greece using almost scientific objectivity and solid facts such as the war, the earthquake and the flood, Plato found himself having to introduce divine forces to conclude the story. Finally, he realized that the western theme of the trilogy was no longer tenable and that his Atlantis story contained no beneficial news for Attika. Troy, of all places, would have become elevated to astronomic heights; something that did not appear desirable so shortly after the Persian War.

THE LAWS 3.676–682: THE EARLY IRON AGE

Plato abandoned the idea of the trilogy and embarked on writing a new book in which he could incorporate at least some of the remaining sources initially intended for the rest of *Critias* and *Hermocrates*. He had clearly learned a lesson from his carelessness with Solon's notes and thus used a different, more cautious approach in this new book.[416] Below are five quotations from the *Laws*, which emphasize Plato's understanding of some of the key issues regarding the Achaean demise: (1) Troy, (2) the flood, (3) civil war, (4) metal shortage and (5) Homer's reports of these events.

1. *Troy.* Since Plato may have realized that Atlantis and Troy are one and the same, it is not surprising that his description of Ilium sounds familiar:

> Ilium was founded, according to us, when men had descended from the hills to a wide and beautiful plain. They built their city on a hill of moderate height near several rivers which poured down from Ida.[417]

2. *The Flood.* Although the flood catastrophe at Tiryns may have been absorbed in the Greek mythology too—in the form of Poseidon's drowning of the Argolid—the Greeks never seem to have connected it with the Achaean demise, probably because they realized that it accompanied a political collapse by chance only.

Thus, Plato remained unable to correlate the flood report from Egypt with the events at the end of the Achaean era; he continued to confuse it with the great deluge, because both were followed by periods of low population density and relatively low levels of technology (Neolithic and Early Iron Age).

> The human race has been repeatedly annihilated by floods and plagues and many other causes, so that only a small fraction survived. Those who escaped the disaster must have been nearly all hill-shepherds. Such men must have been in general unskilled and unsophisticated. So all their tools were destroyed, and any worth-while discovery they had made in politics or any other field was entirely lost.[418]

Obviously, Plato took seriously the notion of periodic setbacks in civilization due to major natural disasters.[419] Although the Atlantis account and the *Laws* describe in this instance the same processes with virtually the same words, the former has thus far been interpreted as a myth and the latter as an historical account.[420]

3. *Civil war*. While the Egyptians thought the Achaean society was flushed away during spectacular earthquakes and floods, the Greeks, including Plato, knew precisely what had caused their downfall. The Greek cities eventually

> mounted an expedition against Ilium. They besieged Ilium for ten years, and during this period the domestic affairs of the individual attackers took a turn to the worse. The younger generation revolted, and the ugly and criminal reception they gave the troops when they returned to their own cities and homes led to murder, massacre and expulsion on a large scale.[421]

Plato's description of a civil war at the end of the Bronze Age fits the archaeological record of the equivalent period (LHIIIC): elimination of aristocrats, demise of artistry and craftsmanship, decimation of population and large-scale emigrations.

4. *Metal shortage*. We have seen that the Achaean economy depended largely on the imports by sea of raw metals and the exports of finished metal products, primarily of bronze. Troy was the place where tin bronze first appeared in the Aegean, and it

has been identified as a major metal–production, refining and trading site. What happened when Troy was destroyed?

> It was virtually impossible to refine fresh supplies of metal. Even if there was an odd tool left somewhere on the mountains, it was quickly worn down to nothing by use. Replacement could not be made until the technique of mining sprang up again among man. During that period all techniques that depend on a supply of copper and iron and so on must have gone out of use.[422]

There was one person who knew Troy and the Trojan War better than anybody else; who, in fact, described it sometimes using the same words as the Egyptian priest. A man who knew about the civil war and the dark age that followed the sack of Troy and who turned all this knowledge into the most fascinating poetry the world has ever seen:

5. *Homer*. When Plato realized that Atlantis and Troy are identical, he also realized how accurate Homer's depiction of the city had been. As a consequence, Plato's appreciation of Homer grew beyond measure:

> He composed these lines . . . under some sort of inspiration from God. And how true to life they are! This is because poets as a class are divinely gifted and are inspired when they sing, so that with the help of Graces and Muses they frequently hit on how things really happen.[423]

The one-to-one comparison between Atlantis and Troy concludes here. It has, I hope, shown that Atlantis does not need to be a mythical continent that was only conceived in Plato's mind. On the contrary, Atlantis has many of the characteristics of a prosperous Late Bronze Age citadel, including some unique parallels with Troy. But even without accepting the analogy of Troy and Atlantis, this line of thought can become a catalyst which could stimulate new ideas that are completely independent of the Atlantis = Troy equation.

From now on, Atlantis will decline in importance, since the story of it seems to be just another version of the same old story of Troy and the Trojan War. What it does lead to, however, is the notion that Troy was much more important in prehistory than was previously thought; that it may have been a very important center for

Bronze Age economics, military life, poetry and literature. For the remaining part of this book I have picked three subjects which may benefit from a new interpretation of Plato's *Timaeus* and *Critias:* Homer's *Odyssey*, the collapse of Achaean society and the topography of the Trojan Plain.

CHAPTER SIX

THE *ODYSSEY* STARTS MAKING SENSE

As we gain a greater knowledge of Mycenaean Greece through archaeology, we gain a greater respect for the accuracy of the Homeric descriptions.[424]

It is remarkable how well you sing the tale of the Achaeans' fate and of all their achievement, sufferings and toils. It is almost as though you had been with them yourself. (8.488)

The following incident happened in a German village called Ankershagen during the winter of 1829. It was Christmastime. The village priest celebrated the holiday with his not-quite-eight-year-old son. Father and son shared a keen interest in history and had had long conversations about the tragic demises of Pompeii, Herculaneum and Troy. Thus the caring father had chosen what he regarded a highly suitable Christmas gift: Dr. Georg Ludwig Jerrer's *World History for Children*. Browsing through his new book, the boy found an illustration of Troy with its huge walls and the Skaean Gate in flames.

"Father, Jerrer must have seen Troy," said the son, "or else he could not have drawn it."

"My son," replied the father, "this illustration rests only on the artist's imagination."

"But did Troy really have such big walls?" asked the boy.

"Yes, my son."

"Dad, if such huge walls ever existed, they cannot be completely lost. They must still be buried under the rubble and dust which accumulated over the centuries. I think, one day, I shall search for these walls and with them I shall find Troy!"

Forty-one years later, the "poor, little boy," as he thought of himself,[425] Heinrich Schliemann, had fulfilled the dream of his childhood. Another ten years later, in 1880, he succeeded—against the explicit advice of his publisher Brockhaus; his collaborator, Virchow; and his translator, Egger—in publishing this self-indulgent story in the monumental volume *Ilios*.[426] One consequence of the publication was that every German pupil ever since has heard this story at some point in school.

Schliemann's affection for myths was paradoxical; he loved them so much that while trying to verify the historicity of ancient ones he created his own. Realizing the effects of myths on his readers, he managed to devote ten percent of *Ilios* to the description of his own legendary life. Much of this autobiography, including the above anecdote, was fabricated;[427] his sixty thousand letters do not contain any hints that he was ever interested in ancient history before concluding his career as a merchant. Although he had invented these stories, obviously to catch the attention of his readers, he nevertheless considered Homer's *Iliad* to be a kind of Baedeker to ancient Greece, in whose accuracy he believed unrestrictedly, without ever contemplating that Homer could have been driven by intentions similar to Schliemann's himself.

What do we know about Homer today, three generations after Schliemann's alleged vindication of the *Iliad*? In brief, we know nothing. Scholars still debate whether Homer existed as an individual, whether he composed both *Iliad* and *Odyssey* or just one of them, whether he was blind or seeing and whether he lived as early as the tenth century B.C.[428] or as late as the seventh.[429] Even Homer's gender was questioned.[430] We cannot say for certain whether he invented the poems or whether they recount genuine old traditions. Yet, the incredible profusion of Homeric scholarship has led to a graphic scenario of what Homer's life and work most likely was like.[431] According to this, Homer was born around 770 B.C. in a rather wealthy family who lived somewhere on the coast of Ionia (today's western Turkey). He probably traveled much before composing the *Iliad* in the middle of his life and the *Odyssey* shortly before his death. Homer's poems made him instantly famous. His work inspired the minds of many ancient Greek and Roman writers. Later, in medieval times, it was temporarily lost. Only the last two hundred years have seen a revival of interest in Homer. In the last century, following the fashionable approaches of those days, the *Iliad* was interpreted as a sun myth, in which the Greeks represent the sun and the Trojans the clouds, while Achilles' wrath was considered an eclipse.[432] This trend of interpretation experienced a sudden end after Schliemann started excavating Ilion. As a result, many scholars felt prompted to adopt a new, nevertheless equally extreme approach: Homer became a "war correspondent," and his words were taken as genuine historic truth. During the last few decades research into Homer has seen still more, sometimes mutually exclusive approaches,[433] including the complete dissection of the author's poems to conclude that they were the composite achievement of several anonymous authors, who strung together a record of oral Greek traditions. Today, the majority of Homer interpretations follow a more moderate avenue of argument: his epics are currently primarily considered to have been written by one author who had gained much experience as a bard before he used the newly discovered art of writing to record the most successful pieces of his repertoire.

Homer's themes rest on much larger oral accounts which were at that time common knowledge throughout the Greek world. At least three such epic cycles existed: the *Argonautika*, the *Herakleia* and the *Trojan Cycle*. Whatever has survived of them was transmuted into Greek legends and vice versa. The *Trojan Cycle*, from which Homer derived his motifs, contained at least half a dozen other oral accounts, such as *The Sack of Ilion* and the *Homecomings*.[434] These oral traditions continued to exist after the composition of the *Iliad* and the *Odyssey*, inspiring other ancient writers to compose further novels and plays based on the same themes which Homer had used but looking from a different perspective, sometimes claiming greater historical accuracy or completeness than Homer had achieved. In recent centuries, however, the excellence of Homer's poems has made his work outshine all other Trojan epics and counterfeit attempts, somewhat regrettably leading to the perception that they are the only ancient Greek traditions that deserve scholarly attention.

The *Iliad* is a tragedy which portrays the events of fifty-one days of the Trojan War from a Greek perspective. For nine years, the Achaean forces have been encamped on the shore before Troy. Numerous times they have fought the Trojans themselves and raided Trojan allies in the vicinity without being able to achieve a decisive victory. As a prize for his successful leadership during an onslaught against a Trojan ally, Agamemnon, the commander-in-chief of the united Greek army, received the girl Chryseis. But when her father, a local priest of Apollo, approached Agamemnon with considerable ransom, the latter refused to release the girl. Angry about Agamemnon, the priest prayed to his god, who subsequently induced a terrible plague in the Greek camp. In order to calm the god's anger, the Greek troops forced Agamemnon to release Chryseis—without asking for ransom. In return, however, Agamemnon confiscates another girl, Briseis, who was Achilles' prize. Achilles is outraged by this latest assault by his archrival and, withdrawing his troops from the battlefield, he refuses to fight for the Greeks in the future. Afterward, an attempt is made to decide the conflict by a single combat between Paris, the seducer of Helen, and Menelaus, her legal spouse, because they are the main contenders in the war. Paris, however, vanishes from the scene, and the battle resumes. Without Achilles and his troops, the Greeks are no longer blessed with superiority. Eventually they are forced to construct a wall and a ditch around their huts and ships, but Hector, the Trojan commander-in-chief, is able to break through the defense system and sets fire to one of the Greek ships. Being worried about an imminent defeat of his fellows, Achilles finally yields to the pleas for support, but he only allows his closest friend, Patroclus, to rejoin the Greek army together with his troops. Patroclus carries the assault too far and is eventually killed by Hector. Achilles, outraged by the loss of his friend, settles the dispute with Agamemnon, rejoins the battle, kills Hector, and—not satisfied with his revenge—maltreats Hector's body by dragging it behind the chariot in front of Troy. At the end of the book, Priam, the ruler of Troy and father of Hector, appears in Achilles' tent to ask for his son's body. Achilles gives in and the *Iliad* ends with an uneasy truce for the funeral of Hector.[435]

Troy and the Trojan War are indivisibly connected with Homer and the *Iliad*; for many centuries they were even considered to be identical. Therefore, a writer who comes forward with a new topographical theory regarding Troy will inevitably look at Homer too. I shall do the same, but instead of analyzing topographic hints in the *Iliad*, I will direct my attention to the *Odyssey*, because, as it turns out, the new interpretation of Plato's *Critias* might have considerable consequences for our understanding of the *Odyssey*.

DEMYSTIFYING THE ODYSSEY

When Schliemann's excavation of Ilion suddenly turned the *Iliad* into a "war report," many people began to search for historic truth in the *Odyssey*, too, often trying to retrace Odysseus' journeys.[436] Since none of these attempts resulted in noteworthy insights, we still lack a comprehension of the geography of the *Odyssey*. It is clear, however, that the book follows a carefully designed scheme.[437] A wealth of admirable and fascinating studies examine this scheme and its poetic merit. The identification of Atlantis as Troy opens the door to yet another, surprisingly novel interpretation of the *Odyssey*.

The places in the book can be divided into those really inhabited during the Late Bronze Age, such as Mycenae, Pylos, Sparta, Troy and Ithaca, on the one hand, and imaginary lands on the other (the country of the Lotus-eaters, the land of the Cyclops etc.). One locality, however, falls in between these categories: Scheria, the land of the Phaeacians, visited by Odysseus just before he returns to Ithaca. It appears as a real country described in abundant detail, just a bit too prosperous perhaps to be genuine. Most scholars today assume that an historic place served as the model for Homer's Scheria, but its location is disputed (Corfu,[438] Sicily,[439] Cyprus,[440] Crete[441] and Calabria[442] are favorite candidates). Others are uncertain[443] or regard Phaeacia as an idealized Ionian state.[444] In any case, name and people are not unique to Homer, since they do occur in the *Argonautika* as well, an oral epic which predates Homer but was written down much later in the third century B.C.[445]

SCHERIA AND ATLANTIS

Homer's Scheria has much in common with Plato's description of Atlantis.[446] These parallels are so striking that they were first realized centuries ago by the Swedish scholar Olof von Rudbeck (1630–1702),[447] and many later writers followed in his track.[448] Today, classicists consider the parallels between Scheria and Atlantis irrefutable.[449] Suspecting plagiarism, they have blamed Plato for "out-Homering Homer," for creating his own imaginary "Scheria" in Atlantis.[450] Such coincidences between individual parts of Greek mythology are not unusual, though, because ancient authors (much like modern authors) liked to make use of well-known and popular themes for their writing. Odysseus' tales about his wanderings in books 9–12, for instance, recollect some of the themes of the *Argonautika* and the oriental epic *Gilgamesh*.[451]

Just as Homer incorporated Near Eastern traditions in the *Odyssey*, Plato was assumed to have taken some characteristics of Scheria and introduced them in his depiction of Atlantis. If, however, the story of Atlantis was not conceived in Plato's mind, a new explanation for the parallels with Scheria must be sought. There is at least a theoretical chance that the coincidences originated from independent oral descriptions of the same place—Troy. Before investigating the consequences of this deduction any farther, one ought to examine some of the parallels between Scheria and Atlantis.

Both the Phaeacians of Scheria and the Atlanteans described themselves as descendants of Poseidon (13.130; 114; 120) and thus akin to the gods. They lived "at the end of the world" (7.23). Instead of being absolute monarchs, their high kings hold councils of the aristocrats (6.54; 7.189; 8.11; 119C), comprising twelve in Phaeacia (8.390) and ten in Atlantis (114A). In both accounts much emphasis is laid on the navigational skills of the people (8.558; 7.320; 117D; 119B), who both live in a rich, fertile plain (6.258; 13.322; 118B), which is nevertheless surrounded by steep cliffs falling sheer into the sea (5.400; 118A). The city, palace and temple lie some way inland from the coast (6.317; 113C), being enclosed by high embankments and a broad harbor (6.262; 7.44; 115D). Both places had excellent ports with a narrow entrance (6.264, 115D), a temple of Poseidon adjacent to royal residences (6.266; 7.85F; 7.135; 115C, 116B) with comparable decoration (6.303; 116B). They both held beautiful parks (6.295; 6.321; 7.112; 117B) with two springs (7.129; 117B) as well as meeting-places and sports stadia (6.266; 8.5; 8.110; 117C). A comparison of the actual descriptions of some of these characteristics, taken from the *Odyssey* and the Atlantis account, accentuates the striking similarities.

SCHERIA

"Our city is surrounded by high battlements; it has an excellent harbour on each side and is approached by a narrow causeway." (6.261)

"Odysseus marvelled at the harbours with their well-found ships, at the meeting-place of the sealords and at their long and lofty walls, which were surmounted by palisades and presented a wonderful sight." (7.44)

"You will see near the path a fine poplar wood sacred to Athene, with a spring welling up in the middle and a meadow all round. That is where my father has his royal park and vegetable garden." (6.292F) "Where trees hang their greenery on high, the pear and the pomegranate, the apple with its glossy burden, the sweet fig and the luxuriant olive." (7.110F)

"The garden is served by two springs, one led in rills to all parts of the enclosure, while its fellow opposite, after providing a watering-place for the townsfolk, runs under the courtyard gate towards the great house itself." (7.128)

Nausicaa went to "the noble river with its neverfailing pools, in which there was enough clear water always bubbling up." (6.86f)

"Here is the people's meeting-place, built up on either side of the fine temple of Poseidon with block of quarried stone bedded deeply into the ground." (6.264)

ATLANTIS

"Beginning at the sea, they bored a channel and thus they made the entrance to it from the sea like that to a harbour by opening out a mouth large enough for the greatest ships to sail through (115D) and after crossing the three outer harbours (117D), full of triremes and all the tackling that belongs to triremes." (117) "They erected towers and gates (116) and the royal palace likewise was such as befitted the greatness of the kingdom, and equally befitted the splendour of the temples." (117A)

"It produced and brought to perfection all those sweetscented stuffs which the earth produces now, whether made of roots or herbs or trees, or of liquid gums derived from flowers or fruits. The cultivated fruit also, and the dry, which serves us for nutriment, and all the other kinds that we use for our meals—the various species of which are comprehended under the name 'vegetables.'" (115A)

". . . bringing up from beneath the earth two springs of waters (133E) and the outflowing water they conducted to the sacred grove of Poseidon and by means of channels they led the water to the outer circles over against the bridges." (117B)

"The springs were of abundant volume, and each kind was wonderfully well adapted for use because of the neutral taste and excellence of its waters." (117A)

"In the centre there stood a temple sacred to Cleito and Poseidon which was reserved as holy ground, and encircled with a wall (115C) and the stone they quarried beneath the central island all round." (116A)

"A kind of radiance, like that of the sun or moon, lit up the high-roofed halls of the great king. Walls of bronze, topped with blue enamel tiles, ran round to left and right from the threshold to the back of the court. The interior of the well-built mansion was guarded by golden doors hung on posts of silver which sprang from the bronze threshold. The lintel they supported was of silver too, and the door-handle of gold. On either side stood gold and silver dogs." (7.83F)

"Finally they made of it an abode amazing to behold for the magnitude and beauty of the workmanship. (115D) All the exterior of the temple they coated with silver, save only the pinnacles, and these they coated with gold. As to the interior, they made the roof all of ivory in appearance, variegated with gold and silver and orichalcum, and all the rest of the walls and pillars and floors they covered with orichalcum." (116D)

A 2700-YEAR-OLD "BACK TO THE FUTURE" SCHEME

If one accepts these parallels as indications of independent descriptions of one and the same place, what would the consequences be for the interpretation of the *Odyssey*? Scheria is the first *polis* visited by Odysseus since he left Troy; hence it would not be all that surprising if he returned to where he was last. But Odysseus and his fellow Achaeans had wiped out this city when they went there before, thus if Homer really wanted Odysseus to see Troy again, he would have to let him travel back in time to a date long before the Trojan War, when both the Achaean states and Troy were at their zenith. Whether one believes in the existence of surrealism in Archaic Greece or not, just for the sake of argument—and for sheer entertainment—this is what the novel would look like from such a perspective.

The *Odyssey* begins with a council of the Olympian gods, ten years after the fall of Troy. All the survivors of the war had reached their homes, except Odysseus who is kept on a remote island as the downhearted lover of the lesser goddess Calypso, a daughter of Atlas (1.54). The gods are sorry for him, except Poseidon, who *"pursued the heroic Odysseus with relentless malice"* (1.20). Nevertheless, Zeus, the king of the gods, decides that the time has come for Odysseus, too, to return home. Once Zeus has made this decision, Homer moves the action away from the gods to the situation back at Odysseus' home in Ithaca. After twenty years of Odysseus' absence, his wife Penelope is being besieged by a horde of vicious suitors, who are lodging uninvited in the royal residence. Her son, Telemachus, being only twenty years old, has no power to expel the impertinent swarm from their home. A messenger of the gods, Hermes, visits Telemachus, proposing to him a journey to the palaces of Sparta and Pylos on the mainland, whose rulers, Menelaos and Nestor, both comrades of Odysseus at Troy, may have some news regarding his father's fate. Many books later Telemachus returns from this journey with no more knowledge about his father but impressively grown in character.[452]

After four books dedicated to Telemachus' travels, Zeus returns to pronounce his judgment about Odysseus' fate. Although the hero is finally allowed to return home, Zeus does not want this voyage to be direct and effortless. He demands that Odysseus make one essential stop in Scheria, the land of the Phaeacians, before he is free to see his family in Ithaca.

Most people think that the main theme of the *Odyssey* is the endless and aimless wanderings of the lost seafarer after the sack of Troy. In reality, however, very little traveling goes on. Telemachus' return trip to Pylos and Sparta and Odysseus' journey from Calypso's island to his home with a stopover in Scheria are all there are in terms of traveling activities; two straight journeys, each interrupted by one stopover. The rest, Odysseus' trip to the underworld, his encounter with the Sirens and with the cannibalistic Cyclops—all these adventures only occur in stories he recounts during his visit to Scheria. How unreliable these tales are is emphasized by the goddess Athene upon Odysseus' arrival on Ithaca:

> Odysseus . . . does not propose even in his own country to drop his sharp practice and the lying tales that he loves from the bottom of his heart. (13.294)

The real journeys of the *Odyssey* are saturated with metaphorical meanings. Odysseus' first trip (from Calypso to Scheria) is excessively long: he has to sail for seventeen days, a journey that can hardly be accommodated within the Achaean sphere of seafaring. Although he is alone and sails through the nights—something keenly avoided by prehistoric helmsmen—his trip runs smoothly without the slightest complications as long as he is returning from his mythical spheres. By letting Odysseus travel for such a long time, Homer portrays the hero's descent from one imaginary world to another, semi-imaginary one.[453] In the same way Homer lets Odysseus sink into a deep sleep, *"the very counterfeit of death"* (13.81), on his second and final voyage from the semi-imaginary Scheria back into the real world.

Why is Odysseus required to go to Scheria? Until now, we have neither found the reason for this detour nor really understood the significance of the events at the Phaeacian court. What is the moral dimension that Homer is hiding behind the metaphorical journeys? Perhaps Zeus' justification of Odysseus' visit to Scheria will provide some hints:

> On his twentieth day he should reach Scheria, the rich country of the Phaeacians, our kinsmen, who will take him to their hearts and treat him like a god. They will convey him by ship to his own land, giving him copper, gold and woven materials in such quantities as he could never have won for himself from Troy, even if he had come away unhurt with his share of the spoil. (5.30)

The mention of Troy in a description of the Phaeacians appears abrupt and dissonant; to be more harmonic, this paragraph could say:

> He should reach Scheria, the rich country of the Phaeacians. They will convey him by ship to his own land, giving him [presents] in such quantities as he could never have won for himself from THEM!

Poseidon, in conversation with Zeus, repeats the same phrase later in the book (13.138).

Although the country, Scheria, and its people, the Phaeacians, bear names, Homer completely avoids using a name for their remarkable city. *Schera* was a Phoenician word for market,[454] and "Scheria" could be interpreted as a market city or a place of trade[455] which would, of course, have suited Troy. The Phaeacians are described by Howard Clarke as living

> far apart from other peoples "in the wash of the great sea" (6.204). Alcinous states that they live in an area where east meets west (8.29), but the Phaeacians, like most of the people Odysseus visits, are themselves contradictory, their name suggesting "darkness," their island perhaps once a legendary island of the dead, their ships conveying souls at night.[456]

If Homer wanted to depict the Trojan souls after their defeat, could he have invented a more suitable metaphor than these dark characters living in a legendary place of the dead—in a city near "the wash (or outflow) of the great sea," where east meets west? There were not many places in Homer's world which would have fitted such a description as much as Troy, lying at the outflow of the Dardanelles where the Black Sea and the Mediterranean worlds meet.

Only once in the whole *Odyssey* does Homer provide reasonably precise sailing directions. In order to arrive at Scheria, Odysseus was advised always to keep the Great Bear on his left—meaning he was heading east-north east.[457] A similar hint for the location of Scheria on an eastern shore of the Mediterranean was given when Athene left *"the pleasant land of Scheria, crossed the barren seas, and came to Marathon"* (7.79)—a plain on the eastern side of Greece near Athens. Yet another time, the king of Scheria, Alcinous, declares that his people would take Odysseus wherever he wishes to go, even

> if the spot is more remote than Euboea, which is said to be at the world's end by those of our sailors who saw it. They not only saw it I must tell you, but finished the return trip also in one and the same day without fatigue. (7.320)

The world cannot have been very big in those days if the sailors could make it to Euboea and back in one day. Euboea lies on the western side of the Aegean diametrically opposed to the Dardanelles and Troy. The only way to travel directly to Euboea across a sea would be from the Anatolian side of the Aegean. If this interpretation is correct, Euboea was regarded as the end of the world from an Anatolian perspective, much the way the straits at Troy were considered the end of the world from a Greek point of view.

When Odysseus arrives near the shores of mythical Scheria, his boat shatters in a storm instigated by Poseidon. "So much for you!" said the god:

> Now make your miserable way across the sea, until you come into the hands of a people whom the gods respect. Even though you reach them, I do not think you'll be in any mood to scoff at the buffeting you will have had. (5.375)

It is two days before stalwart Odysseus is washed ashore—by a strong breeze from the north (5.384). Incidentally, this north wind plays the same prominent role in Scheria that it had played in both

Atlantis and Troy. The topography of the coastline sounds familiar too:

> The land looked like a shield laid on the misty sea. (5.281)
> There were no coves, no harbours that would hold a ship;
> nothing but headlands jutting out, sheer rock, and jagged
> reefs. (5.402)

Steep cliffs are typical for many Aegean shores, but the most prosperous settlements, like that of the Phaeacians, were near coastal plains, which provided fertile land and natural harbors. Only in Troy a coastal plain and *"sheer rocks and jagged reefs"* occur in the same area. Moreover, the coastline at Troy looks literally *"like a shield laid on the misty sea,"* as is evident from a sketch drawn by William Gell in 1806.

When Odysseus reaches the Phaeacian shore, he has suffered hypothermia and exhaustion. He has also been stripped of the only thing he possessed: his clothes. Odysseus realizes that he can survive and recover from fatigue if he buries himself under a pile of leaves. When he wakes from a deep sleep under the leaves, he has been transformed into a young man. Homer used the twenty-day voyage from Calypso and the sleep to describe a metaphorical journey through time, bringing Odysseus to a point in the past when he was a young man. This rejuvenated Odysseus is now being rescued by the beautiful, marriageable princess Nausicaa, who discovers him at the beach. The scene between Nausicaa and Odysseus is one of the most enchanting pieces in world literature. According to Stephen Tracy, two of the main themes of the *Odyssey*, rebirth and rejuvenation, are expressed here more clearly than anywhere else in the novel:

> Homer reinforces the idea that Odysseus' stay with Calypso has
> been a kind of living death by casting the journey away from
> her island in terms that strongly suggest rebirth. Nausicaa is far
> from inevitable. By telling the story as he does, Homer follows
> up the symbolic rebirth of his hero in book five by giving him in
> books six to eight the adventures of a young man. The parallels
> between his short journey [from the shore to Alcinous' palace]
> and Telemachus' journey to Pylos and Sparta are significant,
> and, however lightly, they reinforce the notion that Odysseus
> here in Phaeacia has the experiences of a young man. Each of
> these journeys is fraught with symbolism of death and
> rebirth.[458]

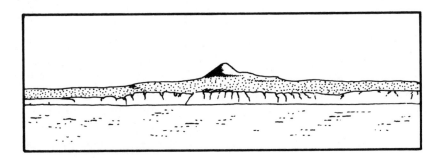

This sketch is drawn after an illustration by William Gell (1806, 32, Plate 13) showing the coast at Troy looking "like a shield laid on the misty sea."

If Scheria and Troy are identical, Odysseus would have traveled back in time to experience an episode in a golden age, one that truly existed a few decades before the legendary war, when both Troy VI and the Achaeans saw their political and economic peaks. By returning the hero to the Troy of the time before the great destruction, Homer expressed most vividly one moral of the *Odyssey*: the futility of war. His aim is to show that the splendid city and people of Troy did not deserve eradication and that the Achaeans gained no triumph. Many noble men were killed during the war, others upon their return. No wonder Odysseus cannot enjoy his stay in Scheria. *"Even though you reach them,"* said Poseidon, you will not really reach them physically, because they do not exist any more, and *"you'll [not] be in any mood to scoff at the buffeting you will have had,"* because your own hands have for ever destroyed these people.

Having been taken to the palace, Odysseus requests a ship from the king, Alcinous, who generously grants the favor even before the visitor has revealed his identity. For the Phaeacians have a reputation that they will provide *"any stranger who lands on their coasts with his passage home."* They are exceptionally skilled sailors who

> pin their faith on the clippers that carry them across the far-flung seas, for Poseidon has made them a sailor folk, and these ships of theirs are as swift as a bird or as thought itself.
> (7.33)

The Phaeacian *"lords of the sea and champions of the long oar"* (8.189) bear unusual, maritime names: Coxswain, Swiftsea, Seaboard, Launcher, Shiprich, Pilot, Sailor, Boatchampion etc.[459] They employed ships with no sails but fifty-two oarsmen (8.36),[460] whereas Telemachus in Ithaca only requested a ship with twenty.[461] The one place in the Mediterranean where outstanding navigational skills and fast ships are of paramount importance is the Black Sea passage. As argued before, the Trojans are likely to have provided pilot services through the Dardanelles and Bosporus, escorting strangers safely home just like the Phaeacians. Tim Severin recently demonstrated how Late Bronze Age galleys could have been rowed upstream through the Bosporus even with only twenty men on the oars.[462] Accurate knowledge of the straits is now and was then essential to utilize the countercurrents along the shore. Thus, experienced local pilots and fast ships would have been one of the most valuable assets of Troy, or Scheria, or Atlantis.

Alcinous realizes that his visitor has come a long way across the sea, but he cannot tell whether he came from west or east. Thus Scheria must have been in maritime contact with both spheres—like Troy. At the same time, the Phaeacians are said to live *"far from the busy haunts of men"* (6.8) with no neighbors of their own (6.279), just as the Trojans represented a distinctive, separate culture, isolated from the nearby Hittites.[463] Furthermore, the Phaeacians represent a society which was hostile to strangers, strategically and economically oriented toward the sea and derived from Poseidon and the Giants[464]—like the Trojans;[465] their talent at handling the oars was said to be *"rivalled by the dexterity of their womenfolk at the loom"* (7.106), once again paralleling the Trojans, whose exceptionally prolific weaving is demonstrated by thousands upon thousands of spindle whorls found during excavations.

The Phaeacians give Odysseus an impressive reception: in his honor they hold endless banquets, compete in athletic games and perform acrobatic dances. These ceremonies start off with the blind bard Demodocus, who sings a passage about a quarrel between Odysseus and Achilles. The first phrase of this poem seems to be a direct allusion to the first line of the *Iliad*: *"The wrath of Achilles is my theme."*[466]

Since the *Iliad* and the Trojan War are events that are yet to come, the songs are meaningless to the Phaeacian lords. But they enjoy Demodocus' song and encourage the lyricist to continue.

They cannot imagine that anybody would set hostile feet on their land:

> There is no man living—there never will be—who could come in enmity to the Phaeacian land; we are loved too well by the immortals. (6.201 Shewring)

But Odysseus breaks out in tears. He had been assured that he will receive his *"full measure of agony"* in Scheria. While the Phaeacians have no notion of the tragedy, Odysseus is forced to realize the splendor of the place and the hospitality of the people he had ravaged. He manages to hide his tears from everybody except King Alcinous. Noticing his guest's discomfort, the king suggests a change of activities: athletic contests. After a few rounds of running, wrestling, jumping, throwing and boxing—the Phaeacians love sports—one of the king's sons eventually invites Odysseus to join in, but Odysseus refuses because he feels *"sick at heart."* Another young Phaeacian, Euryalus, suddenly starts insulting Odysseus for declining such an invitation, calling him a wimp, or worse: a merchant! Odysseus explodes, saying *"You have the brains of a dolt,"* he rushes to pick up a discus of enormous weight and throws it way beyond all other markers. Afterward he challenges his hosts in whatever sport they favor. But Alcinous interrupts again, suggesting a return to more peaceful music and dances. The moral of the intermezzo on the sports ground is clear: Odysseus has been provoked, thoroughly and unnecessarily. Although the cause of the offense was a trifle, its magnitude was sufficient to incite a fierce counterattack. A similar trifling incident may have triggered the quarrels leading to the Trojan War. Homer is now showing how such quarrels could be resolved in a more civilized and mutually beneficial manner.[467] Demodocus, the bard, joined by expert dancers, presents a comedy about the love of Ares and Aphrodite, who was married to the god Hephaistos (nevertheless she conceived three children by Ares). When Hephaistos discovered their cheating, he caught them *in flagrante delicto* in a net which he had installed over the bed. Then he presented them, still in the net, to all his fellow gods (only the goddesses stayed away out of embarrassment). Hephaistos was persuaded by Poseidon to release the cheaters, imposing the condition that Ares should pay a fine. The moral of this comedy is the need for forgiveness— especially in connection with adultery.[468] Once again, this episode may allude to the trifling incidents which led to the Trojan War—

Paris' seizure of Helen. Homer demonstrates how such a conflict could have been resolved among gentlemen without any bloodshed.[469]

After the song, Odysseus raises his voice for the first time since the dissension on the sports ground to praise the marvelous skills of the Phaeacian dancers. Alcinous is so delighted by this tribute that he invites a generous donation to the friendly guest from everybody present. Euryalus, the young man who had insulted Odysseus so badly, apologizes for his blunder, passing his marvelously crafted sword to him as a gift of reconciliation. Odysseus replies,

> May the gods bless you! And I only hope you will not one day miss the sword you have given me here with such conciliatory words.

Homer has saturated all these events and dialogues at the Phaeacian court with an affluence of symbolism, perhaps culminating in Odysseus' tribute to Demodocus' songs of the Trojan War:

> It is remarkable how well you sing the tale of the Achaeans' fate and of all their achievement, sufferings and toils. It is almost as though you had been with them yourself.

Finally, Odysseus requests from Demodocus a song of the wooden horse, his own cunning invention that brought the ultimate Greek victory over the Trojans. The bard fulfilled the request of the noble guest willingly and

> went on to sing how the Achaean warriors, deserting their hollow ambuscade, poured out from the Horse to ravage Troy; how they scattered through the steep streets of the city leaving their ruin in their wake; and how Odysseus, looking like Ares himself, went straight to Deiphobus' house with the gallant Menelaus. And there, sang the bard, he rushed into the most terrible of all his fights. (8.516)

Strangely enough, Demodocus does not sing about Odysseus' cunning idea; instead he concentrates on the dramatic destruction that this invention brought. While Demodocus sings of the terrible slaughtering which happened at the very place where Odysseus is now being spoiled, the latter wept as a woman weeps when she throws her arms round the body of her beloved husband, fallen in battle before his city and his comrades, fighting to save his home-town and his children from disaster. She has found him gasping in the throes of death; she clings to him and lifts her voice in lamentation. But the enemy come up and belabour her back and shoulders with spears, as they lead her off into slavery and a life of miserable toil, with her cheeks wasted by her pitiful grief. (8.527)

The victor, Odysseus, has to suffer the pains of the most pitiable loser, to realize that his remarkable exploit brought nothing but distress. The *Odyssey* is above all a book about the futility of war and the insuperable role of happy family life.

Alcinous, once again, interrupts the performance because he has noticed Odysseus' sorrow. He would prefer everybody, hosts and guest, to be merry, for *"to any man with the slightest claim to common sense, a stranger and suppliant is as good as a brother."* The Phaeacians had relaxed while listening to the tragedies—thinking that they had nothing to lose. As it turns out, however, they are not only wealthy, isolated, hospitable, mysterious sailors, athletes and weavers (like the Trojans)—they are also doomed like the Trojans. Again assuring Odysseus of a safe jorney home, Alcinous impatiently requests his visitor finally to reveal his name. Before Odysseus can reply to Alcinous' request, however, the king introduces a new subject:

At the same time, I must tell you of a warning I had from my father Nausithous, who used to say that Poseidon grudged us our privilege of giving safe-conduct to all comers. He prophesied that some day the god would wreck one of our well-found vessels out on the misty sea as she came home from a convoy, and would overshadow our city with a great mountain-wall. (8.563)

The request for Odysseus' name is directly linked to the prophecy of the Phaeacians' ruin. Rightly so, because the ship that will be wrecked and trigger the catastrophe will be the one that will bring Odysseus to Ithaca. Such prophecies generally come into existence only after the predicted event has taken place.[470] Therefore, in the case of Scheria, the demise must have predated the composition of the poem.

193

Odysseus finally reveals his identity:

> I am Odysseus, Laértës son.
> Men know me for my stratagems.
> My fame has reached the heavens. And my home
> is Ithaca, an island bright with sun.
>
> (9.20 Mandelbaum)

Surprisingly, this revelation leaves no impression on the Phaeacians whatsoever. Although they had been hearing stories about Odysseus and his feats all evening, the identity of their guest inspires not a single remark. Instead, Alcinous reiterates again Poseidon's impending threat *"to teach them to hold their hands and give up this habit of escorting travellers"* (13.150). Meanwhile, Odysseus embarks on the prolonged recollection of his aimless wanderings after the sack of Troy which have made the *Odyssey* so famous.

On the next day he and his crew have to wait until after dusk before they can depart to Ithaca. Bronze Age seafaring, however, was strictly limited to daylight. The mysterious travel through the night, once again, verifies the impression of time travel, especially since Odysseus falls into an extremely deep sleep, only comparable with death. The Phaeacian sailors have to carry him ashore, and even there he continues sleeping. All the details of Odysseus' last voyage to Ithaca let the Phaeacians appear as ghosts, visitors from a different world who arrive at night, quietly and without leaving any traces.[471]

When Poseidon finally realizes that the Phaeacians have even escorted his adversary, Odysseus, back home, the god of the sea decides to take revenge by turning the ship into a rock shortly before it reaches the shore of Scheria. Zeus even encourages Poseidon:

> Choose the moment when all eyes in the city are fixed on the ship's approach to turn her into a rock offshore, and let this rock look like a ship, so that all the world may wonder. (13.154)

There are some small islands off the coast of Troy, but recognizing the shape of a Bronze Age ship in them requires a lot of imagination.

Alcinous, watching the ship becoming petrified, cries:

Was Homer thinking of one of these small islands off the coast of Troy, when he described how the Phaeacian ship was transformed into a rock by Poseidon? (After a panorama engraving by Henry W. Acland 1849.)

> Alas! . . . Poseidon resented our giving safe-conduct to all and sundry . . . and he will overshadow our city with a ring of high mountains. . . . But listen: I have remedies to suggest . . . For the future give up your custom of seeing home any traveller.

In order to escape the disastrous prophecy, Alcinous wants his people to give up their habits of welcoming and piloting foreign travelers. This directive might allude to what could have been the real trigger of the dissensions leading to the Trojan War: a closure of the Black Sea passage for trade vessels, cutting off the Aegean from markets and suppliers in the east.

In the above retelling of the first part of the *Odyssey*, I have neglected the central piece, where the hero speaks about his incredible adventures after the sack of Troy. I regard these stories as sea yarns, possibly current in Homer's days, but largely derived from older traditions such as the *Argonautika* and *Gilgamesh*. Throughout these tales Odysseus claims to be Cretan (13.256; 14.199; 19.172), associating himself with people famed for being the best liars in the world.[472] His stories are not at all essential to comprehend the main themes of the epic, although the encounter with the dead in book eleven provides Odysseus with an opportunity to hear about the destiny of his former commander-in-chief, Agamemnon. The Achaean leader tells how he reached Mycenae soon after the fall of Troy only to be butchered by his wife, Clytemnestra, and her lover, Aegisthus (11.405). Because of this fatal reception Agamemnon warns Odysseus not to sail openly into port when he returns to Ithaca (11.455). He had already been given such a warning, though, by the prophet Teiresias, who had informed Odysseus that he would find trouble in his house upon his arrival (11.117).

THE END OF THE ACHAEANS: LATE HELLADIC IIIC

When Odysseus finally arrives in Ithaca, he has returned not only from distant worlds but also from distant times and encounters with the dead. Soon after awakening from his deathlike sleep, he meets Athene, who grants him further information about the situation in the palace. She tells him that the royal residence is in chaos like the rest of Greece. The Achaeans' victory at Troy has brought nothing but disaster (13.319). The land is broken and ruined; very few admirable aristocrats are still in power, and only those who fought at Troy (Nestor and Menelaus) are considered praiseworthy. Many of the royal princes died at Troy or went astray during their return journey. Fifteen out of twenty-four books describe the miserable state of Greece after the Trojan War, again emphasizing the futility of war.[473] The Trojan War, mentioned in many dialogues throughout the *Odyssey*, is only remembered with bitter feelings, e.g. when Menelaus says:

> How happy could I be, here in my house, with even a third of my former estate, if those friends of mine were still alive who died long ago on the broad plains of Troy. (4.95)

Odysseus, too, shows his resentment over the conflict with Troy (and the role played by the queens in aggravating it):

> It was for Helen's sake that so many of us met our deaths, and it was Clytaemnestra who hatched the plot against her absent lord. (11.438)

Even the swineherd Eumaeus repents the Trojan War. Speaking about Odysseus, he laments:

> But he is dead and gone. And I wish I could say the same of Helen and all her breed, for she brought many a good man to his knees. (14.67)

Homer now reveals that many Achaeans had entered the Trojan War with extreme reluctance and lacking understanding of its necessity. Agamemnon admits that he and Menelaus needed a full month to persuade Odysseus to join forces in the naval expedition. Odysseus recalls this time with bad feelings:

> The time came, however, when Zeus . . . let us in for that deplorable adventure which brought so many men to their knees; and they pressed me and the famous Idomeneus to lead the fleet to Ilium. There was no way of avoiding it: public opinion was too much for us. (14.238)

Looking back to the outcome of the war, Homer has arrived at the conclusion that it was futile—more than that, disastrous—not only for the losers but also for the victors. While the Achaean lords were fighting overseas, their places had been taken over by deputies of less competence. Once the commander had gone to war, many aristocrats took advantage of the power vacuum, trying to raise their own standing. Odysseus' departure from Ithaca increased the number of male aristocrats in the palace from one (Odysseus) to 108 (the suitors), bringing in chaos and anarchy for the rest of the country, in exchange for a formidable, carefree and decadent life for the new, self-appointed rulers.

One indication of the lack of political leadership was the total absence of aristocratic assemblies after Odysseus had left (2.26).[474] The suitors felt powerful because of their large number (2.243); and they made clear that they would not give up their new privileges just because of the king's return. In Agamemnon's case, this threat was turned into reality. When he came home, after ten years of fighting, he was naturally looking forward to a rare welcome from his children and servants (11.426). Instead of being acclaimed for leading such a successful mission, he and all the warriors accompanying him (11.388) were butchered by the man who had replaced him on the throne and in his wife's bed. Later, Aegisthus' and Clytemnestra's brutal murder was avenged by Orestes, the legitimate prince, who slaughtered not only his natural mother and stepfather but also their servants and followers. Lawlessness had taken over Greece, and the country fell into the hands of *"rogues and criminals"* (24.279). The impending civil war was aggravated further by interfering gods. Athene candidly encouraged Telemachus to murder the suitors (1.295) and to seek *kleos* such as Orestes had obtained by killing his father's murderers (1.297). *Kleos* ("fame on the lips of men") was the goal *par excellence* in the heroic age.[475]

All these events are described in the part of the *Odyssey* which plays in the real world. Nothing supernatural overshadows Homer's description of postwar Greece. Even divine activities dropped to a minimum, with Athene only interfering occasionally. Places and protagonists are familiar from the *Iliad*, and many of the cities mentioned in the *Odyssey* are known to have been inhabited in the Late Bronze Age. Because of that, it should be possible to correlate the archaeological record with Homer's depiction of Greece a few years after the sack of Troy.

Archaeologists have only occasionally speculated that the absence of Achaean lords during the Trojan War could have played a role in the collapse of the political system in Greece.[476] One indication supporting this notion is the nearly simultaneous occurrence of the Trojan War and the Achaean demise. If there was a connection between the two phenomena, the time span described in the *Odyssey* would fall into the final phase of the Bronze Age: Late Helladic IIIC.

When Odysseus arrived in Ithaca, some of the Achaean palaces had already fallen to rogues and criminals, while others, such as Pylos and Sparta, continued to be administered by their traditional sovereigns. The archaeological record confirms this picture of a step-by-step collapse of the Late Bronze Age palaces, although Pylos has thus far been considered to have fallen first. The Late Mycenaean architecture even reflects the milieu of Aegisthus in Mycenae and of the 108 suitors beleaguering Odysseus' palace in Ithaca, because the phase of demise was paradoxically accompanied by an increase in noble residences. While the palace at Tiryns was nearly abandoned, new *megara* were built in the lower town, and at least one of those was disrespectfully attached to the citadel walls.[477] Other very large residences arose quite far away from the citadels at isolated places which had thus far been avoided. One might arrive at the conclusion that the collapse of the palace system allowed an increased proportion of the society to act, if not like kings, at least like dukes.

Homer depicts his country on the brink of civil war, describing precisely the kind of upheavals which currently rank as the prime explanation for the Mycenaean demise. Outlawed murderers, such as Theoclymenus from Argos (15.273), roam across the country. The whole society seems to have been turned upside down—aristocrats, the *only* protagonists of the *Iliad*, are described as criminals and murderers, while herdsmen and shepherds rank as the most loyal compatriots of Odysseus. The hero has to team up with a swineherd, Eumaeus, and a cattle-herdsman, Philoetius, to fight against his fellow aristocrats. Homer emphasized this irony, describing them as two king's men, the cowman and the swineherd (21.186), addressed by Odysseus as *"the only two of all my men who will be glad to see me back"* (21.211).

Almost half of the *Odyssey* deals with the subtle preparation of the hero's revenge for the rogues' abuse of Greek hospitality in general and his absence in particular. Eventually Odysseus, together with his son, Telemachus, and the two herdsmen, slaughter every single one of the suitors. Only the bard and the herald are saved from the bloodshed, because they had to transmit these events to subsequent generations.

Odysseus admits that they have killed *"the pick of the Ithacan nobility, the mainstay of our state"* (23.120). Such dramatic conflicts between Achaean aristocrats have made their way into the Greek legends, too, for instance in the case of "Seven Against Thebes," where an attack eventually resulted in the eradication of a whole city. A more selective elimination of aristocrats is indicated in the archaeological record from this period. An outbreak of violence seems to have accompanied the end of the heroic age. When the dust from the burning palaces had settled, the aristocrats and their elite culture had vanished.

Odysseus' retaliation has further aggravated the situation. When he is finally reunited with his wife, Penelope, he points out that the biggest difficulties are yet to come. Eupeithes, the father of the leading suitor, Antinous, has denounced *"Odysseus as the inveterate enemy of our race"* (24.425), and Odysseus realized what that meant:

"I have a horrible fear now that the whole forces of Ithaca will soon be on us here, and that they will send urgent messages for help to every town in Cephallenia." (24.353)

The Linear B tablets from the last days of Pylos record defense preparations against an attacker. Who the enemy was, nobody can tell, but that he succeeded in raiding the city is evident. The same fear of an imminent attack is reflected in Homer's words:

Standing here, he saw the whole hostile force at no great distance, and called excitedly to Odysseus: "See! They are on us." (24.494)

Odysseus and his few followers fight back, carrying the man-slaughter outside the palace walls. The second half of the *Odyssey* sees a continuous escalation toward civil war, and its pace gains more and more momentum toward the end of the book. Only the last sentence of the *Odyssey* claims to establish peace between the contenders, but it appears in such a contrast to the whole development of the plot that it might well have been the attempt of an Alexandrian librarian to introduce a happy ending.[478]

Homer may have given us the long-sought-after explanation for the disappearance of the Mycenaean civilization. Maybe the *Odyssey* concludes at the point when the situation was getting completely out of control, shortly before the Argolid was hit by terrible natural disasters, which struck the final blow to what the Egyptian priest had called "the most perfect race among men."

> "There is a sound of mourning in the air; I see cheeks wet with tears. And look, the panels and the walls are splashed with blood. The porch is filled with ghosts. So is the court—ghosts hurrying down to darkness and to Hell. The sun is blotted out from heaven and a malignant mist has crept upon the world." (20.353)

CHAPTER SEVEN

RECONSTRUCTING TROY

If Hissarlik was neither the producer of raw materials nor the main center of early metal, it was the world market where the raw material and finished products were bought and sold.[479]

Troy remains unique; a century of archaeological exploration has failed to turn up anything comparable. The range of finds from Troy simply cannot be duplicated at any other Bronze Age site in the eastern Mediterranean.[480]

Bronze Age seafaring was as precarious as Russian roulette, if one can trust Odysseus' tales. No Bronze Age crew could ever be sure of surviving the next trip, for their helmsmen were barely in control of the boat. Until shipbuilding was revolutionized, during the seventh century B.C., sailing close-hauled to the wind was impossible. The original rig, having a central mast with a single, square sail on a horizontal yard across it, did not permit such maneuvers.[481] Hence, not only wind force but also wind direction was of fundamental importance for Bronze Age sailors, restricting sailing to daylight and to the summer season. Although the helmsmen would have navigated along the coast and pulled ashore at night, all these precautions could not eliminate the risks involved. Rapid weather changes could turn the proximity to the shore into a threat, because in rough sea the vessels ran the risk of being shattered on reefs or cliffs. Even if the weather was perfect, the crew, while camping ashore, was under permanent danger of enemy attacks. At least some Aegean coasts must have been controlled from watchposts, making a hostile reception of unannounced visitors more likely than a cordial one.

All these obstacles should be remembered when speaking about "long-distance trading" as one of the essential prerequisites of Achaean prosperity. Yet, transportation by sea must have been far more desirable than by land, since commodities could be shipped by sea with much less time and effort spent.[482] Consequently, large-scale long-distance trade largely involved sea transport. To enable undisturbed conveyance of goods by sea, however, some protected havens must have existed where crews could find shelter during storms, where fresh water and food storage could be replenished, broken gear fixed and advice on weather and sailing conditions sought.[483] In recent years, it has become increasingly accepted among archaeologists that Troy was such a naval service station, perhaps the most prominent one in the Bronze Age Mediterranean.[484] Several leading scientists, including Manfred Korfmann, the current excavator of Ilion, have concluded that the Late Bronze Age passage through the Bosporus into the Black Sea was possible and that Troy had a function comparable to today's "last petrol station before the motorway."[485]

Troy would have provided protected harbors where trading vessels found shelter while they were waiting for the right wind conditions; it would have supplied drinking water and stocks, advice on sailing conditions and perhaps pilot services for the passage into the Black Sea. At the same time, Troy served as a trading center in its own right, reached by merchants from eastern Mediterranean and Black Sea shores. The principals of Troy had a strong incentive to bring the city's services to the highest standards: the larger and better equipped the harbor basins were, the higher was the toll that could be exacted from foreign merchants. But the rulers of Troy may have wanted to keep their residences well protected and at some distance from port quarters and trade districts, for the large number of foreigners could produce a volatile atmosphere.

This chapter aims to reconstruct the landscape around the city of Troy from the time when people first settled there to the present day. It will show how the people may have increasingly altered their natural environment until it perfectly suited their needs in the Late Bronze Age. We shall also reexamine the topography of the plain at the time of the Trojan War and during Homer's life, when Trojan grandeur had decayed to insignificance.

THE EVOLVING PLAIN OF TROY

The Trojan Plain has probably been the subject of more geographic studies than any other place in the world, yet the paleotopography of the area remains disputed. Despite the large number of previous studies, no one has ever analysed the many remarkable features in the plain that indicate human interference with the natural environment. Geographic investigations conducted during the last century, especially those by Forchhammer, Spratt, Schliemann and Virchow, have revealed paleo-stream channels, artificial canals, blocked riverbeds, quarries and sand heaps. These phenomena are evidence of human impact on the environment and were most likely part of a general landscape-control system. Furthermore, the natural landscape and human land use have changed with time, and each phase of this evolution must have brought advantages to the people who utilized the landscape. The fact that nobody has thus far been able to produce a comprehensive and satisfactory landscape reconstruction of the Trojan Plain, in combination with the many indications of human interference, indicate an unusually complex environmental history.

Previous reconstructions of the Trojan Plain generally fall into two categories: (1) those which imagine a deep marine bay to have stretched far inland, and (2) those which suspect the plain looked pretty much the same as today with only a minor marine bay at its northern end. The latest geoarchaeological project at Troy came to the conclusion that there was indeed an inlet extending up to eight miles during the Neolithic.[486] According to this model the Late Bronze Age shoreline was still four miles from the present coast.[487] This reconstruction, however, rested on just six cores, which were placed over four miles apart. Consequently only two cores fell into the alluvial plain right in front of Troy; with some bad luck these could even have hit one of the many channels in the floodplain. Also, the relevant strata and chronological periods for which the landscape was reconstructed yielded no dates. Moreover, the whole model rested on the assumption that the global sea level at 6000 B.P. was higher than today, a premise not tenable anymore. Therefore, the possibility of a quite different environmental evolution from the one suggested recently cannot be completely dismissed. In fact, the relief within the coastal plain argues strongly against a recent, extensive regression. Already in 1850, Forchhammer asserted convincingly:

We reject as utterly erroneous the theories that the lower plain may have been formed by a post-Homeric alluvium, and that the latter may have covered up a pretended port, which once extended for a long distance into the land. It would be perfectly inexplicable how vertical banks, from 6 to 10 ft high, could have been built up by the alluvial soil on the sides of the rivers after their prolongation and at the eastern end of the strand, while the lagoons were not filled up by them but were nevertheless separated from the Hellespont by a sandbank.[488]

Producing a satisfactory reconstruction of the landscape evolution of Troy requires decades of field and laboratory research involving the examination of drill cores and excavations, satellite images and aerial photographs, topographic maps and historic accounts, microfossils and botanic remains, soils and quarries. Such a long-term geoarchaeological study is currently being carried out as part of the new excavations at Troy.

The following reconstruction of the Trojan landscape complies with Forchhammer's thinking that the alluvial plain looked much like today when humans first settled in the area. The data utilized for this model were mainly derived from nineteenth-century maps, SPOT and Landsat satellite images and field observations.

NEOLITHIC/EARLY BRONZE AGE

The earliest known settlement in the Troad at Kumtepe may have been established when the Scamander and the Simois rivers both exited on the eastern side of the plain near Intepe, where they had accumulated a small delta.[489] Reconstructions of prehistoric environments in Greece have shown that the preferred sites for early human settlements were in shallow coastal bays where the sea reached farthest inland.[490] Kumtepe may have been located in just such a bay stretching two miles inland of the present shore.

When people began to settle on Hisarlık at around 3000 B.C. their site would have been surrounded by streams. The alluvial plain itself was several feets lower than it is today, and it was certainly full of swamps and marshes, making it a rather hostile environment for human occupants. The preference for Hisarlık over the

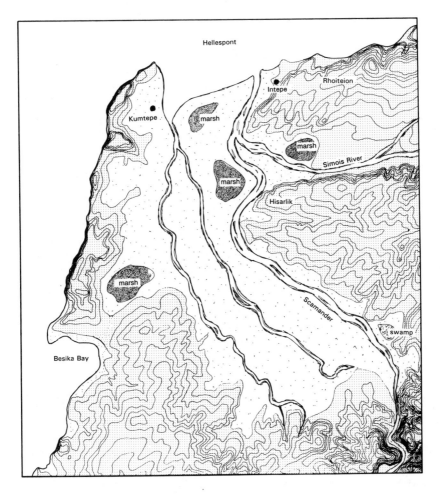

A hypothetical reconstruction of the plain of Troy in the Neolithic period when people first settled the landscape.

sea-oriented site of Kumtepe may reflect the people's desire to be
closer to arable land and perhaps to precious freshwater springs.
Nevertheless, in order to exploit fully the potential of the environment around Hisarlık, the landscape needed significant changing.

MIDDLE/LATE BRONZE AGE

The natural surroundings produced a number of problems for the people of Troy. First of all, their site was quite far from the shore, it lacked a natural harbor and the streams were probably not navigable either. Secondly, the presence of freshwater swamps was a permanent malaria threat. Virchow's anthropological studies of forty-five skeletons from Troy have shown that most of these people died of malaria at an early age.[491] Thirdly, the Trojans would have preferred to increase the proportion of arable land by draining some of the marshes.

Probably the first grand plan to alter the landscape involved the construction of an improved port basin. The best place for such a port would have been near the only natural cove on the steep Aegean shore, Beşik Bay. The bay itself has already been considered a perfect harbor for Troy,[492] because it provided shelter from wind and current, and there was precious fresh water on its shores. Yet these promising natural conditions were not beyond improvement. At one point in the past an artificial canal was dug leading from Beşik Bay through the coastal ridge into the Trojan Plain. This construction has never been dated, and the possibility that it dates to the Bronze Age cannot be excluded. Today, an extensive swamp covers the inland side of the canal. A few thousand years ago this basin could have provided an extremely protected and defensible harbor. Furthermore, the Scamander River could have been diverted through the artificial outlet into the sea, thereby filling port basin and canal with water. At the same time the river diversion would have dried up the coastal swamps at the Hellespont.

This first engineering feat may have been such a success that the Trojan nobles ordered further constructions. What had worked for the Scamander should work for the Simois too. The original bed of the Simois River used to encircle the ridge of Rhoiteion in the far northeastern corner of the plain, using the bed that is now called Intepeh Asmak. The Trojans planned to redirect the entire river to the south, so that it would use the same exit in Beşik Bay as the Scamander. This way the whole coastal plain would be disconnected from further river-water supplies; it would dry up and produce arable land instead of breeding grounds for mosquitoes. Furthermore, the diverted Simois provided a perennial waterway from the palace to the ports

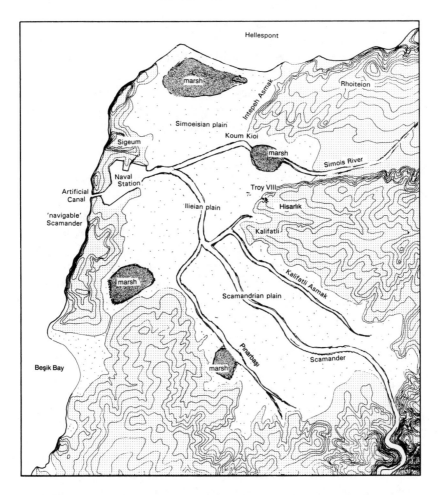

By the Middle Bronze Age, the people of Troy may have begun altering the landscape by excavating artificial channels. The first of these constructions could have been the canal to and from Beşik Bay in combination with a port basin on the inland side of the coastal ridge.

and the coast. Hence, the Trojans excavated a relatively narrow canal, just wide enough for a single boat, between the place where the village of Kalifatli lies today and the port basin inland of Beşik Bay.[493] The remaining waterway between Kalifatli and the former village of Koum Kioi needed no excavation, for the Simois could use an old bed of the Scamander there. It would, however, have to flow upstream for two miles. That presented a problem, because the Simois is already sluggish where it enters the valley between Rhoiteion and Troy. The easiest way to ensure a permanent connection between the citadel and Beşik Bay was to excavate the canal so deep that it would largely be filled by seawater.

Next, the Simois' original bed which led to the Hellespont had to be blocked. In order to achieve that, the Trojans dumped an enormous amount of sand at Koum Kioi (Village of Sand)— material that had become readily available through the channel excavations. The abrupt beginning and end of the infill of the Simois' bed, which prevented the stream from turning north to the Hellespont, was noticed and carefully described by Schliemann.[494] He dug a small trench into the heap of sand and found the clayey alluvial plain surface at its bottom. Schliemann concluded that the massive and well-defined infill at Koum Kioi must have been a sand dune. An alternative explanation, however, for the sizable pile of sand is artificial dumping. Once the Simois' bed was blocked, the stream filled the old Scamander bed below the citadel and continued southwest to exit at Beşik Bay. A very close approximation of this reconstruction, but lacking the artificial blockade at Koum Kioi, was provided in a topographic map by Acland.[495]

There is even a poetic description of the Simois' unusual (man-made) course. In its present form it was written in the mid-1180s A.D. by Joseph of Exeter, an English monk. His *Iliad of Dares Phrygius* is a rendering in Latin verse of what appears to be a free sixth-century-A.D. translation of an anonymous first-century-A.D. Greek original, allegedly describing the Trojan War from an eyewitness's perspective.[496] Much of Dares' original report has been preserved to the present day, but the part below was lost and is therefore only known from the medieval edition.[497] Joseph's verses provide a vivid illustration of the artificial redirection of the Simois:

> The river Simois irrigates nearby countryside as it travels from another world to see Troy. By its long journey through so many kingdoms and cities it would like to have earned the right to flow out into the sea finally as a Trojan river. And while it gazes in unending amazement at Troy it delays its faltering course, slows down its already sluggish flow, and causes the whole city to be encircled. The sea is angry at the delay to its waters and presses in more violently, forcing the

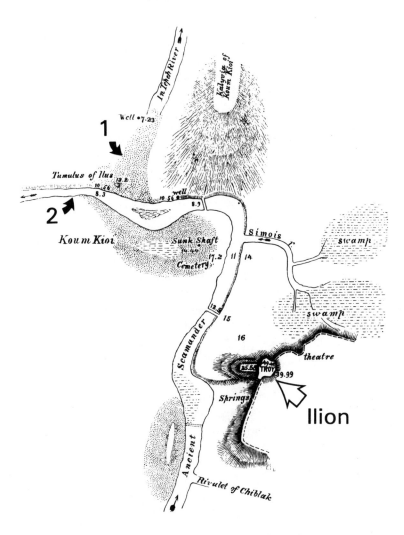

Heinrich Schliemann considered a paleo-stream channel below Ilion to have been the course of the ancient Scamander. This map (Schliemann 1880, 82) shows how the river used to pass at the foot of the fortress and then united with the Simois just north of Ilion. Originally, the Simois River encircled the ridge in the northern part of the map, utilizing the bed of the Intepeh River. This channel, however, eventually became filled with sand (1), redirecting the river to the south, through the bed of the ancient Scamander. At some point the sand barrier was also carved out and a deep and narrow canal dug (2) to divert the Simois again, this time to the west toward Sigeum.

smaller river to move away so that it can get right up to the city. You would think they were striving to see who could get closer, such was the meeting of the two currents, such the continual roaring of the mutual strife.[498]

The Trojans kept digging. They opened a second artificial canal to the Aegean, three miles north of the one at Beşik Bay. There too, a large basin was created on the inland side of the ridge, serving as a second port, perhaps to keep Trojan galleys separate from foreign merchant ships. The two main port basins were then connected with another channel.

If this reconstruction is correct, an approaching Late Bronze Age vessel would not have had the impression of arriving at a well-protected haven. *"The land looked like a shield laid on the misty sea"* (5.181), said Homer and *"the whole region rose sheer out of the sea to a great height"* (118A), said the Atlantis account. Whether or not these remarks are meant to describe the view of the Troad, they are certainly very applicable to this region. All that was visible from the sea were steep and dangerous cliffs at the shore and Mount Ida in the hinterland. A strong current from the outflow of the Dardanelles made the approach to Beşik Bay even more difficult. At a short distance from the bay, however, these currents dropped and guard- and light-houses became visible, but there were still no hints of a protected port. Instead, there was a small cemetery on a promontory, where some well-to-do foreign merchants who had lost their lives at sea were buried.[499] The approaching ship would have been requested by local guards to moor at a quay so that they could check the nationality and intent. Finally, when permission to enter the harbor was granted, the ship was pushed into a narrow channel, leading toward an opening in the cliff, a tunnel, just wide enough for the boat to enter. Because the tunnel was curved, its opposite end was not visible from the entrance. After a 1,600-foot passage through the tunnel, the boat finally reappeared on the inland side of the coastal ridge in a different environment: right at the end of the channel was a large port basin with hundreds of vessels from all over the then-known world. Separate basins for navy vessels were visible in the distance, and there were many channels connecting these basins with each other. A wide coastal plain stretched from here in three directions. Finally, on the opposite side of the plain, some miles from the port, was the

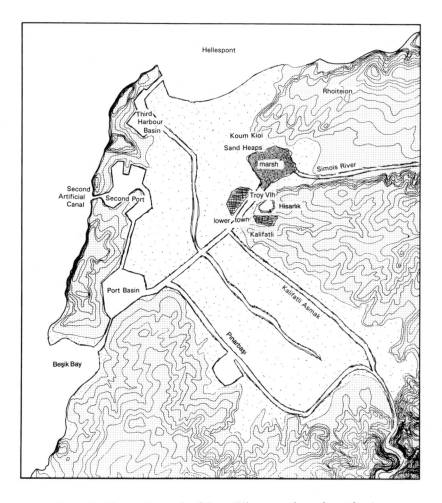

Conceivably, at the peak of Troy IVh, a number of port basins, each connected by channels either to the Aegean, the Hellespont or to the domestic rivers, existed along the inland side of the coastal ridge. There is no reason why the lower town of Troy VI, i.e. the plebeian quarters, should not have extended into the alluvial plain itself. In this hypothetical model, this would have been the appearance of the landscape during the Trojan War. Accordingly, the Greeks could have camped all around the northern and western side of Troy from Rhoiteion to Beşik Bay and they would have been able to use the second port near Sigeum as a "Naval Station."

royal residence of Troy: Ilion, *"amazing to behold."* To the sailor who arrived at Troy the view must have been breathtaking, like a scene from a fairy tale. Considering this majestic view and the sudden disappearance of all this splendor, it is not surprising that Troy contributed more to ancient lore than any other site of the ancient Mediterranean.

By the time Trojan engineering reached its zenith, there was little to improve for marine navigation, so the Trojans turned their attention inland to enhance the quality of the soils in the plain. Apart from the Scamander the plain was traversed by two more rivers: the Pinarbaşi Su on the western side and the Kalifatli Asmak on the eastern side. In order to render these streams navigable and to produce as much arable land as possible, the Trojans began to channel the rivers. They also directed more water into the channels on the edge of the plain, to prevent the Scamander from flooding their fields. Forchhammer noted that the paleo-bed of the Pinarbaşi Su is deeply incised, much wider than necessary and at places linked to very old, man-made drainage canals which run at right angles to it.[500] A third harbor basin, perhaps for domestic purposes, may have been excavated halfway down the Pinarbaşi Su.

In the lower plain, the blockage of the Simois at Koum Kioi was broken at some point and the river redirected once again. While its original bed went north to the Hellespont and then south toward Hisarlık and Beşik Bay, this third course directed the Simois due west toward the northern artificial canal into the Aegean.[501] The new trench was unusually narrow and deep and perhaps not intended as a navigable waterway. It may even have been part of the Mycenaean defense system mentioned by Homer. The idea of excavating a trench and erecting a wall to prevent the Trojans from attacking the Greek ships appears quite obvious, considering the ubiquitous presence of artificial ditches in the plain.

The lower town of Troy could have occupied parts of the central plain between the fortress itself and Beşik Bay. The Atlantis account describes a hippodrome and living quarters for soldiers from this area. This part of the city as well as the whole landscape-control system must have been abandoned during the war, when the Trojans retreated into the citadel. The Greeks probably razed the outer quarters too. During the three thousand years since the Fall of Troy, these extramural districts were buried below alluvium, but traces of them should still be detectable several feet below the present surface.

According to Strabo, the Greeks were using a naval station near Sigeum during the Trojan War, a description that would suit the northern port basin.[502] The southern channel and basins to Beşik Bay may have been rendered useless during the first waves of destruction. For instance, if the channel was roofed over with large rock slabs, these slabs would have blocked the whole waterway once they had fallen down. If this reconstruction is correct, the Greeks' camp could have extended all around Troy: from the northern coastal plain between Rhoetium and Kumtepe to the inland side of Beşik Bay. At the same time, there could have been a headquarters or naval station right in the center at Sigeum.

POST–BRONZE AGE

After the fall of Troy the human landscape control collapsed completely, leaving the streams again to the forces of nature. The Simois may have continued using its artificial bed toward the west for several centuries including the time of Homer. The poet probably lived somewhere on the West Anatolian coast, and some scholars even believe that, at least for some time, he lived and worked at Troy.[503] In any case, it is more than likely that Homer knew the area around Troy from his own observations. If he had looked at the plain during the eighth century B.C., for instance, from the coastal heights at Sigeum, he would have found it to be divided by river channels into three slices:[504] the Simoeisian plain in the north, the Ilieian plain in the center and the Scamandrian plain in the south. Homer knew from ancient oral traditions about a Greek defense system consisting of a wall and a trench, but nothing of it remained in his day. Thus Homer realized that the landscape had changed significantly since the war and that this was largely due to the streams which had meanwhile returned to their original, natural beds:

> Poseidon and Apollo decided to destroy the wall by turning against it the united waters of all the rivers that run down from the range of Ida to the sea. The Earthshaker himself

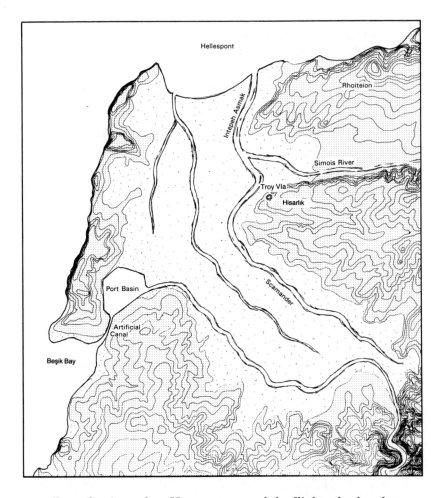

From the time when Homer composed the *Iliad* to the fourth century B.C. the former "Naval Station" of the Greeks could still have been accessible, providing the port for the thriving town of Sigeum. At that time the artificial canal toward Sigeum had long been filled up with sediment from the Scamander. Homer, looking at Troy from the coastal heights, would have seen it divided into three slices: the Simoeisian plain at the Hellespont, the Ileian plain in the center and the Scamandrian plain in the south. The Simois and Scamander rivers could have united in front of Sigeum, just as Strabo said, providing the "navigable Scamander" Pliny had described.

directed the torrent, washed out to sea all the wooden and stone foundations that the Achaeans had laid down with such labour, and levelled the shore of the fast-flowing Hellespont. When the wall had disappeared, he covered the wide beach once more with sand, and turned the rivers back into the channels down which their limpid streams had run before. (XII.18–33)

When Homer completed the *Iliad*, Troy itself was a minor settlement, probably with some of the ancient citadel walls still jutting out of the ground. There may have been a very few remarkable elements in the landscape: a large oak tree, a fig-tree, the "tomb of Ilus," the ford of the Scamander at Sigeum, a rise or hillock in the plain and perhaps one or two big washing basins in front of the city walls. Homer used these topographical features to structure the poem and the sequence of acts,[505] but he clearly put the emphasis on dialogues and activities, not on geography.

The Trojan topography may have remained stable for several centuries after Homer, with the Scamander continuing to use the northern artificial exit near Sigeum. The Roman scholar Pliny, traveling by ship around the Troad during the first century A.D.,[506] described the *"navigable"* Scamander, then the hills of Sigeum with the town of the same name, then the port of the Achaeans which was fed by the combined Xanthos and Simoeis.[507] Roughly at the same time the Greek geographer Strabo produced a similar description, although his rested on observations made by Demetrius of Skepsis and not on firsthand knowledge.

> After Rhoeteium comes Sigeium, a destroyed city, and the Naval Station and Harbour of the Achaeans and the Achaean Camp and the Stomalimne, as it is called, and the outlets of the Scamander; for after the Simoeis and the Scamander meet in the plain, they carry down great quantities of alluvium, silt up the coast, and form a blind mouth, lagoons and marshes.[508]

Strabo has been criticized for crowding together all the features of the landscape in this paragraph.[509] These observations would be plausible, however, if the city of Sigeum was erected in the vicinity of the northern artificial harbor basin, an idea that was first put forward by Brückner.[510] In that case, the city of Sigeum, which was raided and abandoned during the third century B.C.,[511] would have been right next to the naval station and harbor of the Achaeans and the outlet of the Scamander.

Strabo continued describing the length of the coast *"on a straight voyage from Rhoetium to Sigeium to have been sixty stadia"* (about seven miles), whereas the *"Harbour of the Achaeans is about twelve stadia distant from Ilium."* A sea voyage from the ridge at Sigeum to Rhoetium would indeed have passed along sixty stadia of coast, while the artificial harbor basin itself was only around twelve stadia from Ilion. After Sigeum had become deserted, the last artificial port basin and its man-made exit silted up, too, releasing both the Scamander and the Simoeis to meander again throughout the whole alluvial plain. At that point the Trojan Plain had been transformed back into the shape it possessed before human interference with the landscape began.

CHAPTER EIGHT

CONCLUSIONS

The one common denominator among all the various theories that have been put forward is the singular lack of detachment shown by the theorists. Instead of beginning with Plato, most begin with a hypothesis and develop their ideas with an enthusiasm that often verges on fanaticism.[512]

Extremist scholars usually maintain that their position is so obviously correct, so clearly superior, that only a grand conspiracy has kept it from gaining general acceptance. The feelings of neglect and rejection that fuel the drive and determination of extremist scholars give their works an unmistakable aura of paranoia.[513]

NEAR HITS

Since Atlantis has been located all over the world, it should not be surprising that somebody should have seen it in Troy too. Indeed, many books on Atlantis also mention Troy, but usually only to underline the author's conviction that a mythical locality can overnight become archaeological truth. Troy and Atlantis are in many aspects so similar that Atlantologists and traditional scholars often mention them in one breath. For instance Benjamin Howett, one of the more influential disbelievers, compared Atlantis with Homer's tale of Troy—and the romance of Arthur.[514] This book appeared in 1892, years after the existence of Troy was proven. Dušanić noticed that the apparent incompleteness of the Atlantis account recalls the apparent incompleteness of the *Iliad*, where the destruction of Troy is foreshadowed but not narrated.[515] Rhys Carpenter found that, *"like the Homeric Troy inflated too large for tiny Hisarlık, Atlantis grew in Plato's thoughts into a continent too large for the Mediterranean."*[516] Now we know that the real Troy may have extended way beyond "tiny Hisarlık" while Atlantis was probably much smaller, as described by Plato. The analogy between the Trojan War and the war in the Atlantis legend has been recognized before but was considered *"farfetched,"* because the Trojan War was a long siege not a *"blow,"* and nothing sank into the sea afterward.[517] This interpretation overlooks the fact that the mentioning of *"greatest perils"* and the desertion of the Greek forces by their foreign allies imply that some time elapsed during the conflict between Greeks and Atlanteans. The closest coincidence that I am aware of between the reconstruction of the Atlantis legend presented here and previous interpretations may be found in Katherine Folliot's small book *Atlantis Revisited.*[518] Folliot, too, came to the conclusion that the story described the Mycenaean world in the thirteenth century B.C.; she also recognized the many Anatolian components in the account, but then looked for Atlantis in Andalusia.

Troy appears as one of the suggested locations for Atlantis in a map in Zdeněk Kukal's thorough scientific treatment of the legend, but there is no reference to the source,[519] and I was unable to find any previous identifications of Atlantis in Troy.[520] Atlantologists occasionally claim that Troy had been in contact with Atlantis, rather than being Atlantis itself. This idea might be based on what is considered to be one of the most inglorious hoaxes of Atlantis research. In 1912, Paul Schliemann, a man who declared himself to be Heinrich Schliemann's grandson, although family records later disproved the existence of such a grandson,[521] wrote an article for the *New York American* entitled, "How I Discovered Atlantis, the Source of All Civilization." Paul Schliemann claimed that his grandfather had left an envelope which was only to be opened by a member of the Schliemann family who would be willing to devote his life to the matters discussed inside. The envelope was accompanied by an ancient owl-headed vase. After making the pledge Paul Schliemann broke the seal of the envelope. The papers inside first instructed him to break open the vase too. He discovered some square coins of platinum-aluminum-silver alloy in it as well as an inscribed metal plate which said in the Phoenician language *"Issued in the Temple of Transparent Walls."* The papers included a description of a large bronze vase, found at Troy, containing coins and other artifacts of metal, bone and pottery. This vase and some of the items were inscribed *"From King Cronos of Atlantis."* Full of enthusiasm about his discovery, Paul Schliemann announced the publication of a book which would reveal all the details, but unfortunately it never appeared, nor were the objects ever shown in public.

PREREQUISITES FOR THE DECIPHERING

The parallels between Atlantis and Troy are so obvious—one being the most famous legendary place in the western world, the other the most famous archaeological site—that it appears strange that nobody has compared the two before. In reality, however, a number of prerequisites had to be fulfilled before the analogy between Troy and Atlantis could be drawn. First of all, the Bronze Age culture and the site of Troy had to be discovered. This information has been available only during the last hundred years, after Schliemann's excavations. From then on, one could have argued that Atlantis and its opponent must be sought in the Late Bronze Age Aegean. K.T. Frost unfortunately directed his attention to the then current excavations of the Middle Bronze Age palace of Knossos on Crete, and diverted scholarly concern in the wrong direction for several decades. After the Atlantis discussion had been spoiled by popularists, it required new, sound, scientific observations to arouse anybody's interest in the topic. These became available with the establishment of the new discipline of geoarchaeology, the science of reconstructing ancient landscapes, and with the discovery that earthquakes had occurred at the end of the Mycenaean era.

When Charles MacLaren's (1822) purely theoretical investigations brought him to the conclusion that Troy existed and that it was located on the hill called Hisarlık, his discovery had no impact whatsoever. Fifty years later, however, the archaeological world was turned upside down by Schliemann's excavations of the site. Although MacLaren's deductions were later vindicated by Schliemann's work, he had initially been uncertain whether it was a wise idea to *"give it to the press."* My deductions are theoretical, too, much like MacLaren's and—at least for the moment—some of the arguments I use are disputable.

COUNTERARGUMENTS AND SHORTCOMINGS

1. *If Plato's account is taken literally, my theory does not fit the most vital characteristics of Atlantis in terms of date, location, island character and size.*

As far as I know, there is not a single ancient text whose information, including absolute measurements, can be transferred into modern terminology without any adjustments and interpretations. Providing such interpretations, establishing a historic framework and exercising source-criticism are among the most important tasks of historical sciences. If we would accept every detail in ancient texts as being correct, ancient history as a discipline would become redundant. Therefore, a literal interpretation of an ancient Greek text must be considered more dubious than an interpretation that just seeks a core of historic truth in the text. Furthermore, although Troy does not match the description of Atlantis in terms of date, location, size and island character, it does fit virtually the whole of the rest of the story, at least as far as one can judge it, given the incompleteness of the archaeological record.

2. *The ancient Greek opponent of Atlantis is said to have come from Attika, suggesting a Classical framework. The Argolid, the center of political power in Greece during the Late Bronze Age, is never mentioned. Furthermore, Atlantis seems to have been the initial aggressor, whereas the Trojan War is generally assumed to have resulted from Greek assaults.*

The first point, the confusion of Attika and the Argolid, is negligible if one assumes that the legend originated in Egypt several centuries before it was told. From an ancient Egyptian perspective the two neighboring districts are virtually indistinguishable. The second point, the conventional belief that the Achaeans commenced the aggressions that led to the Trojan War, rests exclusively on impressions gained from Homer, since there is no other evidence for the war. Homer, however, never describes the events that led to the Trojan War in much detail.

The remaining shortcomings of my case are not genuine counterarguments, since they do not speak against an identification of Troy with Atlantis. My hypothesis, however, still lacks support from indisputable scientific evidence in several instances.

3. *The supposed earthquake which damaged Mycenae and Tiryns around 1200 B.C. is not accepted as fact by everybody. Not all archaeologists believe that there is sufficient evidence to support the earthquake assertion.*

Unfortunately, there is no unambiguous technique today to reconstruct earthquakes. The only reliable way to detect and date earthquakes in ancient periods is from historic descriptions. But archaeological interpretations cannot always wait until the right techniques have arrived.

4. *Even if there was an earthquake at Tiryns, the flood may not coincide with it. Neither archaeological nor geological dating techniques are sufficient to claim a simultaneous occurrence of both events.*

Even if the flood at Tiryns neither coincides with an earthquake nor with the LH IIIB/C boundary, the remarkable parallels between Atlantis and Troy are still there.

5. *There is no evidence for a larger LH IIIB town at Tiryns that might have been destroyed and buried by the flash-flood. The auger cores, only 10 four inches in diameter, are nothing but needle-stitches into an area that would require decades of excavation to determine its true archaeological content.*

The currently known extent of the LH IIIB city, however, coincides perfectly with the limits of the flash flood deposits. Hence it is more than likely that constructions continue below the flood deposits at least at some places.

6. *My reconstruction of the Trojan coastal plain, inspired by the Atlantis legend and derived from surface observation only, contradicts the most recent geoachaeological reconstruction of this area.*

A proverb, often heard among scientists, says, "*If you need sweeping theories, introduce them before there are too many facts.*" The most recent reconstruction of the Trojan landscape is just one of many—and it, too, contradicts many competent observations that were made in the past, which is why it has generally been received with skepticism.

7. *When interpreting Plato I am willing to accept many of his assertions as correct; others however subjectively chosen, I totally reject. In a similar manner, I often refer to Frost, Carpenter, Luce, Bernal and many other authors although my conclusions differ completely from theirs.*

I said, deciphering the Atlantis account is like solving a very complicated puzzle: some pieces belong to it, others do not and again others have been altered. I have considered the many hundreds of individual arguments that I derived from learned archaeologists to be individual puzzle pieces that might usefully be assembled in a new context.

8. *The analogy of Scheria and Atlantis in particular is extremely disputable. The Phaeacians of the* Odyssey *are almost exclusively described as a maritime folk, while the Trojans in the* Iliad *lack this attribute completely. Moreover, the phenomena found in the archaeological record of the* LH IIIC *period can be interpreted in numerous ways.*

Absolutely! Nevertheless, the analogy of Troy and Scheria as well as the comparison between the *Odyssey* and the LH IIIC period show, if nothing else, that genuinely novel and refreshingly original ideas are still possible in a discipline that is increasingly threatened by the prolificness of its own protagonists. This book was not written to replace old dogmas with new ones, it was written to inspire the reader, to encourage the disregarding of conventional beliefs and to pursue new lines of thinking. Even if one accepts that the Atlantis enigma is now decoded, new and unsolved problems will arise as a consequence. Trying to find the answers to the problems of the future in a true-false way of thinking or a black-and-white way of arguing will only inhibit the progress of science—and worse, it will take the fun out of it.

KATSINGRI

Among the most pleasant places to enjoy a sunset in Greece are the mountaintops on the eastern side of the Argive Plain. Archaeologists who work in the Argolid know this, of course. Thus, every once in a while we take a car to the village of Agios Adrianos, formerly called Katsingri, and beyond, on a road that leads to nowhere apart from a peak, called Profitis Ilias. Sometimes when I went to this peak, I was in the company of some leading Bronze Age archaeologists.

The last time a few of us went this route, a farmer had blocked our way with his pickup truck, because he had to collect tobacco leaves which were drying in the sun. He was not alone; his mother or grandmother was helping him get on with the work. The two had evidently chosen the timing of their task so that they would be able to finish it just before dusk. Acclimatized to life in Greece, we watched them for a minute or two, but then we decided to take over their work, not just out of comradeship but also because we wanted to save our view of the sunset. We got out of the car, shouted a few words in Greek and swiftly but carefully transferred the long wooden sticks with the tobacco leaves onto the bed of the truck. The shouting intensified when the job was done. *"Kaló taxídi"* (*bon voyage*) and *"stó kálo"* (go to the good) cheered the couple, without ever asking who we were and where we planned to go. For they knew it.

Moments later we reached the small place just below the summit where the car can be parked and turned. A few steps higher up on the top of the mountain sits a white chapel. If it was not open when we came, one of us knew where to find the key. Yet, rather than going inside the chapel, it was far more appealing to us to sit outside, leaning against its white-painted wall and enjoying the silhouette of the Arkadian mountains under the descending sun. I had brought a bottle of retsina and some water, someone else a plate with appetizers which were especially prepared for our little excursion by a local *Kafenion* owner. It may be outside my literary abilities to describe the ambience of total tranquillity emitted by the view from there, combined with the taste of retsina and the peaceful sound of cheeping cicadas. But I know this: it was one of the moments for which we became involved in Greek archaeology.

Below us lay the valley where the fate of Greece was determined more than once in the past few thousand years, the valley which became the center of the first civilization on the entire European continent. There was Tiryns sitting on the flat plain near the coast, over to the right lay Midea and Mycenae, and at the foot of the mountains opposite rested Argos. Inevitably our minds were contemplating what this view might have been like over three thousand years ago. Surely, the Achaeans were up here, too; some remains of buildings even document their presence.

Half to himself and half to me, somebody remarked,

"Perhaps they did not use all that land for agriculture. They may have conducted chariot races down there too."

Perhaps, I thought. But I was more attracted by the view of the Mycenaean dam just below us. Pondering the engineering feat from this bird's-eye perspective, I said,

"They must have had an incredible understanding of landscape-forming processes to have placed it right there. If they had put the dam a little higher upstream, the artificial canal to the next riverbed could have been two-thirds shorter. Yet, they dug the longer trench just to include a few more tributaries in the redirection. They must have had maps!"

"Oh, no," said another Mycenaean archaeologist. "They didn't have maps."

After a little while, when the sun, the retsina and the appetizers had disappeared and our conversation had expanded from local to global problems, I asked:

"And what about the Trojan War? Could it be possible that two events of such magnitude as the Trojan War and the Mycenaean demise occurred almost simultaneously but completely independently of each other?"

"Forget Homer," said someone else.

"What if the whole political structure collapsed because the kings and leading aristocrats withdrew from their realms to fight in this prolonged war?"

Silence.

"Maybe I should write something about this idea," I said.

"You'd better not!"

NOTES

1. Cherniss 1947, 252
2. Lee 1965, 156
3. Bernal 1987, 6
4. Carpenter 1966, 18
5. Kuniholm 1990, 653
6. Baillie & Munro 1988, 345; Baillie 1988a, 72
7. Neumann & Parpola 1987
8. Pang *et al.* 1988
9. Baillie 1988b, 155
10. The story of Atlantis should not be called a myth, because that would require *supernatural* beings, ancestors or heroes in a primitive view of the world. Instead it should be designated a legend ("an unverified popular story handed down from earlier times") or an account ("a narrative or record of events"). Plato himself never considered this story a *muthos* but always a *logos* (20D, 21A, 21C, 21D, 26E, 27B, 108C).
11. Plato was not inclined to accept ancient myths as truth. He realized that in the absence of accurate historical knowledge, ancient tales are bound to be literally false (*Republic* 382D). Nevertheless, misrepresentations could be turned into "useful" information by "assimilating them to the truth" (Gill 1980, xiv).
12. Bernal 1987, 3
13. Rosenmeyer 1956, 172, speaking about the odd placing of the Atlantis account in *Timaeus*.
14. Muck 1976, 10
15. Kukal 1984, 1
16. Luce 1969, 43
17. Lee 1965, 15
18. Becher 1986, 7
19. Muck 1976, 37
20. Pischel 1982, 99
21. de Camp 1970
22. Lewis Spence quoted by Lee 1965, 157
23. Muck 1976, 112
24. Velikowsky 1950
25. Forsyth 1980, 70
26. Ramage 1978, 30; Muck 1976, 53
27. Muck 1976, 53
28. Frost 1909
29. Frost 1913; Balch 1917. Frost states that his *Times* letter was published on 19 January 1909, but he is mistaken; it appeared a month later, on 19 February.
30. Frost 1913, 192

31. Galanopoulos & Bacon 1969; Luce 1969; Mavor 1969; see Vitaliano 1971 for review
32. Bernal 1987, 107; Bernal 1991, 304; Pellegrino 1991
33. Ramage 1978, 41
34. Archer-Hind 1888, 78
35. Taylor 1928, vii
36. Taylor 1928, vii
37. Lee 1965, 158
38. Cornford 1937, 18
39. e.g. Robin 1913; Termier 1916; Schuchert 1917; Schuller 1917; Hennig 1925; 1927; Borchardt 1927a; 1927b; Schulten 1927; Herter 1928; Stella 1932; Heidel 1933; Gidon 1934; Bramwell 1937
40. Taylor 1928, 56; Frutiger 1930, 248; Herter 1944, 238; Giovannini 1985
41. Aristotle, *Meteorologica* A.8.343; B.8.368; Pausanias 7.24
42. Taylor 1928, 51; Pallottino 1952, 231; Skemp 1952, 85
43. Rudberg 1917; Wilamowitz-Moellendorff 1948, 471; Corbato 1953, 235
44. Vidal-Naquet 1964; Dušanić 1982
45. Dušanić 1982, 29
46. Bury 1929, 4
47. Gill 1977, 292
48. Welliver 1977; Fredericks 1978, 92; Gill 1980
49. Gill 1977, 298
50. Hennig 1925, 8 pointed out that Atlantis would be the only fictional country in the literature whose description is linked to genuine geographic places.
51. Gill 1977, 287 & 292
52. Gill 1980, xxii: "It is remarkable—in a Platonic narrative—how unsymbolic, and how purely descriptive, the account seems."
53. Taylor 1928, 53
54. Herodotus, *Histories* 2.143
55. Wilamowitz-Moellendorff 1948, vol. 1: 242–5; Bidez 1945, 21
56. Brandenstein 1951, 46–9
57. Ramage 1978, 13
58. Ramage 1978, 13
59. see Ramage 1978, 85. Nevertheless some references to a pre-Platonic Atlantis do exist. For instance, Hellanicus of Lesbos, a fifth-century B.C. scholar who worked on mythology, chronology, local history and ethnology, published a work entitled *Atlantis*. Although it has been lost, there are several references to it (Jacoby 1923, 109f, 139; fragments 5, 134, 135; Jacoby 1954, 2).
60. Diodorus Siculus 3.56–61 speaks in some detail about a tribe called Atlantians, whom he described as most civilized men possessing great cities in a fertile territory on the edge of the ocean.
61. Taylor 1928, 23; Rosenmeyer 1949, 405; Davies 1971, 332; Luce 1978, 76
62. Lee 1965, 149
63. Forsyth 1980, 31

64. Forsyth 1980, 33
65. Forsyth 1980, 32
66. Diodorus Siculus 15.7
67. Kukal 1984, 5; Ramage 1978
68. Strabo, *Geography* 13.1.36
69. Theophrastus, *Doctrines of Natural Philosophers*, fragment 12; Luce 1978, 51
70. Strabo, *Geography* 2.102; de Camp 1970
71. Pindar, *Paean* 4.27–44
72. Proclus, *In Timaeum* 61A (Diehl 1965, vol I: 197)
73. Proclus, *In Timaeum* 24D
74. Proclus, *In Rempublicam* I.18.17
75. Taylor 1928, 45
76. Taylor 1928, 17
77. Burnet 1914, 338 and 351; Taylor 1928, 23; Luce 1978, 76
78. Taylor 1928, 23; Cornford 1937, 1
79. Bury 1929, 3
80. Taylor 1928, 23
81. Taylor 1928, 14
82. Archer-Hind 1888, 63
83. Forsyth 1980, 42
84. De Camp 1970, 208
85. Taylor 1928, 15
86. Taylor 1928, 23; Luce 1978, 77
87. Barker 1918, 268; Cornford 1937, 1; Hackforth 1944, 7
88. 108A: "Hermocrates . . . later on, when it is his duty to speak will make the same request." 108C: "You, my dear Hermocrates, are posted in the last rank."
89. after: Platon, *Sämtliche Werke* 5, Rowohlt, Hamburg 1989
90. Frank 1923; Lee 1965, 24
91. Bury 1929, 5
92. Taylor 1928, 11
93. Archer-Hind 1888, 18; Taylor 1928, ix and 9; Lloyd 1968, 84
94. Lloyd 1968, 81
95. Taylor 1928, ix; Lloyd 1968, 89
96. Bury 1929, 13
97. Taylor 1928, 10; Bury 1929, 15
98. Eucken 1983, 188, 193 and 207
99. Proclus, *In Timaeum* 24 A/B
100. Lee 1965, 147
101. Taylor 1928, 11 and 19
102. Taylor 1928, 51; Bury 1929, 4
103. Cornford 1937, 8
104. Gill 1980, xvii describes Plato's style in the *Timaeus* as "very historical," reminiscent of the introduction of Herodotus' and Thucydides' histories.
105. Lee 1965, 149
106. Cornford 1937

107. Luce 1978, 73
108. Cornford 1937, 1
109. Archer-Hind 1888, Taylor 1928; Cornford 1937; Lloyd 1968
110. Zangger 1992
111. Valladas *et al.* 1987; 1988
112. Runnels 1988
113. van Andel & Runnels 1987
114. Shackleton & van Andel 1986
115. Jacobsen 1976; Hansen 1980
116. Cherry 1981, 45; Perlès 1987
117. Payne 1975
118. Jacobsen 1976
119. Angel 1972
120. Angel 1972
121. Angel 1972
122. Halstead 1981, 192
123. Ammerman & Cavalli-Sforza 1984, 47; Halstead 1989, 70
124. Runnels 1983
125. Halstead 1989, 70
126. Halstead 1989, 70
127. Angel 1972
128. Zangger 1991a
129. Pullen 1992
130. Zangger 1991a
131. Muhly 1988, 10
132. Chadwick 1976, 139
133. Pernicka *et al.* 1990
134. Strabo, *Geography* 13.1.23; Wagner *et al.* 1985, 77; Wagner *et al.* 1989, 299
135. Stos-Gale *et al.* 1984, 27; Seeliger *et al.* 1985, 597; Wagner *et al.* 1989, 304; Pernicka *et al.* 1990
136. Knapp 1986; 1988
137. Muhly *et al.* 1991
138. Konsola 1984
139. Halstead 1989, 77
140. Zangger 1992
141. Konsola 1984; Hägg & Konsola 1986
142. Marinatos 1986, 14
143. Chadwick 1976, 4
144. Aitken 1988; Manning 1988; Baillie & Munro 1988; Dietz 1991, 316
145. Kilian 1988
146. Sandars 1978, 65
147. Demakopoulou 1988, 25
148. Hammond 1986, 46
149. Bass *et al.* 1989
150. Taylor 1983, 31
151. Chadwick 1976, 141
152. Wells, Runnels & Zangger 1990

153. Demakopoulou 1988, 37
154. Sandars 1978, 65
155. Siebler 1990, 101
156. Easton 1990, 443
157. Siebler 1990, 106
158. Mee 1984: IIIB1 instead of LH IIIA2/B
159. Rapp 1982, 55
160. Easton 1985; 1990, 443; Siebler 1990, 182
161. Mee 1978; but LH IIIB2 pottery is relatively rare anywhere outside the Peloponnese and central Greece (see Sherratt 1980).
162. Blegen *et al.* 1958, 12; Blegen 1975, 162; *contra* Finley 1974, 5
163. Taylor 1983, 160; Mellaart 1984, 66; see also Luce 1975, 182
164. Chadwick 1976, 141
165. Carpenter 1966; Lamb 1967; Bryson *et al.* 1974; Lamb 1977, 421; Weiss 1982, 197; *contra* Shrimpton 1987
166. Shear 1987, 154
167. Kilian 1982, 193
168. Podzuweit 1982, 68 and 70
169. Comparable Mycenaean constructions have been found at several places in Greece, see Knauss 1989
170. Sandars 1978, 10; James 1991
171. Thucydides 1.12; Plato, *Laws* 3.682
172. Desborough 1975, 669
173. Starr 1962, 79
174. Thucydides 1.6.3
175. Herodotus, *Histories* 1.28
176. Aristotle, Diodorus Siculus, Plutarch, Diogenes Laërtius
177. Herodotus, *Histories* 2.179; Hammond 1986, 125
178. Luce 1978, 60
179. Diogenes Laërtius 1.50
180. Plutarch, *Life of Solon* 31
181. Plutarch, *Life of Solon* 26.1; Diehl, *Anthologica Lyrica Graeca*, fragment 6
182. Luce 1978, 60
183. Taylor 1928, 52
184. Knapp 1988, 212: "Whatever befell the Bronze Age kingdoms, the bulk of the people—farmers and laborers—lived on."
185. Kemp 1989, 8 and 20
186. Knapp 1988, 30
187. A further hint might be provided in the clause, that "the water pours *over the fields*," for soil erosion triggered by agricultural over-exploitation is today considered to have been the most important factor of prehistoric landabuse (van Andel, Zangger & Demitrack 1990).
188. Luce 1969, 193; Sandars 1978, 105
189. Millard 1984, 1
190. Luce 1969, 194
191. Sandars 1978, 47

192. Pischel 1982, 51
193. Knapp 1988, 14
194. Knapp 1988, 53
195. Taylor 1983, 33
196. Carpenter 1966, 31
197. Chadwick 1976, 182
198. The flood, mentioned in the Egyptian account, may have made its way into the Greek mythology, too, which says that Poseidon drowned the Argolid after he had been defeated by Hera.
199. Lee 1965, 36
200. *"in eurem Lande entsproß, dem du entstammst und euer gesamter jetzt bestehender Staat."* Platon, *Sämtliche Werke* 5, Rowohlt, Hamburg 1959
201. Hammond 1986, 68
202. Chadwick 1976, 180
203. Taylor 1983, 135
204. Chadwick 1976, 49
205. Chadwick 1976, 180; Snodgrass 1987, 170
206. Luce 1975, 36
207. Ramage 1978, 19; *contra* Settegast 1990
208. Gidon 1934; Spanuth 1979, 32; Galanopulos & Bacon 1969, 30
209. Diodorus Siculus 1.26
210. Parker 1950, v and 56; Rice 1990, xvi
211. Spanuth 1979, 22: 1252–1175 B.C.
212. Herodotus, *Histories* 2.142–5
213. Folliot 1984, 48
214. Folliot 1984, 48
215. Chadwick 1976, 103: 57 or 83 lb
216. In a non-Homeric account of the Trojan War (Dictys of Crete 6.4) Menelaus reports that, while in Egypt, he built a magnificent tomb for his pilot, Canopus, who had been killed there by serpents.
217. Demakopoulou 1988, 62
218. Chadwick 1976, 73
219. Taylor 1983, 131
220. Chadwick 1976, 136; Taylor 1983, 132; Knapp 1988, 210
221. Luce 1975, 110
222. Herodotus, *Histories* 2, 164
223. Knauss 1989; 1990
224. Nilsson 1932
225. Odysseus admits that the Achaeans were deeply involved in all kinds of plundering and strife (14.222–233), but considering the attention given to the Trojan War by ancient Greek writers, this conflict must have been the most outstanding military event of that time.
226. Barnett 1975, 359
227. Pritchard 1969, 262; Gardiner 1971, 284; Barnett 1975, 371; Sandars 1978, 119; Millard 1984, 7
228. Sandars 1978, 124
229. Carpenter 1966

230. Borchardt 1927, 19
231. Stubbings 1975, 343
232. Sommer 1932, 270; Starke 1981; Easton 1985, 192
233. Luce 1975, 63
234. Jones 1924, 44, 109; Vercoutter 1954; Edel 1966; Luce 1975, 63; Haider 1988, 56
235. Hennig 1927, 80
236. Strabo, *Geography* 3.5.170
237. Hennig 1927, 85
238. Servius on Vergil's *Aeneid* 11.262
239. Babcock 1917, 391; Hennig 1927, 85; Heidel 1933, 205
240. Ehrenberg 1973, 18
241. Heidel 1933, 203
242. Ehrenberg 1973, 182
243. Haider 1988, 147
244. Brandenstein 1951, 75–7
245. Herodotus, *Histories* 1, 202
246. Kukal 1984, 188
247. Brandenstein 1951, 70
248. Luce 1975, 63
249. Becher 1986, 13
250. Aristotle, *Meteorologica* 2.1.354a
251. Pischel 1982, 114
252. Korfmann 1988, 52; Koromila 1991, 32
253. Luce 1969, 169
254. Pischel 1982, 18 and 29
255. Pischel 1982, 32
256. Spanuth 1979, 21
257. Labaree 1957
258. Carpenter 1948
259. Koromila 1991, 32
260. Luce 1969, 49
261. see also Robert 1917
262. Bryant 1799a; 1799b
263. Bryant 1776, vol. 3: 437
264. Millard 1984, 2
265. Gell 1804, 119
266. Demakopoulou (ed.) 1988, 25. Graves 1960, 265 describes a federal government for Troy and considers it a "usual arrangement in the Bronze Age."
267. Barnett 1975, 360; Haider 1988, 49
268. Hammond 1986, 52
269. Korfmann 1986a, 13
270. Finley 1974
271. Archer-Hind 1888, 80
272. Starr 1962, 110
273. Plato, *Laws* 3
274. Wilamowitz-Moellendorff 1919, vol. 1: 597; Arrigoni 1967, 267; 1969

275. Shackley 1979: 429; Butzer 1982
276. Kukal 1984, 19
277. Kukal 1984, 19
278. Platt 1890, 136
279. Pope & van Andel 1984
280. Rothmaler 1943; Beuermann 1956
281. Angel 1972, 90
282. Kukal 1984, 22
283. Lohmann 1983; 1985; 1987
284. Wells, Runnels & Zangger 1990
285. Chadwick 1976, 66
286. Luce 1975, 184
287. Luce 1975, 168
288. Chadwick 1976, 96
289. Schliemann 1880, 167
290. Forchhammer 1850, 1
291. "Meander" is the ancient name for the Turkish river "Menderes," a name borne also by Troy's most prominent stream, the "Skamandros."
292. Very few scholars have noticed this coincidence, e.g. Herter 1928, 42; Schulten 1939, 343
293. Forchhammer 1850, 15
294. Strabo, *Geography* 13.1.2; 13.1.7
295. Schliemann 1880, 132
296. Podzuweit 1982, 65
297. Brandenstein 1951, 73; Schubart 1982, 227; Niemeyer 1989
298. Hammond 1986, 63 considers the wealth of Troy VIIa consistent with the sphere of Priam's and his allies' influence stretching from the Axios in the west to the Propontis in the east, from Mt. Ida in the south to Thrace in the north.
299. Hammond 1986, 53
300. Combellack 1968, 472
301. Combellack 1968, 358
302. Hammond 1986, 53
303. Brückner 1925, 230; Korfmann 1988, 48; Easton 1990, 440
304. Braudel 1972, 110
305. Hammond 1986, 53
306. Blegen *et al.* 1953, 15; Podzuweit 1982, 65
307. Blegen 1963, 37
308. Saherwala 1985, 34
309. Lee 1965, 138
310. Wagner *et al.* 1989, 299
311. Muhly *et al.* 1991
312. Frankfort 1927, 148
313. Gell 1804, 120
314. Strabo, *Geography* 13.1.23; Zengel 1990, 54
315. Borchardt 1927b, 281; Kukal 1984, 31
316. Strabo, *Geography* 13.1.56

317. Hesiod, *Shield of Heracles* 122
318. Leaf 1923, 285
319. Cook 1973, 264 n. 5
320. Mentioned in the ancient literature for instance by Pausanias 5.12 and Pliny 23.23.
321. Neuburger 1919, 20; Netolitzky 1926, 51
322. Neumann 1902; Borchardt 1927b, 281
323. Herodotus, *Histories* 5.49 described Phrygia (central western Anatolia) as the richest country in the world for flocks.
324. see also Pischel 1982, 128; Zengel 1990, 54
325. Blegen *et al.* 1953, 17: "In the remains examined by the Cincinnati Expedition nothing has been observed that is not consonant with the conclusion that the Sixth Settlement [i.e. Troy vi] enjoyed a long era of prosperity and peace." Latacz 1986, 102: "Between Troy i and vi the fortified area continuously expanded until it reached roughly 20,000 square metres [5 acres]. This expansion of the citadel despite repeated destructions by fire and earthquake, implies steadily increasing prosperity and population, indicating rising economic success and political power from the early late bronze periods."
326. Schliemann 1880
327. Blegen 1963, 121
328. Cook 1973, 14
329. Korfmann 1986, 11
330. Forchhammer 1850, 20
331. Schliemann 1880, 98
332. Mauduit 1840, 132 and 215
333. see also Cook 1973, 146
334. Schliemann 1880, 98. Later geological investigations have shown that the sediments in Beşik Bay are derived from the Scamander (Mey 1926, 19).
335. Pliny, *Natural History* 5.30: "*amnis navigabilis*"
336. e.g. Gell 1804
337. Cook 1973, 167 n. 1
338. Kukal 1984, 27
339. Knauss 1989; 1990
340. Schliemann 1880, 99
341. Forchhammer 1850. Cook 1973, 166 thinks Forchhammer's measurements seem excessive—I disagree.
342. Already in *Timaeus* it was said, that "all that we have here, lying within the mouth of which we speak, is evidently a haven having a narrow entrance."
343. Brückner 1925
344. Such citadels surrounded by concentric rings are frequently called "troy towns" in English and *Trojaburgen* in German and there is a traditional story connected with them, that a virgin is held prisoner within them.
345. Luce 1975, 177
346. Schliemann 1875, 13 and 109

347. Leaf 1912, 54
348. Schliemann 1875, 140
349. Wood 1985, 89
350. Blegen 1963, 13
351. Blegen 1963, 122
352. Hesiod, *Theogony* 726
353. Hesiod, *Theogony* 734
354. Hesiod, *Works and Days* 150
355. Herodotus, *Histories* 1, 98
356. Herodotus, *Histories* 1, 180
357. Schliemann 1875, 17 and 348
358. Zengel 1990, 74
359. Blegen *et al.* 1953, 10
360. Strabo, *Geography* 8.353
361. Pliny, *Natural History* 36.26; Gill 1980, 64
362. Blegen 1963, 149
363. Blegen *et al.* 1953, 6
364. Blegen 1963, 13
365. Schliemann 1875, 32
366. Gell 1804, 121
367. Schliemann 1880, 81
368. Schliemann 1880, 88
369. Kraft, Kayan & Erol 1980; 1982
370. Forchhammer 1850, 9
371. Zangger 1991a, 1991b, 1992
372. Combellack 1968, 128
373. Schliemann 1880, 153
374. Blegen 1963, 13 and 17
375. Folliot 1984, 83
376. Combellack 1968, 102
377. Folliot concludes "the Anatolians taught love and respect for horses."
378. Hammond 1986, 53
379. Apollonius of Rhodes, *Argonautica*; Labaree 1957; Severin 1986; Koromila 1991; *contra*: Carpenter 1948
380. Severin 1986, 38; Korfmann 1988
381. *Black Sea Pilot* 1908; Leaf 1912, 358
382. Korfmann 1986a
383. Schliemann 1875, 125
384. Schliemann 1875, 185
385. Neumann 1986, 357
386. Blegen 1963, 39
387. Schliemann 1880, 78 citing Eustathius *Ad Il.* 20.74
388. Luce 1975, 172
389. e.g. Napier 1840; Forchhammer 1850
390. Forchhammer 1850, 14
391. Schliemann 1880, 97
392. Gell 1804, 118
393. Schliemann 1880, 80

394. Schliemann 1880, 85
395. Forchhammer 1850, 20
396. Forchhammer 1850, 14
397. Korfmann 1986a, 9
398. Blegen 1963, 138: "They did not neglect to pay careful attention to detail, but at the same time they possessed the vision and capacity to carry out a project of enduring grandeur."
399. Snodgrass 1987, 201
400. Schliemann 1875, 369; Zengel 1990: 53
401. Latacz 1986, 102
402. Hammond 1986, 26
403. Folliot 1984, 82
404. Folliot 1984, 78
405. Chadwick 1976, 185; Wenke 1980, 459
406. Blegen et al. 1953, 249–54
407. Blegen et al. 1953, 253; 1963, 139
408. In Atlantis, however, the most important pillar was said to have been in the center of the temple.
409. Gill 1977, 299; 1979, 153
410. Cornford 1937, 1
411. Ledger 1989, 197
412. Diogenes Laërtius 3.37
413. Plato, Republic 10.595A–608B
414. Plato, Republic 3.390C; Clarke 1981, 9
415. quoted by Rubens & Taplin 1989, 113
416. Kerferd 1961, 31: "In the Laws Plato hangs his web upon more pegs than is usual elsewhere, the pegs being well-known historical events."
417. Plato, Laws 3.682
418. Plato, Laws 3.677
419. Luce 1978, 50
420. Skemp 1952, 85: "Finally, in Laws 3, Plato transfers from fantasy to fact the statement that the earth suffers periodic inundations."
421. Plato, Laws 3.682
422. Plato, Laws 3.678
423. Plato, Laws 3.682
424. Bernal 1990, 132
425. Schliemann 1891, 13
426. Stoll 1989, 337
427. Siebler 1990, 100; Traill 1990, 84
428. Rieu 1950, xv
429. Rubens & Taplin 1989
430. Butler 1897
431. Latacz 1989, 90
432. Clarke 1981, 12 lists a few other bizarre ideas.
433. Sherratt 1990, 807
434. De Camp 1970, 214
435. Rieu 1950, ix

436. Bradford 1963; Lessing 1966; Obregón 1971; Pillot 1972
437. Von der Mühll 1940, 698; Latacz 1989, 193
438. Shewan 1918; 1919
439. Butler 1967; Pocock 1957
440. Obregón 1971
441. Leaf 1915, 183
442. Wolf & Wolf 1968; 1990, 84
443. Forsyth 1980, 111
444. Hammond 1986, 68
445. Apollonius of Rhodes, *Argonautica*
446. e.g. Gill 1980, 64
447. Spanuth 1979, 217
448. see discussion in Kluge 1911; Frost 1913; Hennig 1925; 1927; Borchardt 1927a; Schulten 1927; Spanuth 1956; 1965; 1979; de Camp 1970
449. Vidal-Naquet 1964, 426; Gill 1980, xiii
450. Forsyth 1980, 111
451. Stanford 1968, 9; Griffin 1987, 4
452. Hölscher 1988, 44, notes that Telemachus' journey rests on no mythological background and may therefore have been an invention by Homer. Its purpose may have been to depict the situation in Greece in more detail.
453. Griffin 1987, 47
454. de Camp 1970, 197 furthermore remarked that *Schedia* means "raft."
455. Forsyth 1980, 111
456. Clarke 1981, 261
457. Severin 1986, 217
458. Tracy 1990, 37, 46f
459. Severin 1986, 222
460. Carpenter 1948, 2, argues that sails would be useless for the Black Sea passage. Bronze Age ships would have had to rely on their rowing speed only, which must have exceeded four knots in order to make the passage.
461. Graves 1960, 217: The *Argo*, which had to go up the Bosporus, was also propelled by fifty oars.
462. Severin 1986
463. Blegen *et al.* 1953, 17; Podzuweit 1982, 65
464. Rose 1969, 405
465. Latacz 1986, 101
466. Griffin 1987, 67
467. Book III of the *Iliad* describes how Paris challenged Menelaus to a single combat to avoid the Trojan War.
468. Tracy 1990. Kirk 1970, 174 considers this passage a "sophisticated Ionian development belonging to the latest stage of the true oral tradition."
469. The whole conflict that led to the Trojan War has been compared to "two squabbling farmers" fighting over landownership. See Morris 1986, 102; MacDowell 1978, 11.

470. Luce 1969, 229
471. Rüter 1969, 245; Rubens & Taplin 1989, 125
472. Tracy 1990, 87
473. Rieu 1950, xviii confesses that even "the *Iliad* was written not to glorify war (though it admits its fascination) but to emphasize its tragic futility."
474. Griffin 1987, 69
475. Nagy 1977; Redfield 1975
476. Mellaart 1984, 63; Mee 1984
477. Gercke & Hiesel 1971, 15
478. Griffin 1987, 76 and Siebler 1990, 90 report how the end of the *Odyssey* was adjusted in Alexandria.
479. Frankfort 1927, 148
480. Muhly & Pernicka 1990
481. Carpenter 1948, 1
482. Raban 1981, 40
483. Koromila 1991, 32
484. Carpenter 1948, 6
485. Korfmann 1986; 1988, 48; Latacz 1986, 111; Siebler 1990, 203
486. Kraft, Kayan & Erol 1980; 1982
487. Ps.-Scylax' *Periplus* (fourth century B.C.), on the other hand, describes Ilion as being twenty-five stades from the sea, which still at present is the distance between the sea and the site. If the measurement is correct, how could the coastline have changed so much within a few hundred years? See Cook 1973, 182.
488. Forchhammer 1850, 28
489. MacLaren 1863, 46
490. Zangger 1991a
491. Zengel 1990, 53
492. Latacz 1986, 105
493. To the present day there is an extensive sand ridge along this course.
494. Schliemann 1880, 83
495. Acland 1849
496. Clarke 1981, 33
497. Frazer 1966
498. Joseph of Exeter, *Trojan War* I: 524–36
499. Latacz 1986, 109; Korfmann 1988, 49
500. Forchhammer 1850, 14
501. Cook 1973, 178–86; 1984, 167
502. Strabo, *Geography* 13.1.31 and 36
503. Siebler 1990, 83, mentions Lesky, Pöhlmann, Hölscher.
504. Thornton 1984, 154: "It is plain that the Xanthus, in part of its course, cuts through the plain more or less at right angles to a line connecting Troy and the Achaean ships."
505. Thornton 1984, 150
506. Pliny, *Natural History* 5.30
507. Forchhammer 1850, 26
508. Strabo, *Geography* 13.1.31

509. Cook 1984, 167
510. Brückner 1925, 245
511. Cook 1973, 180
512. Ramage 1978, 42
513. Muhly 1990, 83
514. Jowett 1892, vol. 3: 429–33
515. Dušanić 1982
516. Carpenter 1966, 30
517. Kukal 1984, 41
518. Folliot 1984
519. Kukal 1984, 3
520. Kukal 1984, 13, also mentions an article entitled "Troy and Atlantis" which appeared in the little-known journal *Atlantean Research*—I have seen neither.
521. Reinach 1912, 429; Forsyth 1980, 6

BIBLIOGRAPHY

Acland, Henry W. (1849): *The Plain of Troy—Illustrated by a Panoramic Drawing and a Map*, James Wyatt and Son, Oxford, 1–48.

Aitken, M.J. (1988): "The Minoan Eruption of Thera, Santorini: A Reassessment of the Radiocarbon Dates" in *New Aspects of Archaeological Science in Greece*, Richard Jones & H.W. Catling (eds.), Athens, 19–24.

Ammerman, Albert J. & L.L. Cavalli-Sforza (1984): *The Neolithic Transition and the Genetics of Populations in Europe*, Princeton University Press, Princeton, 1–176.

Angel, J. Lawrence (1972): "Ecology and Population in the Eastern Mediterranean," *World Archaeology* 4, 88–105.

Archer-Hind, R.D. (1888): *The Timaeus of Plato*, Macmillan & Co., London, 1–358.

Arrigoni, Emilio (1967): "Elementi per una ricostruzione del paesaggio in Attica nell'epoca Classica," *Nuova Rivista Storica*, 267–96.

Arrigoni, Emilio (1969): "Elementi per una ricostruzione del paesaggio in Attica nell'epoca Classica," *Nuova Rivista Storica* 53, 265–322.

Babcock, William H. (1917): "Atlantis & Antilla," *The Geographical Review* 3 (5), 392–5.

Baillie, Michael G.L. (1988a): "Irish Oaks Record Volcanic Dust Veils Drama!" *Archaeology Ireland* 2 (2), 71–74.

Baillie, Michael G.L. (1988b): "Marker Dates—Turning Prehistory Into History," *Archaeology Ireland* 2 (4), 154–55.

Baillie, Michael G.L. & M.A.R. Munro (1988): "Irish Tree Rings, Santorini and Volcanic Dust Veils," *Nature* 332 (6162), 344–46.

Balch, Edwin Swift (1917): "Atlantis or Minoan Crete," *The Geographical Review* 3 (5), 388–392.

Barker, Ernest (1918): *Greek Political Theory. Plato and His Predecessors*, Methuen & Co., London, 1–403.

Barnett, R.D. (1975): *The Sea Peoples*, Vol. II Part 2, *Cambridge Ancient History*, Cambridge University Press, 359–78.

Bass, George F., Cemal Pulak, Dominique Collon & James Weinstein (1989): "The Bronze Age Shipwreck at Ulu Burun: 1986 Campaign," *American Journal of Archaeology* 3, 1–29.

Becher, Martin Roda (ed.) (1986): *Geschichten von Atlantis*, Sammlung Luchterhand, Darmstadt, 1–271.

Bernal, Martin (1987): *Black Athena. The Afroasiatic Roots of Classical Civilization*. Vol. I: *The Fabrication of Ancient Greece 1785–1985*, Rutgers University Press, New Brunswick, 1–575.

Bernal, Martin (1990): "Responses to Critical Reviews of Black Athena: The Afroasiatic Roots of Classical Civilization. Vol. I: The Fabrication of Ancient Greece 1785–1985," *Journal of Mediterranean Archaeology* 3 (1), 111–37.

Bernal, Martin (1991): *Black Athena. The Afroasiatic Roots of Classical Civiliza-tion*. Vol. II: *The Archaeological and Documentary Evidence*, Free Association Books, London, 1–736.

Beuermann, Arnold (1956): "Die Waldverhältnisse im Peloponnes unter besonderer Berücksichtigung der Entwaldung und der Auf-forstung," *Erdkunde* 10, 122–36.

Bidez, J. (1945): *Eos, ou Platon et l'Orient*, M. Hayez, Brussels, 1–190 and 1–51.

Blegen, Carl W., John L. Caskey & Marion Rawson (1953): *Troy III: The Sixth Settlement*, 2 Vols., Princeton University Press, Princeton, 1–418.

Blegen, Carl W. et al. (1958): *Troy: Excavations Conducted by the University of Cincinnati 1932–1938*, Vol. IV: *Settlements VIIa, VIIb and VIII*, Princeton University Press, Princeton.

Blegen, Carl W. (1963): *Troy and the Trojans*, Thames and Hudson, London, 1–240.

Blegen, Carl W. (1975): *Troy VII*, Vol. II Part 2, *Cambridge Ancient History*, Cambridge University Press, 161–64.

Borchardt, Paul (1927a): "Platos Insel Atlantis," *Petermann Mitteilungen 73*, 19–31.

Borchardt, Paul (1927b): "Nordafrika und die Metallreichtümer von Atlantis," *Petermann Mitteilungen 73*, 280–82.

Bradford, Ernie (1963): *Ulysses Found*, Hodder & Stoughton, London, 1–238.

Bramwell, James (1937): *Lost Atlantis*, Cobden-Sanderson.

Brandenstein, Wilhelm (1951): *Atlantis; Größe und Untergang eines geheim-nisvollen Inselreiches. Arbeiten aus dem Institut für allgemeine und verglei-chende Sprachwissenschaft*, Gerold Verlag, Vienna, 1–105.

Braudel, Fernand (1972): *The Mediterranean and the Mediterranean World in the Age of Philip II*, Vol. 1, Collins, London, 1–642.

Brückner, Alfred (1925): "Forschungsaufgaben in der Troas," *Archäolo-gischer Anzeiger* 40, 230–48.

Bryant, Jacob (1776): *A New System, or, An Analysis of Ancient Mythology: Wherein an Attempt Is Made to Divest Tradition of Fable; and to Reduce the Truth to Its Original Purity*, T. Payne, P. Elmsly, B. White & J. Walter, publishers, London, 1–601.

Bryant, Jacob (1799a): *Some Observations Upon the Vindication of Homer and of the Ancient Poets Who Have Recorded the Siege and Fall of Troy*, M. Pote & E. Williams, publishers, Eton, 1–96.

Bryant, Jacob (1799b): *A Dissertation Concerning the War of Troy and the Expedition of the Grecians as Described by Homer*, S. Hamilton for T. Payne et al. publishers, London, 1–162.

Bryson, R.A., H.H. Lamb & D.L. Donley (1974): "Drought and the Decline of Mycenae," *Antiquity* 47, 46–50.

Burnet, John (1914): *Greek Philosophy*, Macmillan, London, 1–360.

Bury, R.G. (1929): *Plato*, Vol. IX of The Loeb Classical Library, Harvard University Press, Cambridge, Mass., 1–636.

Butler, Samuel: *The Authoress of the Odyssey*, re-edited by University of Chicago Press, Chicago (1967), 1–275.

Butzer, Karl W. (1982): *Archaeology as Human Ecology: Method and Theory for a Contextual Approach*, Cambridge University Press, 1–364.

Carpenter, Rhys (1948): "The Greek Penetration of the Black Sea," *American Journal of Archaeology* 52, 1–10.

Carpenter, Rhys (1966): *Discontinuity in Greek Civilization*, Cambridge University Press, 1–80.

Chadwick, John (1976): *The Mycenaean World*, Cambridge University Press, 1–201.

Cherniss, Harold (1947): "Some War-Time Publications Concerning Plato," *American Journal of Philology* 68 (270), 225–65.

Cherry, John F. (1981): "Pattern and Process in the Earliest Colonization of the Mediterranean Islands," *Proceedings of the Prehistoric Society* 47, 41–68.

Clarke, Howard W. (1981): *Homer's Readers*, University of Delaware Press, New York, 1–327.

Combellack, Frederick M. (ed.) (1968): *Quintus of Smyrna: The War at Troy— What Homer Didn't Tell*, University of Oklahoma Press, 1–279.

Cook, J.M. (1973): *The Troad—An Archaeological and Topographical Study*, Oxford, Clarendon Press, 1–443.

Cook, J.M. (1984): "The Topography of the Plain of Troy," in *The Trojan War—Its Historicity and Context*, Lin Foxhall & John K. Davies (eds), Bristol Classical Press, Bristol, 163–72.

Corbato, Carlo (1953): "In Margine Alla Questione Atlantidea Platone e Cartagine," *Archaeologia Classica* 5, 232–37.

Cornford, Francis Macdonald (1937): *Plato's Cosmology*, Kegan Paul, London, 1–376.

Davies, J.K. (1971): *Athenian Propertied Families 600–300 B.C.*, Clarendon Press, Oxford.

De Camp, L. Sprague (1970): *Lost Continents*, Dover Publications, New York, 1–348.

Demakopoulou, Katie (ed.) (1988): *Das mykenische Hellas; Heimat der Helden Homers*, Dietrich Reimer Verlag, Berlin, 1–277.

Desborough, V.R. D'A. (1975): *The End of Mycenaean Civilization and the Dark Age*, Vol. II, Part 2, *Cambridge Ancient History*, Cambridge University Press, 658–77.

Diehl, Ernst (1965): *Procli Diadochi in Platonis Timaeum Commentaria*, 3 vols., first published 1903, reprinted by Hakkert, Amsterdam.

Dietz, Søren (1991): *The Argolid at the Transition to the Mycenean Age*, The National Museum of Denmark, Copenhagen, 1–336.

Dušanić, Slobodan (1982): "Plato's Atlantis," *L'Antiquité Classique* 51, 25–52.

Easton, Donald (1985): "Has the Trojan War been found?" *Antiquity* 59, 188–96.

Easton, Donald (1990): "Reconstructing Schliemann's Troy," in *Heinrich Schliemann nach hundert Jahren*, William M. Calder III & Justus Cobet (eds), Vittorio Klostermann, Frankfurt am Main, 431–47.

Edel, Elmar (1966): *Die Ortsnamenliste aus dem Totentempel Amenophis III*, Bonner Biblische Beiträge 25, Peter Haustein Verlag, 1–101.

Ehrenberg, Victor (1973): *From Solon to Socrates*, Methuen, London and New York, 1–505.

Eucken, Christoph (1983): *Isokrates. Seine Positionen in der Auseinandersetzung mit den zeitgenössischen Philosophen*, Walter de Gruyter, Berlin, New York, 1–304.

Finley, Moses I. (1974): *Schliemann's Troy—One Hundred Years After*, Oxford University Press, London, 1–22.

Folliot, Katherine A. (1984): *Atlantis Revisited*, Professional Books Ltd., Abingdon, Oxon., 1–129.

Forchhammer, Peter Wilhelm (1850): *Beschreibung der Ebene von Troja*, Heinrich Ludwig Brönner, Frankfurt am Main, 1–28.

Forsyth, Phyllis Young (1980): *Atlantis—The Making of Myth*, McGill-Queen's University Press, Montreal & Croom Helm, London, 1–209.

Frank, Erich (1923): *Plato und die sogenannten Pythagoreer*, Max Niemeyer, Halle, 1–399.

Frankfort, Henri (1927): "Studies in Early Pottery of the Near East. II. Asia, Europe and the Aegean and Their Earliest Interrelations," *Royal Anthropological Institute London, Occasional Papers* 8, 1–203.

Frazer, R.M. (1966): *The Trojan War: The Chronicles of Dictys of Crete and Dares the Phrygian*, Indiana University Press, Bloomington, 1–185.

Fredericks, S. Casey (1978): "Plato's Atlantis: A Mythologist Looks at Myth," in *Atlantis—Fact or Fiction?*, Edwin S. Ramage (ed.), Indiana University Press, Bloomington and London, 81–99.

Frost, K.T. (1909): "The Lost Continent," *The Times*, London, Friday 19 February 1909, 10.

Frost, K.T. (1913): "The *Critias* and Minoan Crete," *Journal of Hellenic Studies* 33, 189–206.

Frutiger, P. (1930): *Les mythes de Platon*, Paris.

Galanopoulos, A. & Edward Bacon (1969): *Atlantis: The Truth Behind the Legend*, Nelson, London, 1–216.

Gardiner, A.H. (1971): *Egypt of the Pharaohs*, Oxford, Clarendon Press.

Gell, William (1804): *The Topography of Troy and Its Vicinity*, London, 1–124.

Gercke, Peter & Gerhard Hiesel (1971): "Grabungen in der Unterstadt von Tiryns von 1889 bis 1929," *Tiryns* V, Verlag Philipp von Zabern, Mainz, 1–19.

Gidon, F. (1934): "Les submersions atlantiques (irlando-armoricaines) de l'âge du bronze et la question de l'Atlantide," *Mémoires de l'Académie des Sciences, Arts et Belles Lettres de Caen* 8, Caen, 91–114.

Gill, Christopher (1977): "Genre of the Atlantis Story," *Classical Philology* 72, 287–304.

Gill, Christopher (1979): "Plato's Atlantis Story and the Birth of Fiction," *Philosophy and Literature* 3, 64–78.

Gill, Christopher (1980): *Plato; The Atlantis Story: Timaeus 17–27*, Bristol Classical Press, Bristol, 1–95.

Giovannini, Adalberto (1985): "Peut-on démythifier l'Atlantide?" *Museum Helveticum* 92, 151–56.

Graves, Robert (1960): *The Greek Myths*, Vol. II, Penguin, London, 1–412.

Griffin, Jasper (1987): *The Odyssey*, Cambridge University Press, 1–107.

Hackforth, R. (1944): "The Story of Atlantis: Its Purpose and Its Moral," *Classical Review* 58, 7–9.

Hägg, Robin & Dora Konsola (eds) (1986): *Early Helladic Architecture and Urbanization*, Studies in Mediterranean Archaeology 56, Paul Åströms Förlag, Gøteborg, 1–102.

Haider, Peter W. (1988): *Griechenland-Nordafrika: Ihre Beziehungen zwischen 1500 und 600 v. Chr.*, Wissenschaftliche Buchgesellschaft, Darmstadt, 1–262.

Halstead, Paul (1981): "Counting Sheep in Neolithic and Bronze Age Greece," in *Pattern of the Past: Studies in Honor of David Clarke*, Ian Hodder, G. Isaac & N. Hammond (eds), Cambridge University Press, 307–339.

Halstead, Paul (1989): "The Economy Has a Normal Surplus: Economic Stability and Social Change Among Early Farming Communities of Thessaly, Greece," in *Bad Year Economics: Cultural Responses to Risk and Uncertainty*, Paul Halstead & J. O'Shea (eds), Cambridge University Press, 68–80.

Hammond, N.G.L. (1986): *A History of Greece to 322 B.C.*, Clarendon Press, Oxford, 1–691.

Hansen, Julie M., (1980): "The Paleoethnobotany of Franchthi Cave, Greece," unpublished Ph.D. dissertation, Indiana University, Bloomington.

Heidel, W. A. (1933): "A Suggestion Concerning Plato's Atlantis," *Proceedings of the American Academy of Arts and Sciences* 68, 189–228.

Hennig, Richard (1925): "Das Rätsel der Atlantis," *Meereskunde* 14 (5), 1–29.

Hennig, Richard (1927): "Zum Verständnis des Begriff 'Säulen' in der antiken Geographie," *Petermann Mitteilungen* 73, 80–87.

Herter, Hans (1928): "Platons Atlantis," *Bonner Jahrbücher* 133, 28–47.

Herter, Hans (1944): "Altes und Neues zu Platons Atlantis," *Rheinisches Museum für Philologie* 92, 236–65.

Hobson, Christine (1990): *Exploring the World of the Pharaoh*, Thames and Hudson, London, 1–192.

Hölscher, Uvo (1988): *Die Odyssee; Epos zwischen Märchen und Roman*, C.H. Beck, Munich, 1–360.

Jacobsen, Thomas W. (1976): "17,000 years of Greek Prehistory," *Scientific American* 234, 76–87.

Jacoby, Felix (1923): *Die Fragmente der griechischen Historiker*, Erster Teil, Weidmannsche Buchhandlung, Berlin, 1–534.

Jacoby, Felix (1954): *Die Fragmente der griechischen Historiker*, Dritter Teil, E.J. Brill, Leiden, 1–661.

James, Peter (1991): *Centuries of Darkness*, Jonathan Cape, London, 1–434.

Jones, M.E. Monckton (1924): *Ancient Egypt From the Records*, Methuen, London, 1–244.

Jowett, Benjamin (1892): *The Dialogues of Plato*, third edition, 4 vols., Oxford University Press.

Kemp, Barry (1989): *Ancient Egypt: Anatomy of a Civilization*, Routledge, London and New York, 1–356.

Kerferd, G.B. (1961): "Plato As an Historian—Review of R. Weil, *L'Archéologie de Platon*," *Classical Review* 11, 30–1.

Kilian, Klaus (1982): "Zum Ende der mykenischen Periode in der Argolis," *Jahrbuch des Römisch-Germanischen Zentralmuseums* 27, 166–95.

Kilian, Klaus (1988): "Die mykenische Architektur," in *Das mykenische Hellas; Heimat der Helden Homers*, Katie Demakopoulou (ed.), Dietrich Reimer Verlag, Berlin, 30–4.

Kirk, G.S. (1970): *Myth: Its Meaning and Functions in Ancient and Other Cultures*, Cambridge University Press, 1–299.

Kluge, F. (1911): *De Platonis Critia*. Unpublished Ph.D. dissertation, Halle, 19.

Knapp, A. Bernard (1986): "Production, Exchange and Socio-Political Complexity on Bronze Age Cyprus," *Oxford Journal of Archaeology* 5 (1), 35–60.

Knapp, A. Bernard (1988): *The History and Culture of Ancient Western Asia and Egypt*, The Dorsey Press, Chicago, 1–284.

Knauss, Jost (1989): "Mykenische Wasserbauten in Arkadien, Böotien und Thessalien—mutmaßliche Zielsetzung und rekonstruierbare Wirkungsweise," *Kongressband Wasser*, Berlin, 31–70.

Knauss, Jost (1990): *Kopais 3*. Frank GmbH, Munich, 1–288.

Konsola, D. (1984): *Η Πρωιμη Αστικοποιηση Στους Πρωτοελλαδικους Οικισμους*, Athens.

Korfmann, Manfred (1986a): "Troy: Topography and Navigation," in *Troy and the Trojans*, Machteld Mellink (ed.), Bryn Mawr College, Bryn Mawr, 1–28.

Korfmann, Manfred (1986b): "Beşik-Tepe. Vorbericht über die Grabungen von 1984," *Archäologischer Anzeiger* 3, 303–29.

Korfmann, Manfred (1988): "Ausgrabungen an der Bucht von Troia," *Tübinger Blätter*, 47–52.

Koromila, Marianne (1991): *The Greeks in the Black Sea; From the Bronze Age to the Early Twentieth Century*, Panorama, Athens, 1–301.

Kraft, John C., Ilhan Kayan & Oğuz Erol (1980): "Geomorphic reconstructions in the environs of ancient Troy," *Science* 209 (4458), 776–82.

Kraft, John C., Ilhan Kayan & Oğuz Erol (1982): "Geology and paleogeographic reconstructions of the vicinity of Troy," in *Troy—The Archaeological Geology*, George Rapp & John Gifford (eds), Princeton University Press, Princeton, 11–41.

Kukal, Zdeněk (1984): *Atlantis in the Light of Modern Research*, Czechoslovak Academy of Sciences, Prague, 1–224.

Kuniholm, Peter I. (1990): "Archaeological Evidence and Nonevidence for Climatic Change," *Philosophical Transactions of the Royal Society of London* A330, 645–55.

Labaree, Benjamin W. (1957): "How the Greeks Sailed Into the Black Sea," *American Journal of Archaeology* 61, 29–33.

Lamb, H.H. (1967): "Review of Rhys Carpenter's *Discontinuity in Greek Civilization*," *Antiquity* 41, 233–34.

Lamb, H.H. (1977): *Climatic History and the Future*, Princeton University Press, Princeton, 1–835.

Latacz, Joachim (1986): "News From Troy," *Berytus* 34, 97–127.

Latacz, Joachim (1989): *Homer; Der erste Dichter des Abendlandes*, Artemis Verlag, Munich, 1–211.

Leaf, Walter (1912): *Troy. A Study in Homeric Geography*, Macmillan and Co. Ltd., London, 1–402.

Leaf, Walter (1915): *Homer and History*, Macmillan, London, 1–375.

Leaf, Walter (ed.) (1923): *Strabo on the Troad*, Book 13, Cap. 1, with translation and commentary, Cambridge University Press, 1–352.

Ledger, Gerard R. (1989): *Re-counting Plato; A Computer Analysis of Plato's Style*, Clarendon Press, Oxford, 1–254.

Lee, Desmond (1965): *Plato: Timaeus and Critias*, Penguin Books, London, 1–167.

Lessing, Erich (1966): *The Voyages of Ulysses: A Photographic Interpretation of Homer's Classic*, Macmillan, London, 1–275.

Lloyd, Geoffrey Ernest Richard (1968): "Plato As a Natural Scientist," *Journal of Hellenic Studies* 88, 78–92.

Lohmann, Hans (1983): "Atene—eine attische Landgemeinde klassischer Zeit," *Hellenika Jahrbuch*, Bochum, 98–117.

Lohmann, Hans (1985): "Landleben im klassischen Attika—Ergebnisse einer archäologischen Landesaufnahme des Demos Atene," *Jahrbuch der Ruhr-Universität Bochum*, 71–96.

Lohmann, Hans (1987): "Zur Prosopographie und Demographie der attischen Landgemeinde Atene," *Geographica Historica, Stuttgarter Kolloqium zur Geographie des Altertums* 5.

Luce, John Victor (1969): *Atlantis—Legende und Wirklichkeit*, Gustav Lübbe Verlag, Bergisch Gladbach, 1–336.

Luce, John Victor (1975): *Archäologie auf den Spuren Homers*, Bastei Lübbe Verlag, Bergisch Gladbach, 1–283.

Luce, John Victor (1978): "The Sources and Literary Form of Plato's Atlantis Narrative," in *Atlantis—Fact or Fiction?*, Edwin S. Ramage (ed.), Indiana University Press, Bloomington and London, 49–78.

MacDowell, Douglas M. (1978): *The Law in Classical Athens*, Thames and Hudson, London, 1–280.

MacLaren, Charles (1822): *A Dissertation on the Topography of the Plain of Troy—Including an Examination of the Opinion of Demetrius, Chevalier, Dr. Clarke, and Major Rennell*, Edinburgh, 1–270.

MacLaren, Charles (1863): *The Plain of Troy Described: And the Identity of the Ilium of Homer With the New Ilium of Strato Proved*, Adam and Charles Black, Edinburgh.

Manning, Sturt (1988): "The Bronze Age Eruption of Thera: Absolute Dating, Aegean Chronology and Mediterranean Cultural Interrelations," *Journal of Mediterranean Archaeology* 1 (1), 17–82.

Marinatos, Spyridon (1986): *Kreta, Thera und das mykenische Hellas*, Hirmer Verlag, Munich, 1–184.

Mauduit, A.F. (1840): *Découvertes dans la Troade*, Didot Frères, Paris and Roland, London, 1–265.

Mavor, James W. (1969): *Voyage to Atlantis*, Souvenir Press, London, 1–320.

Mee, Christopher B. (1978): "Aegean Trade and Settlement in Anatolia in the Second Millennium B.C.," *Anatolian Studies* 28, 121–55.

Mee, Christopher B. (1984): "The Mycenaeans and Troy," in *The Trojan War—Its Historicity and Context*, Lin Foxhall & John K. Davies (eds), Bristol Classical Press, Bristol, 45–56.

Mellaart, James (1984): "Troy VIIa in Anatolian Perspective," in *The Trojan War—Its Historicity and Context*, Lin Foxhall & John K. Davies (eds), Bristol Classical Press, Bristol, 63–82.

Mey, Oscar (1926): *Das Schlachtfeld vor Troja; eine Untersuchung*, Verlag Walter de Gruyter, Berlin and Leipzig, 1–37.

Millard, A.R. (1984): "Events at the end of the Late Bronze Age in the Near East," in *The Trojan War—Its Historicity and Context*, Lin Foxhall & John K. Davies (eds), Bristol Classical Press, Bristol, 1–15.

Morris, Ian (1986): "The Use and Abuse of Homer," *Classical Antiquity* 5, 81–138.

Muck, Otto (1976): *Alles über Atlantis*, Knaur, Munich, 1–320.

Muhly, James D. (1988): "The Beginnings of Metallurgy in the Old World," in *The Beginning of the Use of Metals and Alloys*, Robert Maddin (ed.), MIT Press, Cambridge, Mass., 2–20.

Muhly, James D. (1990): "Black Athena Versus Traditional Scholarship," *Journal of Mediterranean Archaeology*, 3(1), 83–110.

Muhly, James D. & Ernst Pernicka (1990): Oral presentation at the Schliemann Conference, Berlin, December 1990.

Muhly, James D., F. Begemann, Ö. Öztunali, E. Pernicka, S. Schmitt-Strecker & G.A. Wagner (1991): "The Bronze Metallurgy of Anatolia and the Question of Local Tin Sources," *Archaeometry "90*, Ernst Pernicka & Günther Wagner (eds), Birkhäuser, Basel, 209–20.

Nagy, Gregory (1977): *The Best of the Achaeans: Concepts of the Hero in Archaic Greek Poetry*, Johns Hopkins University Press, Baltimore, 1–392.

Napier, E. (1840): "Remarks on Ancient Troy and the Modern Troad," *United Service Journal* 2, 289–310.

Netolitzky, Fritz (1926): "Das Atlantisproblem," *Wiener Prähistorische Zeitschrift* 13, 43–55.

Neuburger, Albert (1919): *Die Technik des Altertums*, R. Voigtländer Verlag, Leipzig.

Neumann, B. (1902): "Messing," *Zeitschrift für Angewandte Chemie* 15, 511–16.

Neumann, Jehuda (1986): "Wind and Current Conditions in the Region of the 'Windy Ilios' (Troy)," *Archäologischer Anzeiger*, 345–63.

Neumann, J. & Parpola, S. (1987): "Climatic Change and the Eleventh–Tenth-Century Eclipse of Assyria and Babylonia," *Journal of Near Eastern Studies* 46 (3), 161–82.

Niemeyer, Hans-Georg (1989): *Das frühe Kathargo und die phönizische Expansion im Mittelmeerraum*, Vandenhoeck & Ruprecht, Göttingen, 1–34.

Nilsson, Martin Persson (1932): *The Mycenaean Origin of Greek Mythology*, reissued 1972, Cambridge University Press, 1–258.

Obregón, Mauricio (1971): *Ulysses Airborne*, Harper & Row, New York, 1–188.

Pallottino, Massimo (1952): "Atlantide," *Archaeologia Classica* 4, 228–40.

Pang, Kevin, S.K. Srivasta & H.-h. Chou (1988): "Climatic Impacts of Past Volcanic Eruptions: Inferences From Ice Core, Tree Ring and Historical Data," 1988 Fall Meeting of the American Geophysical Union.

Parker, Richard A. (1950): *Calendars of Ancient Egypt*, Studies in Ancient Oriental Civilization, The University of Chicago Press 26, 1–83.

Payne, Sebastian (1975): "Faunal change at Franchthi cave from 20,000 to 3,000 B.C.," in *Archaeozoological Studies*, A.T. Clason (ed.), Academic Press, New York, 120–31.

Pellegrino, Charles (1991): *Unearthing Atlantis*, Random House, New York, 1–325.

Perlès, C. (1987): *Les industries lithiques taillées de Franchthi*, Tome I: *Présentation générale et Industries Paléolithiques*, Indiana University Press, Bloomington.

Pernicka, Ernst; F. Begemann, S. Schmitt-Strecker, & A.P. Grimanis (1990): "On the Composition and Provenance of Metal Artifacts From Poliochni on Lemnos," *Oxford Journal of Archaeology* 9 (3), 263–98.

Pillot, Gilbert (1972): *The Secret Code of the Odyssey; Did the Greeks Sail the Atlantic?*, Abelard-Schumann, London, 1–208.

Pischel, Barbara (1982): "Die atlantische Lehre—Übersetzung und Interpretation der Platon Texte," *Europäische Hochschulschriften*, Reihe 19, Abt. A23, 1–303.

Platt, Arthur (1890): "Plato and Geology," *The Journal of Philology* 18, 134–9.

Pocock, L.G. (1957): *The Sicilian Origin of the Odyssey*, New Zealand University Press, Wellington.

Podzuweit, Christian (1982): "Die mykenische Welt und Troja," in *Südosteuropa zwischen 1600 und 1000 v. Chr.*, Bernhard Hänsel (ed.), 65–88.

Pope, Kevin O. & Tjeerd H. van Andel (1984): "Late Quaternary Alluviation and Soil Formation in the Southern Argolid: Its History, Causes and Archaeological Implications," *Journal of Archaeological Science* 11, 281–306.

Pritchard, J.B. (ed.) (1969): *Ancient Near Eastern Texts Relating to the Old Testament*, Princeton University Press, Princeton.

Pullen, Daniel (1992): "Ox and Plow in the Early Bronze Age Aegean," *American Journal of Archaeology* 96, 45–54.

Raban, Avner (1981): "Die antiken Häfen des Mittelmeeres," in *Strandverschiebungen*, Sonderheft in Ruperto Carola, Heidelberg, 39–83.

Ramage, Edwin S. (ed.) (1978): *Atlantis—Fact or Fiction?*, Indiana University Press, Bloomington and London, 1–210.

Rapp, George (1982): "Earthquakes in the Troad," in *Troy—The Archaeological Geology*, George Rapp & John Gifford (eds), Princeton University Press, Princeton, 43–58.

Redfield, James (1975): *Nature and Culture in the "Iliad,"* The University of Chicago Press, Chicago, 1–287.

Reinach, Salomon (1912): "Une mystification," *Revue Archéologique* 20, 429.

Rice, Michael (1990): *Egypt's Making; The Origins of Ancient Egypt 5000–2000 B.C.*, Guild Publishing, London, 1–322.

Rieu, E.V. (transl.) (1946): *Homer—The Odyssey*, Penguin Books, London, 1–365.

Rieu, E.V. (transl.) (1950): *Homer—The Iliad*, Penguin Books, London, 1–469.

Robert, Carl (1917): "Eine epische Atlantias," *Hermes* 52: 477–9.

Robin, L. (1913): "Platon et la science sociale," *Revue de metaphysique et de morale* 21, 219–21.

Rose, Gilbert P. (1969): "The Unfriendly Phaeacians," *Transactions of the American Philological Association* 100, 387–406.

Rosenmeyer, Thomas G. (1949): "The Family of Critias," *American Journal of Philology* 70, 404–10.

Rosenmeyer, Thomas G. (1956): "Plato's Atlantis Myth: Timaeus or Critias?" *The Phoenix* 10, 163–72.

Rothmaler, Werner (1943): "Die Waldverhältnisse im Peloponnes," *Intersylva—Zeitschrift der Internationalen Forstwirtschaft* 3, 329–43.

Rubens, Beaty & Oliver Taplin (1989): *An Odyssey Round Odysseus*, BBC Books, London, 1–176.

Rudberg, Gunnar (1917): "Atlantis och Syrankusai," *Eranos* 17, 1–80.

Runnels, Curtis (1983): "Lithic Artifacts From Surface Sites in the Mediterranean Area," *British Archaeological Reports—International Series* 155, 143–48.

Runnels, Curtis (1988): "A Prehistoric Survey of Thessaly: New Light on the Greek Middle Paleolithic," *Journal of Field Archaeology* 15 (3), 277–90.

Rüter, Klaus (1969): *Odyseeinterpretationen*, Vandenhoeck & Ruprecht, Göttingen, 1–264.

Saherwala, G. (1985): "Die Ausgrabungen auf Hissarlik-Troja," in *Troja— Heinrich Schliemann's Ausgrabungen und Funde*, Griechisches Ministerium für Kultur und Wissenschaften, Athens, 22–39.

Sandars, Nancy (1978): *The Sea Peoples*, Thames and Hudson, London, 1–224.

Schliemann, Heinrich (1891): *Selbstbiographie*, Ernst Meyer (ed.), F.A. Brockhaus, Wiesbaden, 12. Auflage 1979, 1–144.

Schliemann, Henry (1875): *Troy and Its Remains*, John Murray, London, 1–392.

Schliemann, Henry (1880): *Ilios: The City and Country of the Trojans*, John Murray, London, 1–800.

Schubart, Hermanfrid (1982): "Phönizische Niederlassungen an der Iberischen Südküste," in *Die Phönizier im Westen*, Hans Georg Niemeyer (ed.), Verlag Philipp von Zabern, Mainz, 207–234.

Schuchert, Charles (1917): "Atlantis, the 'Lost' Continent," *The Geographical Review* 3 (1), 64–66.

Schuller, Rudolph (1917): "Atlantis, the 'Lost' Continent," *The Geographical Review* 3 (1), 61–64.

Schulten, Adolf (1927): "Tartessos and Atlantis," *Petermann Mitteilungen* 73, 284–88.

Schulten, Adolf (1939): "Atlantis," *Rheinisches Museum für Philologie* 88, 326–46.

Seeliger, T.C., E. Pernicka, G.A. Wagner, F. Begemann, S. Schmitt-Strecker, C. Eibner, Ö. Öztunali & I. Baranyi (1985): "Archäometallurgische Untersuchungen in Nord- und Ostanatolien," *Jahrbuch des Römisch-Germanischen Zentralmuseums* 32, 597–659.

Settegast, Mary (1990): *Plato Prehistorian*, Lindisfarne Press, Hudson, New York, 1–334.

Severin, Tim (1986): *The Jason Voyage*, Arrow Books, London, 1–263.

Shackleton, Judith C. & Tjeerd H. van Andel (1986): "Prehistoric Shore Environments, Shellfish Availability, and Shellfish Gathering at Franchthi, Greece," *Geoarchaeology* 1 (2), 127–43.

Shackley, Myra L. (1979): "Geoarchaeology—Polemic on a Progressive Relationship," *Die Naturwissenschaften* 9, 429–32.

Shear, Ione Mylonas (1987): *The Panagia Houses at Mycenae*, The University Museum, Philadelphia, Monograph 68, 1–171.

Sherratt, E.S. (1990): "'Reading the texts': archaeology and the Homeric question," *Antiquity* 64, 807–24.

Shewan, A. (1918): "Scherie—Corcyra," *Classical Philology* 13 (4), 321–34.

Shewan, A. (1919): "Scherie—Corcyra," *Classical Philology* 14 (2), 97–107.

Shrimpton, Gordon (1987): "Regional Drought and the Economic Decline of Mycenae," *Classical Views* 6, 137–76.

Siebler, Michael (1990): *Troia-Homer-Schliemann*, Verlag Philipp von Zabern, Mainz, 1–248.

Skemp, J.B. (1952): *Plato's Statesman*, Routledge & Kegan Paul, London, 1–244.

Snodgrass, Anthony (1987): *An Archaeology of Greece: The Present State and Future Scope of a Discipline*, University of California Press, Berkeley and London, 1–218.

Sommer, Ferdinand (1932): *Die Ahhijava-Urkunden*, Abhandlungen der Bayerischen Akademie der Wissenschaften, Philosophisch-historische Abteilung, Munich, 1–469.

Spanuth, Jürgen (1956): *Atlantis—The Mystery Unravelled*, Arco Publishers, London, 1–207.

Spanuth, Jürgen (1965): *Atlantis; Heimat, Reich und Schicksal der Germanen*, Grabert Verlag, Tübingen, 1–676.

Spanuth, Jürgen (1979): *Atlantis of the North*, Sidgwick & Jackson, London, 1–302.

Stanford, W.B. (1968): *The Ulysses Theme; A Study in the Adaptability of a Traditional Hero*, Basil Blackwell, Oxford, 1–339.

Starke, Frank (1981): "Die Keilschrift-luwischen Wörter für 'Insel' und 'Lampe'," *Zeitschrift für Vergleichende Sprachforschung* 95, 141–57.

Starr, Chester (1962): *The Origins of Greek Civilization: 1100–650 B.C.*, Jonathan Cape, London, 1–385.

Stella, L.A. (1932): "L'Atlantide di Platone e la preistoria egea," *Rendiconti del Instituto Lombardo Academia di Scienze e Lettere* 65, 988–90.

Stoll, Heinrich Alexander (ed.) (1989): *Auf den Spuren der Antike; Heinrich Schliemanns Berichte über seine Entdeckungen in der griechischen Welt*, Verlag der Nationen, Berlin, 1–511.

Stos-Gale, Z.A., N.H. Gale & G.R. Gilmore (1984): "Early Bronze Age Trojan metal sources and Anatolians in the Cyclades," *Oxford Journal of Archaeology* 3, 23–37.

Stubbings, Frank H. (1975): *The Recession of Mycenaean Civilization*, Vol. II, Part 2, *Cambridge Ancient History*, Cambridge University Press, 338–58.

Taylor, A.E. (1928): *A Commentary on Plato's Timaeus*, Oxford Clarendon Press, 1–700.

Taylour, Lord William (1983): *The Mycenaeans*, Thames and Hudson, London, 1–180.

Thornton, Agathe (1984): *Homer's Iliad: Its Composition and the Motif of Supplication*, Vandehoeck & Ruprecht, Göttingen, 1–182.

Tracy, Stephen V. (1990): *The Story of the Odyssey*, Princeton University Press, Princeton, 1–160.

Valladas, H., J.L. Joron, G. Valladas, B. Arensburg, O. Bar-Yosef, A. Belfer-Cohen, P. Goldberg, H. Laville, L. Meignen, Y. Rak, E. Tchernov, A.M. Tillier & B. Vandermesch (1987): "Thermoluminescence Dates for the Neanderthal Burial Site at Kebara in Israel," *Nature* 330, 159–60.

Valladas, H., J.L. Reyss, J.L. Joron, G. Valladas, O. Bar-Yosef & B. Vandermesch (1988): "Thermoluminescence Dating of Mousterian 'Proto-Cro-Magnon' Remains From Israel and the Origins of Modern Man," *Nature* 331, 614–16.

van Andel, Tjeerd H. & Curtis Runnels (1987): *Beyond the Acropolis—A Rural Greek Past*, Stanford University Press, Stanford, 1–212.

van Andel, Tjeerd H., Eberhard Zangger & Anne Demitrack (1990): "Land Use and Soil Erosion in Prehistoric and Historic Greece," *Journal of Field Archaeology* 17, 379–96.

Velikowsky, Immanuel (1950): *Als die Sonne stillstand*, Stuttgart.

Vercoutter, Jean (1954): *Essai sur les relations Egyptiens et Préhellènes*, L'Orient ancien illustré 6, Paris.

Vidal-Naquet, Pierre (1964): "Athènes et l'Atlantide," *Revue Etudes Grècques* 77, 420–44.

Vitaliano, Dorothy B. (1971): "Atlantis: A Review Essay," *Journal of the Folklore Institute* 8 (1), 66–76.

Von der Mühll, P. (1940): *Odyssee*, Realencyclopädie für die classischen Altertumswisssenschaften, Suppl.Band 7, Stuutgart and Munich, 696–768.

Wagner, Günter A., Ernst Pernicka, T.C. Seeliger, Ö. Öztunali, I. Baranyi, F. Begemann & S. Schmitt-Strecker (1985): "Geologische Untersuchungen zur frühen Metallurgie in NW-Anatolien," *Bulletin of the Mineral Research and Exploration Institute of Turkey* 101/102, 45–81.

Wagner, Günther A., Önder Öztunali & Clemens Eibner (1989): "Early Copper in Anatolia," *Der Anschnitt*, Beiheft 7, 299–304.

Weiss, Barry (1982): "The Decline of Late Bronze Age Civilization As a Possible Response to Climatic Change," *Climatic Change* 4, 173–198.

Welliver, Warman (1977): *Character, Plot and Thought in Plato's Timaeus-Critias*, Philosophia Antiqua 32, E.J. Brill, Leiden, 1–6.

Wells, Berit, Curtis Runnels & Eberhard Zangger (1990): "The Berbati-Limnes Archaeological Survey—The 1988 Season," *Opuscula Atheniensa* 18 (15), 207–38.

Wenke, Robert J. (1980): *Patterns in Prehistory*, Oxford University Press, New York, 1–724.

Wilamowitz-Moellendorff, Ulrich von (1919): *Platon*, 2 Vols., later edition 1948, Weidemannsche Buchhandlung, Berlin, 1–767.

Wolf, Armin & Hans-Helmut Wolf (1990): *Die wirkliche Reise des Odysseus*, Langen Müller, Munich.

Wolf, Hans-Helmut & Armin Wolf (1968): *Der Weg des Odysseus*, Wasmuth, Tübingen, 1–244.

Wood, Michael (1985): *In Search of the Trojan War*, BBC Books, London, 1–272.

Zangger, Eberhard (1991a): "Tiryns Unterstadt," *Archaeometry '90*, Ernst Pernicka & Günther Wagner (eds), Birkhäuser, Basel, 831–40.

Zangger, Eberhard (1991b): "Prehistoric Coastal Environments in Greece: The Vanished Landscapes of Dimini Bay and Lake Lerna," *Journal of Field Archaeology* 18 (1), 1–15.

Zangger, Eberhard (1992): *Geoarchaeology of the Argolid*, German Archaeological Institute in Athens (in press).

Zengel, Eva (1990): "Troy," in *Troy, Mycenae, Tiryns, Orchomenos—Heinrich Schliemann: The 100th Anniversary of his Death*, Katie Demakopoulou (ed.), Ministry of Culture of Greece, 51–77.

INDEX

Achaeans:
  Argive Plain, on 75–7; aristocratic
  rule 95; armaments 104; Black Sea,
  navigation into 113; centre,
  reconstruction of 82; civil war 174;
  craftsmanship 105; early, dating
  73–4; end of 196–200; engineering
  feats of 105; first, knowledge of 74;
  gods, affinity for 105; metal
  shortage 174–5; political and
  economic success 74; population,
  dispersion of 86–7; pottery 101;
  realm of 100; society, information
  about 75; states, collapse of 79–80;
  Troy, war against 78; writings 98
Acropolis 87, 129
Aegean people:
  Qadesh, at battle of 116
Aegean Sea:
  map of 2
Agamemnon 107, 180, 195–6
Anatolia:
  Bull Cult 165; iron objects,
  fabrication of 166; ore deposits,
  distribution of 71
Archaic period 100
Archer Hind, R. D. 41
Argive Plain 13:
  defence on 77; deposits on 126;
  kingdoms of 75–7; Late Bronze Age
  settlements 4; limestone slopes, soil
  on 71
Argolid 3, 220, 223:
  Achaean centre, reconstruction of
  82; Artemisian mountain range 64;
  flood in 122; inhabitation of 66; Late
  Bronze Age settlements 6
Argos, plain of 127
Aristotle 48–9, 111
Athenian State:
  predecessor of 100
Athenians:
  Achaean community, as 131
Athens 1:
  Atlantis, war with 120; class strife 88
Atlantic Ocean:
  references to 111–13

Atlantis:
  animals 140–1; architecture and
  landscape management 141, 143;
  area of influence 115–16; believers in
  37–40; books dealing with 38; canal,
  boring 145; channels of water
  surrounding 148; characteristics of
  107; confederation of kings 115, 136;
  construction techniques 150–1;
  Critias, and 131–73; customs,
  description of 167–9; derivation of
  name 114; description of 59–62;
  description of plain 160–1;
  destruction of 117–18; exercising in
  157; foreign names mentioned 107;
  fruit and vegetables 141; gardens
  155; Helike, representing 42;
  Homer's Scheria, and 181–4, 222;
  horses 157; interpretation of legend
  105–7; interpretations, history of
  38–9; kings of, sphere of influence
  113; land, fertility of 138; locations,
  possible 38–9; manpower and
  engineering 163–4; measurements
  102; metals, production of 138–9;
  Minoan civilization, impressions of
  40; myth, basis of 5, 10–11, 90;
  mythology, place in 45; neutral
  approach to 42–5; non-believers in
  40–2; plain, size of 158–9; Plato's
  trilogy, place in 57–9; political
  system 164–5; Poseidon as creator of
  132–4; quarry, conversion to
  shipyard 151; research, dangers of
  11–14; rural surroundings 160;
  spearmen, ranking 157; story of
  12–13; summary of attributes 119;
  temple of Poseidon 154; Troy, as
  description of 114–15; Troy, obvious
  parallels with 219; vegetation 140;
  water conduits, system of 155
Atlas 114
Attika 100:
  boundaries of 123–4; description of
  120–1; forest cover, disappearance
  of 127; soil erosion in 126
Aurichalcit 140